KENSINGTON

KENSINGTON

BY

GEOFFREY EVANS

ST. MARTIN'S PRESS
NEW YORK

First published in Great Britain 1975
by Hamish Hamilton Ltd
90 Great Russell Street London WC1

SBN 241 89107 8

Printed in Great Britain by
WESTERN PRINTING SERVICES LTD, BRISTOL

Contents

List of Illustrations

Endpapers
Engraving of Kensington Palace by John Rocque, 1736

Map of Kensington
(*drawn by Patrick Leeson*)
facing page 158

Illustrations 3, 5a, 5b, 6b, 7a, 7b, 8a, 8b, 9a, 10a, 11a, 11b, 12a, 12b, 13a, 13b, 14a, 14b, 15, 16, 22a, 22b, 23a, 23b, and the endpapers are reproduced by kind permission of the Kensington and Chelsea Public Libraries; 1a, 1b, 4 and 9b by kind permission of the Trustees of the British Museum; 24a and 24b by kind permission of the Radio Times Hulton Picture Library; 2a, 6a and 20b by kind permission of the Guildhall Library, City of London; 2b, 17a, 19c and 21a by kind permission of Mrs. Barbara Denny; 19a, 19b and 20a by kind permission of Harrods Ltd.; 18 by kind permission of the Curator of the Watts Gallery; and 17b by kind permission of the Greater London Council Photograph Library. Illustrations 1a, 1b, 2a, 3, 4, 5a, 5b, 6a, 6b, 7a, 7b, 8a, 8b, 9a, 9b, 10a, 11a, 11b, 12a, 12b, 13a, 13b, 14a, 14b, 15, 16, 20b, 22a, 22b, 23a and 23b were photographed by John R. Freeman & Company; 10b by Sydney W. Newbery; 18 by Jeremy Marks; 21a by John Roden and 21b by John Laing and Son Ltd.

ACKNOWLEDGMENTS

My warm thanks are due to the many who have taken so keen an interest in the preparation of this book and who have gone out of their way to an extent I could hardly have hoped for, to assist me with material or advice.

There are some, however, to whom I owe a special debt of gratitude.

To Mr. Ronald Ryall, for his generosity in putting his splendid library on the history of Kensington, including his unique scrap books of press cuttings, articles and illustrations going back over a hundred years, at my disposal.

To Mr. S. C. Holliday, recently Chief Librarian of the Kensington Central Library, and his staff. Particularly do I wish to express my sincere thanks and appreciation to Miss Rita Ensing, Principal Reference Librarian, and Mr. R. B. Curle, in charge of Local History, for the endless trouble they have taken on my behalf. Their comments on the text (any errors are my responsibility), and their help in the selection of illustrations, have been invaluable. Miss Patricia Meara and the staff of the Chelsea Reference Library have also given me every assistance as have the Librarians of the Westminster Abbey and Lindley Libraries.

To Dr. Stephen Pasmore, for sparing me his valuable time and for allowing me the full use of his fascinating essays on Edwardes Square and Thomas Henshaw.

To Mr. John Yeoman, for his personally conducted tour of Leighton House and to Miss Evelyn Brown and Mr. D. A. Boyd for supplying me with documents on the bird life of Kensington.

To Officers of the Victoria and Albert, the Natural History, the Science and Geological Museums for their kind co-operation at all times.

To Mr. Alan Sanders, Planning Control Officer of the Borough of Kensington and Chelsea and members of the staff of the Kensington and Notting Hill Housing Trusts, for discussing the environmental problems of the Borough with me.

To Councillor Mrs. M. Gumbel, Mayor of the Royal Borough of

Kensington and Chelsea at the time this book was first suggested, for her hospitality and continued interest.

I also acknowledge with gratitude the assistance I received from:— Miss Jessie Dobson, lately Curator of the Hunterian Museum, The Royal College of Surgeons; Mrs. John Blaker of Brompton Square; Mr. J. H. Malyon, the Secretary of the General Cemetery Company, Kensal Green, and Mr. Burthon, the Superintendent; the Public Relations Departments of Messrs. Harrods and Biba, and Mrs. Enid Venables; Mr. Lodge, one-time gardener to the roof garden of the old Derry and Toms; various shopkeepers and stall-holders in the Portobello Market and those house-holders and individuals whom I have met casually and talked with, in the streets of the Borough.

As ever, I owe much to my wife for patiently bearing with my hand-writing, alterations and deletions when typing the manuscript.

Finally, I wish to express my warm thanks to Mr. Christopher Sinclair-Stevenson and Miss Helen Thomson of Messrs. Hamish Hamilton for their friendly advice and co-operation throughout.

London 1974   G.C.E.

INTRODUCTION

THE ROYAL BOROUGH

*'A handsome populous place, well set in fine ground
and esteemed of very good air.'*

IT IS no easy task to keep within bounds a story of a part of Greater London so rich in history as Kensington, in which so many stirring events of national interest have taken place and so vast a number of celebrated persons have lived through the centuries—Royalty, the Peerage, Statesmen, Artists, Men of Letters, Surgeons, Industrialists and distinguished Soldiers—to name some.

A full and comprehensive history would fill many volumes and occupy many years; even then, because of the plethora of controversial statements made by well-known historians of the past, together with a considerable confusion of dates, there is no guarantee that the story would be accurate in all its parts.

If W. J. Loftie began his monumental *Kensington, Picturesque and Historical*, published in 1888, with the words: 'My greatest difficulty has been to decide what should be included and what left out. The material has been so abundant', and went on to say, 'I have endeavoured to pick and choose things which, so far as I know, have not appeared in any other book', how much harder is it to-day, when almost a century has gone by since Loftie put pen to paper.

Much has happened and many changes have occurred since the Broad Walk was the scene of fashionable parades in which Kings and Queens, Dukes and Duchesses and other celebrities of the day took part and since Kensington was the rural town of Thomas Faulkner's time when he wrote *The History and Antiquities of Kensington* in 1820. The days when the muffin man rang his bell in Holland Street, and carried his wares on his head in a basket covered with a spotless cloth, have passed; the picture that some connect with Kensington in the Victorian and Edwardian eras of an ultra-respectable residential area, of impeccably dressed elderly ladies with snuffling pug-dogs at their heels, doing their shopping in the fashionable stores, and of stiffly starched nursemaids pushing their well-scrubbed charges in prams through the gardens, has also faded.

Consequently, this book is an attempt to bring to life subjects which have an interesting bearing on the life and development of Kensington from the time of the coming of William and his Normans, when the Saxon tribes of Chenesi and Cnottinga lived in their stockades, grazing their cattle and sheep in the environs of the High Street and herding their swine in the woods of modern Notting Hill in which deer, wild and and other game abounded, to the amalgamation of Kensington boar Chelsea in 1964 (together with a look at the Royal Borough since that event); and in so doing to introduce, as far as possible, the people, customs and incidents connected with its history which, until now, have not been included in one single book on the Royal Borough.

In other words, it could be termed an Anthology and its contents and style summed up in the words of the seventeenth-century biographer, John Strype: 'In what I have writ, I have endeavoured to follow the track of truth; and have recalled things as I found them. I may perhaps be censured for this plain and impartial way of writing, and blamed that I have not put some veil or varnish on some things and been wholly silent on others.'

*

Looking back over the years, it is apparent that the gradual evolution of a small village into an important part of the maelstrom of activity of Greater London came about in a series of cycles of which the first is that period between 1066 and the middle of the seventeenth century. It was in the latter part of this era that such noble mansions as Holland House, Campden House and Nottingham House were built and the drift of City magnates from the congested and unhealthy surroundings of London to the salubrious environment of Kensington began.

The next cycle, during which the drift to Kensington was even more noticeable, started with the purchase of Nottingham House by William III in 1689 and the move of his Court to what was to become Kensington Palace, where it remained until 1760 when George III, on ascending the throne, transferred himself and the Court to St. James's Palace.

It was fortunate for those who, by virtue of their connections with the Court, had to fall in with William's move and find new accommodation, that the building of so delightful a square as Kensington Square had begun three years before and was shortly to be followed by areas such as Holland Street.

Some idea of the appearance and popularity of Kensington in 1705, in the early years of Queen Anne's reign, is obtained from John Bowack's *Antiquities of Middlesex*: 'about a mile from Chelsea to the north . . ., stands Kensington upon a gentle ascent, a handsome populous place, well set on fine ground and esteemed of very good air. This town has ever been resorted to by persons of quality and citizens who, for many years, have honoured it with several fine Seats.' Of course he was referring only to that part of Kensington south of Campden Hill for, then, both the Hill and far beyond it to the Harrow Road was sparsely inhabited, and comprised open country, woods and farm land.

For the next half-century, that is to say until the early part of the nineteenth century, little expansion took place, but the years that immediately succeeded saw a remarkable burst of activity in Kensington, Brompton and Campden Hill, with the erection of a number of elegant squares, among them Edwardes Square, Brompton, Alexander and Campden Hill, the development of the Phillimore Estate westwards and northwards from the High Street, and the emergence of Notting Hill as a residential area. The charming Pelham and Egerton Crescents, the palatial houses of Onslow and Hereford Squares and Kensington Gate and the exclusive Kensington Palace Gardens, came a little later.

Throughout the reign of Queen Victoria expansion continued and while the developers were busy erecting the dignified houses of Lansdowne Road and Crescent and the stately Royal Crescent, in the Ladbroke and Norland Estates of Notting Hill, the Great Exhibition of 1851 gave a tremendous impetus to the growth of residential and public buildings in South Kensington and in Kensington itself.

Particularly was this so between the Fulham and Kensington Roads, west of Queen's Gate and Onslow Square and as far as the Earls Court Road, the building of Onslow, Stanhope and Cromwell Gardens, and Redcliffe Square, brought some relief to the urgent demand for housing.

It was in this period, too, that Kensington began to rival the West End as a popular shopping district, when Charles Harrod laid the foundations for the world-famed store in Knightsbridge and Barkers, Derry and Toms and Pontings opened in the High Street. Exhibition Road, also, was prominent in the cultural field when work began on the South Kensington Museum (now the Victoria and Albert) in 1856 to mark the first of what was to become an enclave of museums second to none in the world.

*

But among all the events and comings and goings of well-known personalities which have followed one another in kaleidoscopic fashion, without doubt, the grant of the pre-fix 'Royal' to the Borough in 1901 must be one of the most important occasions in its history.

It is a greatly prized honour for, although the granting of the title
'Royal' does not carry with it any special precedence or privilege,[1] there
are only three English Boroughs[2]—Kensington, Kingston-upon-Thames,
the place of crowning of the Saxon Kings, and Windsor—on which the
Sovereign has conferred the title.

To determine how it came about, one has to go back two years, to 1899
and the passing of the London Government Act, as a result of which
Kensington became one of the Metropolitan Boroughs of London. In his
Minutes for the year ending November 1901, Sir Henry Seymour King,
the first Mayor of the new Borough, gave an account of the events that
ensued:

'One of the earliest points which excited interest in the Council and
generally throughout the new Borough was the title or designation which
should in future be applied to the old Court suburb, and after due consideration the Council resolved in December last to present an Address to
her late Majesty [Queen Victoria died in January 1901] alluding to the
fact that Kensington Palace had been her birth place and praying that she
might graciously be pleased to confer upon the Borough some special
distinction which should for all time perpetuate the memory of Her
Majesty's former close association with Kensington.

'Although unhappily Her Majesty passed away before definite action
had been taken on the Council's memorial, she had, it afterwards transpired, given expression to a wish favourable to a granting of the Council's
petition, and I was privileged in July last to receive a communication from
the Secretary of State for the Home Department, officially intimating that
the King had, in accordance with the expressed wish of Her late Majesty,
that her birth at Kensington Palace should be so commemorated, been
pleased to command that the Borough should in future be designated
"The Royal Borough of Kensington".

'It is unnecessary for me to say how grateful the Council were to receive
this mark of favour at the hands of His Majesty. Their views being formally
expressed in a resolution passed by them when the communication was
submitted at their meeting on 24 July, directing that the Secretary of

---

[1] A miscreant, arrested in 1913, did put it to his advantage demanding to be taken
to the Police Station in a cab, for he claimed this was a privilege accorded to all offenders
arrested in a 'Royal' Borough. Although his demand was met, later enquiries revealed
no authority for such a claim and, alas for residents in Kensington who may clash with
the law, this privilege is no longer recognized.

[2] To avoid confusion it should be made clear that the titles of such towns as
Leamington Spa and Tunbridge Wells, are the Boroughs of *Royal* Leamington Spa
and *Royal* Tunbridge Wells.

State be asked to convey to His Majesty the dutiful and grateful appreciation of the Council, as the representative Municipal Authority of
Kensington, of the honour which His Majesty had so graciously conferred
upon the Borough.'[1]

To celebrate this outstanding occasion a banquet was held of which the
Kensington News, 19 July 1901, gave the following account:

'The popular Mayor of Kensington (Sir Henry Seymour King) invited
a large and distinguished company to dine with him at the Kensington
Town Hall on Wednesday evening to meet the Rt. Hon. The President of
Local Government Board. The arrangements were most complete in every
way, and the banquet a great success. Of course, there were many interesting speeches but the acoustic properties of the hall are not of the best
under the most advantageous conditions, and as the temperature was
excessively high, it was necessary to have all the ventilation that the
windows would provide and the speakers thus had the additional difficulty
thrust upon them of having to contend with the great noise from the
street traffic.'

It then went on to give the names of those at the Top Table—Peers,
Members of Parliament, Bishops, Admirals, Generals and Mayors of
other Boroughs—and also a list of the other important people present.
It continued:

'The Mayor proposed "The King", saying that he did so with peculiar
pleasure, because that day Kensington had received a special token of
Royal favour. He had been privileged to receive a letter, every word of
which had been approved by His Majesty the King, which it was his
privilege to read to the distinguished company before him as follows.'
(He then read the letter from the Home Office, the gist of which is
contained in the Mayor's Minutes.)

'He was sure it would be as agreeable to them as it was to him that the
day should be marked out for an event so commemorative of their ancient
and royal suburb. He, therefore, asked them to drink with peculiar
enthusiasm and heartiness the toast to him who had so graciously granted
this distinction, this honour on the Borough.

'The toast was drunk with enthusiasm, the National Anthem was
sung and three hearty cheers were given for the King on the call of the
Mayor.

'During the dinner which was catered by Messrs. Spiers and Pond,
the "Red Band" played a classical selection of music and the speeches

---

[1] Since the grant of the title is the only modern example of its kind, it is set out in
full in Appendix I together with a description of the Borough Arms in Appendix II.

interspersed with vocal selections by . . .'—and the report concluded by giving the names of the singers.

*

Since that memorable event took place, two World Wars have been fought bringing both death and destruction to Kensington as it did to other Boroughs of London, and whereas the first may have done little structural damage to the old Court suburb, and although families were bereaved by the casualties to relatives fighting in the field, the second brought a number of casualties and considerable damage to the buildings.

Overall, out of a total of 2,718 casualties incurred, just over 400 persons lost their lives in bombing attacks, which fortunately was a surprisingly small number, considering that more than 12,500 bombs, of which 600 odd were high explosive, fell in the Borough. But the buildings suffered severely in that no less than 33,341 houses were hit, and of these over 4,000 were either completely demolished or severely damaged,[1] Holland House being one of them. But, once hostilities were ended, Kensington vigorously set about putting its house in order again and to-day to the ordinary visitor there are few visible signs of the wounds that were inflicted.

[1] These casualty figures have been taken from the records of Captain E. J. Holmes, Air Raid Precaution Officer for Kensington during 1939–45 War.

CHAPTER ONE

THE FOUR MANORS

WHY KENSINGTON and whence is this name derived? The answers to these questions are veiled in a cloud of controversy for, over the years, historians have offered a number of clues, Chenesitun—Chensnetune—Kingsentona—Kinsnetuna being some of the variations. One can take one's choice, but in Domesday Book it was certainly scheduled as Chenesinton, a name still remembered in Cheniston Gardens.

Writing in 1820, Thomas Faulkner, the eminent historian, tells us that Chenesi was a proper name in the time of Edward the Confessor (1042–66) and that the town or village of the time might have been known as Chenesitun or town of Chenesi.

Conversely, in 1880, W. J. Loftie wrote that a Saxon tribe settled between the East and West Saxons and came to be known as the Middle Saxons—hence Middlesex. He went on to say that one, Oswulf, a Saxon or a Dane, acquired a large area, named Oswulfs Town, or Oswulf's Stone,[1] in which lay a parish inhabited by a Saxon family, the Kensings or Kemsings, who resided in the hilly, fertile land enclosed on the north by what is now the Bayswater Road, Notting Hill High Street and Holland Park Avenue and on the south by Kensington High Street: in Roman times this southern boundary followed the edge of the marshes brought about by the periodical flooding of the river Thames over the present sites of Chelsea and Fulham.

Before the arrival of William the Conqueror, very little is known of the early history of that part of Middlesex which now makes up the modern Kensington, except to note an incongruous situation caused by an island of Chelsea—Upper Chelsea, St. Luke's Chelsea or 'Chelsea Outland'—springing up in the north-west corner of Kensington, south of Kensal Green on the Harrow Road and no less than two miles from Chelsea.

Until recently, it has always been accepted that this phenomenon arose

---

[1] The name is partially retained in Ossington Street, north of the Bayswater Road, the boundary between Kensington and Paddington.

in the reign of Edward the Confessor when the then master or chamberlain
of the King's household, Thurstan by name, presented his Manor of
Chelsea to the King's religious foundation at Westminster, a gift which
included some 130 wooded acres of the great forest of Middlesex, in and
around to-day's Kensal, Bosworth Road and the northern end of Ladbroke
Grove. It was Thurstan's intention that these woods should provide
faggots to stoke the Abbey fires and supply acorns to feed the abbot's herd
of swine.

But now, the argument has been put forward that this story is inaccurate,
that the document from which it was taken refers to Chalkhill in the
manor of Kingsbury and not Chelsea and that the mistake occurred
because of a misreading of the two names—Csalchythe (Chelsea) for
Csalchylte (Chalkhill). Experts on the subject agree to differ, so how and
when Chelsea 'Outland' originally came to be in Kensington until 1899
must remain a mystery.

With the advent of the Norman invasion great changes took place in the
ownership of land in England, since William hastened to reward his
Barons and the Church for their services in the conquest. To Geoffry,
Bishop of Coutances, went the Manor of Chenisinton, ten caracutes[1] in
extent made up of arable land, pasture for cattle, pannage for 200 swine
and three arpents[2] of vineyards, the whole amounting to approximately
1,200 acres.

But the Bishop never took possession in person and instead it was held
under his lordship by the de Vere family whose head, Alberic or Aubrey
de Vere, a close friend of William, had come to England with him: on the
death of the Bishop in 1093, the Manor of Chenisinton passed entirely
into the hands of the de Veres, who became tenants-in-chief to the Crown.

Without the help of contemporary maps it is impossible to describe
the boundaries of the estate in exact detail, but in broad terms it was that
area contained by the Harrow Road on the north, the Fulham Road on
the south, on the west by 'The Creek' (a stream which later became the
Kensington Canal and is now the railway), and finally the eastern boundary
followed an arbitrary line from the point where Ladbroke Grove joins the
Harrow Road, thence south to Kensington Palace Gardens, onwards down
Queen's Gate including the Science, Natural History and Victoria and
Albert Museums, along Knightsbridge to the northern end of Sloane
Street where it turned eastward to join the Brompton and Fulham Roads.

[1] A caracute was as much as could be tilled by one plough and eight oxen, normally
120 acres. In the reign of Edward III it was adjudged to be 112 acres.
[2] A variable measure, about one acre.

In all the Manor was three and a half miles wide by two miles long with boundaries measuring six miles.

As in the case of the Bishop, there is no record of the de Veres having resided in Kensington despite the fact that fourteen generations were Lords of the Manor, that is to say until 1526, when their connection with Kensington ceased; but no doubt they visited it from time to time to hold their 'courts' and give judgement in matters affecting the tenants. The silver star on a red ground in the Borough Arms taken from the de Vere Arms, de Vere Gardens and Hotel are reminders of the family's connection with the Borough.

The history of this great family is one of ups and downs as they backed the successful or unsuccessful claimant to the throne of England. Their estates were often confiscated and then restored; some held high command and fought with distinction in Aquitaine for Edward I, at Creçy with the Black Prince and with Henry V at Agincourt; some met their end on Tower Hill.

In 1142, the third Aubrey de Vere was created Earl of Oxford, a title held by the family until 1703, when the twentieth Earl died without an heir. Macaulay wrote: 'He derived his title through an uninterrupted male descent when the families of Howard and Seymour were still obscure, when the Nevilles and Percies enjoyed only a provincial celebrity and when the great name of Plantagenet had not yet been heard in England.'

The career of Robert, ninth Earl of Oxford, favourite of Richard II, 'a young man full of vivacity whose youthful sallies were very pleasing to his master', was a stormy one. Created Marquess of Dublin, a new title, in 1385, and later Duke of Ireland (the marquessate having been revoked in 1386), and Knight of the Garter, he was accused of treason by the Royal Dukes and following his defeat by Henry Bolingbroke, later Henry IV, at Radcote Bridge, Oxon, he only escaped with his life by swimming the river; fleeing to Holland, he died in agony in 1392 from wounds received when hunting wild boar. By the King's command his body was brought back to England for burial in 1395, and Richard attended his funeral in person.

The thirteenth Earl, John, spent twenty-four years of his fifty-one in prison either in the Tower or in Hammes Castle near Calais, yet rose to high office in the reigns of Henry VII and VIII: said to have been the architect of victory at Bosworth, he became Lord High Admiral of England, Ireland and Aquitaine under Henry VII and Lord Great Chamberlain by command of Henry VIII.

But whatever claims to fame the various de Veres may have had, the only one to have had a direct influence on Kensington was Aubrey, the first of the line in England and who died in 1088. His eldest son, Geoffry, while still a young man, contracted a fatal disease which was at least temporarily allayed by the ministrations of Fabritius, Abbot of Abingdon, and in gratitude, the boy, as he lay on his death bed, persuaded his father to make the Abbot a grant of the Church of St. Mary and of land amounting to about 250 acres between the modern Church Street and Addison Road. The name accorded to this estate was 'The Manor of Abbots Kensington' and, by virtue of its position, it separated the southern part of the parish from the north: beyond, to the west, there were a few farms within the Kensington boundary and this area came to be known as 'The Manor of West Towne'.

By the twelfth century, the Kensington estate comprised the following four manors—the Manor of Earlscourt,[1] the southernmost, in the centre, around the church of St. Mary Abbots, the Manor of Abbots Kensington and, west of this, the Manor of West Towne. Lastly, beyond Notting Hill High Street, lay the Manor of Knotting or Nutting Barns, but this was forfeited by the de Veres in the fifteenth century and never restored to them, passing through the hands of Henry VIII, who acquired it to add to his already vast hunting lands, of Edward VI and of William Cecil, Lord Burghley, on whom it was conferred by Elizabeth I.

There now appeared on the scene a man who was to leave an indelible mark on the history of Kensington—Sir Walter Cope.

*

The Cope family had come to prominence during the reign of Richard II and had their residence in 'a very pleasant and gallant house near Banbury'. One held the appointment of Cofferer to Henry VII, an office which brought him a large amount of money, and among his sixteenth-century descendants were two brothers, Anthony of Bramshill, the elder, and Walter 'of the Strand' in London, the younger; it is the latter with whom we are concerned.

On the accession of James I to the throne, Walter Cope rose rapidly in royal favour being appointed successively Gentleman of the Privy Chamber, Chamberlain of the Exchequer and Master of the Court of Wards and Liveries, all very lucrative appointments, and to which he added a baronetcy. Being a shrewd man he invested much of his capital in property and set about acquiring the four Manors of Kensington, his first venture being to obtain possession of the Manor of West Towne,

[1] The Manor House stood approximately on what is now Earls Court Station.

then held by Queen Elizabeth's printer, Christopher Barker. This he purchased for £1,300 in 1591. Following Aubrey's example of bestowing benefits on the Church, Robert, fifth Earl of Oxford, in 1284, had leased forever the Manor of West Towne enclosed by Holland Park Avenue, Kensington High Street, Holland Walk and Holland Road, to 'his dear and faithful Chaplain, Simon Downham', but since then it had changed hands many times.

The Manor House, 'the Ould House in Kensyngton'—comprising the house itself, some farm buildings and fields—stood at the corner of Melbury and Addison Roads, just east of St. Barnabas' Church, and here Walter Cope may have lived while he was planning and building Cope's Castle,[1] the future famous Holland House. In order that he should have an ample supply of fish for his table here and later at his new house, he caused some ponds to be made in the grounds, stocked them with carp and pike and christened them 'The Moats'.

A letter of 1609 in the Public Records Office refers to a social evening during which the ponds were used to entertain the guests as well as to provide food: 'I was the last week with my wife at a solemne dinner at Kensington [Holland House]—where we encountered much good companie and besides good cheere and the fair shewe of the house newly trickt and trimmed for the purpose. We had a morrice dance and the King's Cormorants to entertain us.'[2] Evidence that in 1722 these ponds were still fulfilling the purpose for which they were designed is a notice in the press of that year offering a reward of five guineas for information concerning the poaching of fish one night in September by dragging the ponds with nets.

On Sir Walter's removal to Cope's Castle, the Henshaw family obtained the leasehold of the manor house and Thomas Henshaw, Envoy Extraordinary to Christian V, King of Denmark and Norway in the time of Charles II, distinguished scholar of chemistry, alchemy, natural history and philosophy, friend of John Evelyn and one of the first twenty Fellows elected to the Royal Society, lived there for fifty years until his death in 1700.

During his travels, he made a large collection of various objects of which Lord Yarmouth wrote, 'Mr. Henshaw has brought over with him

[1] It is believed he had a house on Campden Hill, the location of which is not accurately known.

[2] The Chinese had long used cormorants to fish for them. Tethered by a string, they were launched into the water with their throats so bound that they could not swallow their catch which was retrieved from their beaks to be eaten or sold. James I kept such a pair at his Court.

many curiosities the principle of which lies in the unicorn's horn in which he has as much as he prices at four or five hundred pounds.'

Gardening, too, must have been one of Henshaw's interests for in 1690 we find him writing to Sir Hans Sloane. 'You were pleased to promise me some melon seeds and some of the seeds of ye great gourd of Jamaica. The season of sowing is now and my hot bed is ready.' His confidence in the efficiency of the Post Office of the day was profound for he continued, 'You need onely inclose them in a piece of paper and superscribe it for me at my house neare Kensington, the penny post will bring it as safe as if you delivered it with your own hand.'

*

The year 1599 was a busy one for Cope since in those twelve months he purchased the Manors of both Knotting Barns and Abbots Kensington. The first he obtained from the trustees of Lord Burghley, who had died the previous year, at a cost of £2,000, but resold in two years to a London Alderman and Sheriff, Sir Henry Anderson, which transaction brought him a handsome profit of £1,400. Had he retained Knotting Barns he would have eventually owned the whole parish as it existed before Aubrey de Vere's gift to the Abbot of Abingdon.

When buying Abbot's Manor, Cope was unable to obtain possession of the manor house itself, which stood on Palace Green, the sitting tenant being unwilling to vacate it, and it was for that reason decided to build Cope's Castle.

The last remaining Manor, Earls Court, in more modern times celebrated for its many Exhibitions and the Motor Show, lay between 'The Creek', Kensington High Street, the Old Brompton Road and as far east as what was known as Brompton Park, the whole amounting to 770 acres; in 1608, it was the property of the Earl of Argyll and his wife (the latter, as a descendant of the de Veres, having received the Manor as a marriage settlement).

Negotiations went ahead the following year, resulting in the Argylls obtaining a licence to sell to Cope 'all that Manor or Lordship of Earls Court and all messuages, lands etc in Kensington, Chelsey and St. Margarets, Westminster, called or known by the name of the Manor of Earls Court'. The Manor House, Hale House,[1] was excluded from the sale, as had happened in the case of Abbots Manor, and remained reserved to the heirs of the old Earls.

[1] The house may at one time have been occupied by Henry Cromwell, fourth son of the Protector, and the name changed to Cromwell House.

From the frequent references to him in the parochial history, Walter Cope appears to have exerted much influence in the parish and to have taken a deep interest in improving the lot of the poor and destitute. Sadly, he was not destined to see the completion of Cope's Castle for he died in 1614, leaving the house and grounds to his wife during her widowhood and thereafter to his only child, Isobel, as sole heiress. Isobel, who had married Henry Rich, second son of the first Earl of Warwick, and Penelope, sister of Robert Devereux, Earl of Essex, inherited the property in 1621, when her mother remarried, and Kensington reached another milestone in its history, for the event marked the beginning of the fascinating story of Holland House.

*

To-day one has become so accustomed to the conglomeration of monster concrete buildings in Kensington, the jostling crowds on the pavements of the High Street and the continuous roar of buses, taxis and cars, that it requires a wide stretch of imagination to visualize the Borough in the early years of Elizabeth I when the population was only a few hundred and, for example, the ground between Brompton and Chelsea as far as 'The Creek', the boundary between Kensington and Fulham, was 'sandy and waste, partly serving as a rabbit warren'. And it was not until towards the close of her reign that big houses began to appear with a resultant rise in population. This was in no small measure due to the numerous outbreaks of plague in the City and the law, not always effective, forbidding the building of houses within a certain distance of the City in order to prevent the spread of the disease.

In consequence, the wealthy, whose professions obliged them to live within easy reach of the City, sought for a healthy place to which they could escape and yet be within an hour's ride of their place of business.

Thus Kensington began to expand and prosper, the poorer taking advantage of the move of the wealthy into the area not only for the work it provided but also for the better protection of life and property, since in those days and for many years to come it was unsafe for individuals to move into or out of the City during darkness, owing to the activities of the many footpads. The poorer people who still had to go to and fro were able, therefore, to join up with the rich and their escorts for the hazardous journey.

Places of entertainment also sprang to life and, in 1668, Samuel Pepys seems to have spent an hilarious and somewhat expensive evening with Mrs. Knepp, the actress, at 'The Grotto' where they 'had admirable pleasure with their singing and fine ladies listening to us. . . .' He also expended 16s. 6d., a large sum for those days, in the tavern, which may have accounted for his description of the return journey—'mighty merry and sang all the way to the town'.

As time passed, so more and more people began to reside in Kensington and the purchase of Nottingham House by William III as a Royal residence 'gradually led to its [Kensington] becoming the best and most fashionable, the most secure and most healthy of Middlesex villages'.

CHAPTER TWO

THE GRAND MANSIONS

HENRY RICH, Baron Kensington, Earl of Holland in the County of Lincolnshire and Knight of the Garter, continued with the building of Cope's Castle, or Holland House as it now became, where his father-in-law had left off, devoting a substantial sum to the project.

'Handsome, gallant in behaviour and of courtly address', he is purported to have made a great impression on Queen Henrietta Maria and to have been one of her favourites. Yet his public life was one of vacillation, for at one moment he was espousing the Royalist cause, the next, giving his support to Parliamentarians, and then again changing sides so that he had the trust of neither. In 1648 he was in the service of the King, and while attempting to raise the siege of Colchester he was taken prisoner by Cromwell's men: carried to London, he was tried by the High Court in February of the following year and sentenced to death.

Unstable though Rich may have been in his allegiances, his loyalty to the Crown came to the surface at the end and he, like many others of that era, went to his death with courage and calm. On 9 March 1649, resplendent in white satin waistcoat and a lace cap on his head, he stepped on to the scaffold at Westminster Hall to follow the Duke of Hamilton, whose body had just been carried off, and to precede Lord Capel. Without showing any sings of emotion, he gave his executioner £10 not to touch his body nor take his clothes or the lace cap from his head when it was severed. Then, after addressing the assembly and wishing happiness to the Kingdom, he placed his head on the block and himself gave the signal for the axe to drop. A man of great charm and good looks, he died bravely, and was buried in Kensington Church the next day.

Almost immediately Holland House was taken over by General Fairfax as his headquarters and tradition has it that Cromwell once paced the garden with General Ireton, discussing the problems of the day; because Ireton was almost stone deaf and Cromwell was compelled to shout, it had to be the garden so that their conversation could not be overheard.

The Parliamentary occupation was short and Lady Holland was soon allowed to return. She was to spend much of her remaining years adding to the house and encouraging the theatrical profession to give performances in her home when all the theatres had been closed by the Puritans. Her son, Robert, besides succeeding to his father's title, also took that of fifth Earl of Warwick through his grandfather, the first Earl.

Fifteen years after the death of Edward, sixth Earl of Warwick, in 1701, his widow, Charlotte, married as her second husband Joseph Addison, Secretary of State, essayist, poet and man of letters, whose statue stands in Westminster Abbey and of whom it was written 'no other Englishman has influenced the social development of his country more powerfully'. Thus another illustrious name was added to the role of occupants of Holland House.

From all accounts Addison had long been in love with the Countess and, before the marriage, when he lived in Sandford Manor, Fulham (where the gas works now stand), he was tutor to her son, the seventh Earl, to whom he wrote delightful letters encouraging his charge to instruct himself in natural history, particularly birds and their nests.

His own interest in the subject and the rural character of Kensington at the time is plainly shown in extracts from a letter written by Addison to the Earl in 1708.

My dear Lord,
I have employed the whole neighbourhood in looking after birds' nests. . . . This morning I have news brought to me of a nest that has a abundance of little eggs, streaked with red and blue veins. . . . My neighbours are very much divided in their opinions upon them: some say they are skylarks; others will have them to be canary birds; but I am much mistaken in the turn and colour of the eggs if they are not full of tom-tits. If your Lordship does not make haste, I am afraid they will be birds before you see them.
Since I am so near your Lordship, methinks, after having passed the day among the more severe studies, you may often take a trip hither and relax yourself with these little curiosities of nature. [1]

It has been said that his married life with the Countess was not a happy one; referring to their marriage, Dr. Johnson remarked: 'At length the lady was persuaded to marry him in terms much like that in which a Turkish princess is espoused, to whom the Sultan is purported to pronounce "Daughter, I give thee this man as thy slave".'

But Joseph Addison did not live long in Holland House, for he died of asthma and dropsy three years after the marriage, having spent much of

[1] As Mr. Derek Hudson observes, 'he could well have added "and bring your mother too"'.

that time in the great hundred-foot-long library. The story goes that he used to pace up and down the room, with a bottle of wine at each end, stimulating his thoughts by taking a swig from each bottle on the turn, and that his illness was brought on by his penchant for alcohol. But as Loftie sums up, 'It is certain that no one whose health was disordered by excess could have written Addison's pure, sweet, lucid essays in The Spectator.'

*

Until 1726, when Henry Fox, created Baron Holland in 1763, leased Holland House from William Edwardes, Baron Kensington (a distant cousin of the Earls of Warwick, to whom the estate had descended), it was occasionally let. Among the reputed lessees was William Penn who colonised the province of Pennsylvania and built the town of Philadelphia; King William III also looked over the house as a possible residence to which he could escape from the polluted air of London, but decided against it. Then, in 1768, Henry Fox, Baron Holland, bought the house outright, together with much of the land north of Kensington High Street, and thus began an ownership of the Holland estate by the Fox family which was to last for just short of two hundred years.

Despite his ungainly figure, an awkward manner, and somewhat forbidding features, plus the fact that he was inclined to stutter when speaking in public, Henry Fox, like his father before him, rose to the rank of Paymaster General, an appointment he held for eight years until 1765.

The father, Sir Stephen Fox, said by some to have started life as a choirboy, by others as a footman, had risen high in the world entirely by his own efforts and when he contracted his second marriage at the age of seventy-six, Henry Fox and his elder brother, Stephen, later Earl of Ilchester, were the result of the union.

Again like his father and some of his Paymaster General predecessors, Henry Fox took advantage of his official position to acquire considerable wealth, to the extent of being named as 'a public defaulter of unaccounted millions', and in the cartoons of the day he was portrayed as a fox decamping with bags of gold. In fact, he was universally regarded as entirely unscrupulous and made himself the object of deep public hatred.

But that was only one side of his character and, in private life at Holland House, he was a very different man. Devoted husband, over-indulgent father to his three sons, he was an excellent host and delighted in entertaining his friends in lavish manner; he also took a close personal interest in improving his garden.

The elopement of Lady Georgina Caroline Lennox, daughter of the Duke of Richmond, and her marriage to Henry Fox in 1744, was one of the great scandals of the day. Such a furore did it cause that Lord Carteret recalled that, in passing through the rooms of Kensington Palace, he came upon two statesmen discussing 'the unfortunate affair' in such a manner as to make him fancy that 'our fleets and armies had been defeated'.

Because Lady Caroline's parents planned to marry her to a more eligible suitor, to evade the introduction she temporarily disfigured herself by removing her eyebrows and then, hiding herself from public gaze, she slipped out of the house to marry Henry Fox. Twenty years afterwards and twelve months before her husband was made Baron Holland of Foxley, Wiltshire, she was created a Baroness in her own right, taking the title of Baroness Holland in the County of Lincolnshire, so that had she died before Henry, there would have been two Lord Hollands, her husband and son, in the House of Lords; as it happened she died in the same month as her husband so the situation did not arise.

Of Henry Fox's three sons, the eldest, Stephen, held the title for only six months, dying in 1774, the same year as his parents, leaving as heir to the baronies his one-year-old son, Henry Richard, who was to turn Holland House into the famous political and cultural centre of the times. The second son, Charles James—eminent Statesman, superb orator, Leader of the Opposition during Pitt's long administration, Foreign Secretary twice and Napoleonist—although not born in Holland House, spent much of his spoilt youth there. Described by his nephew as of medium height, of sallow complexion, thoughtful brow and kind countenance, with a slovenly but not ungraceful gait and a corpulent figure, which was not ungainly, Charles James Fox was a popular member of society, a clever amateur actor and a keen sportsman.

As a result of his heavy drinking and gambling habits,[1] he incurred colossal debts and to pay them off he, at one period, toyed with the idea of marrying an heiress, to which his father's reaction was that he hoped it was true because he would have to go to bed for at least one night in his life. Other than the burden the debts brought about, late nights and alcohol do not appear to have affected him to any extent and, writing of them in 1803, when he was fifty-four years old, Thomas Creevey recalled in a letter: 'I supped last night with Fox at Mrs. Bouverie's. . . . You would be perfectly astonished at the vigour of body, the energy of mind, the innocent playfulness and happiness of Fox. The contrast between him

[1] Lord Holland paid over £140,000 for the bad debts of Stephen and Charles.

and his old associates is the most marvellous thing I ever saw—they having all the air of shattered debauchees, of passing gaming, drinking, sleepless nights, whereas the old leader of the gang might really pass for the pattern and the effect of domestic good order.'

While still in office, he contracted dropsy and died of the disease, like his elder brother before him, at Chiswick in 1806, attended affectionately to the last by his nephew and disciple Henry Richard. The statue to commemorate the great man occupies a prominent position at the west end of Westminster Abbey.

The third son, Henry Edward, entered the Army and after reaching the rank of general was Governor of Gibraltar from 1804–10, dying a year after vacating the appointment.

*

Left an orphan on the death of his mother Mary, daughter of the Earl of Upper Ossory, when he was five years old, Henry Richard, third Baron Holland, spent his early years in the care of his uncle, Lord Upper Ossory, while his other uncle, Charles James Fox, kept a watchful eye on his education. In the meantime Holland House was let for the next twenty years until Henry was ready to occupy it.

Throughout his nine years at Eton, followed by a further two at Oxford, Henry Holland showed no signs of exceptional brilliance, but instead began to display those qualities of charm of manner, patience and cheerfulness in adversity (for he suffered great pain from hereditary gout), which were to earn him universal respect and affection.

To further his education he spent the ensuing three years after leaving the university in travelling through Europe, meeting and making friends with many notable men and women who were to be frequent visitors to Holland House in the years to come.

In 1794, when he was twenty-one, he found himself in Naples and here an event took place which was to have a great influence on the rest of his life for, in this romantic city, he met, for the first time, Lady (Elizabeth) Webster, who was touring Europe with her fast-living, bad-tempered husband Sir Godfrey.

Well-read and heiress to a fortune, the beautiful Lady Webster, though only twenty-three, had already presented her husband with five children, but the marriage was an unhappy one and the gaiety and charm of the young Lord Holland quickly attracted her.

One wonders whether the domineering characteristics which she was to exhibit later in life were apparent then; if they were, they made no difference to Holland, who fell in love immediately with this talented woman.

The result was inevitable; the Webster marriage broke up and, in early 1796, Elizabeth was expecting a child by Lord Holland. On returning to England, the divorce having gone through, the couple were married in 1797 and took up residence in Holland House, to live there happily for forty years, despite the complete contrast in their respective natures.

Shunned by the Court and slighted by society ladies because of the scandal in which she had been involved, this amazing woman was determined to be the great hostess of the day, while her husband, a strong supporter of the Whigs (like his uncle), entered a political life in which he was to occupy the offices of Lord Privy Seal and Chancellor of the Duchy of Lancaster, and to champion the abolition of slavery. And so began an era in which Holland House became the rendezvous of the leading Whig politicians, the outstanding literary men, intellectuals and wits of the day, among them eminent men and women from abroad.

Dinner was a splendid occasion. The fine long dining-room shone with elegance, the crimson damask walls making a rich setting for the innumerable portraits; above, an immense chandelier shone down on to the table and on the gleaming silver on the sideboard, and at one end of the table, leading the conversation, sat the commanding and watchful hostess, of whom it was once said, 'a centurion did not keep his soldiers in better order than she did her guests'.

'Mr. Allen,[1] there is not enough turtle soup for you: you must take gravy or none' or 'Mr. Luttrell, make room!', to which Henry Luttrell, celebrated conversationalist and diner out, replied, 'It must certainly be made for it doesn't exist', were some of the utterances that issued from the imperious lady.

In the course of time, Lord Holland, because of his affliction, did not appear until the dessert and his arrival in a wheel chair had an immediate soothing effect on his guests. 'He sets me more at ease than almost any person that I know,' wrote Macaulay. Whereas these occasions may have been soothing to some, they only increased Lady Holland's anxiety for her husband's health, since the sight of the exotic fruit and other good things on the table, all very bad for Henry Holland's gout, were an undeniable temptation to him. Melon was one of his particular delights and once, when Lord Grey was present, he pleaded to be allowed a slice, but his wife

---

[1] John Allen, physician and writer, lived in the house and acted as adviser and personal assistant to Lady Holland. A kind-hearted man and 'the best informed and one of the ablest men I know', according to Lord Byron.

was adamant until Lord Grey successfully intervened, at which point his host gratefully exclaimed, 'Ah, Lord Grey, I wish you were always here: it is a fine thing to be Prime Minister.'

Very few of the celebrities of the period failed to put in an appearance at dinner or the salons at Holland House at one time or another. The Prince Regent and the Duke of Clarence, afterwards William IV, dined there, as did the Duke of Wellington; among the statesmen were Lords Grey, John Russell, Moira, Macartney and Canning; the law was represented by such personalities as Brougham and Romilly; Byron, Moore and Rogers were numbered among the poets, while Sydney Smith and Sheridan enlivened the conversation with their witticisms; of literary men, Lord Macaulay, Sir Walter Scott and Charles Dickens were frequent guests, as were foreign visitors, for example Talleyrand and Madame de Staël; the stage, too, was not omitted and Banister and Kemble were often in evidence.

At one period the social life at Holland House was disrupted, when Lady Holland acquired a cat which was hardly ever permitted out of her sight, and to whose vagaries she demanded unqualified submission from all her visitors. 'Rogers, it seems, has already sustained considerable injury in a personal affair with this animal; Brougham only keeps *him* or *her* at arm's length by snuff and Luttrell has sent in a formal resignation of all further visits till this odious new favourite is dismissed from the Cabinet,' wrote Creevey in 1822.

Imperious as she was as hostess in her own home, Lady Holland seems to have been equally so as a guest in the houses of others. Dining with the Earl of Essex one night in 1835, she began by complaining that there was no fire; then that she was very badly helped to turtle and condemned it as being both bad and ill-dressed, and when her host helped her to venison, she said it was too tough for her digestion and sent it away. As the ladies left the table, turning to Lord Essex, she enquired if he had ordered a fire to be lit in the next room and, on his replying that he had not, she said, 'Then I shall light it myself.' When the men returned to the ladies a fire was burning brightly and it was discovered that Lady Holland had used some of her host's notes in the card-rack on the chimney-piece to light it.

Strangely, thunderstorms, however slight, put her in so great a panic that, even when she was entertaining, at the first clap or flash of lightning she would rush from the room to her bedroom where she stayed with the curtains drawn and candles lit until it abated.

Much attached to her house and garden she did a great deal to maintain

and improve both and was the first successful importer of the dahlia into
England in 1804. These multi-coloured flowers were a source of great
pride to her and her husband, so much so that Holland wrote the following
verse to her:

> The Dahlia you brought to our isle
> Your praises forever shall speak
> 'Mid gardens as sweet as your smile
> And in colours as bright as your cheek.

By 1840, Lord Holland's health and the strain of political life were
beginning to take their toll, yet his gaiety and wit remained undiminished,
as for instance when hearing that his eccentric friend, George Selwyn, a
man with a morbid interest in funerals, corpses and executions, had called
to enquire after his health, he remarked: 'If Mr. Selwyn calls again, let
him in: if I am alive I shall be glad to see him and if I am dead, he will be
glad to see me!'

His end came abruptly for after appearing as well as he ever was one
day, he was dead two days later—22 October 1840—at the age of sixty-six.
'A public life more consistent is not to be found in our annals' and 'the
most gracious and interesting countenance that was ever lighted up by the
mingled lustre of intelligence and benevolence', was Macaulay's summing
up.

Lady Holland survived her husband by five years, but never lived
again permanently in Holland House, though she continued to entertain
her friends there until the faithful Dr. Allen died, after which she could no
longer face staying in the house. As each year passed so her circle decreased
as old and intimate friends died; she herself followed them in 1845.

*

The fourth and last Lord Holland suffered from delicate health and, like
Lord Byron, his idol, was crippled in one leg. Artistic in outlook, he
spurned an offer to enter politics and spent much of his early youth in
Italy, indulging in many love affairs, until he was persuaded to take up a
diplomatic career: in this he was singularly successful in assignments in
Austria, Germany and Italy until he resigned from the service in 1840.

Although he was deeply attached to Holland House, the English climate
and his unsatisfactory relations with his mother kept him out of the
country for long intervals. Even when he succeeded his father, he lived
for only short periods in England but, nevertheless, spent a large amount
of money on altering the great house.

His wife, Lady Mary Augusta, daughter of the Earl of Coventry, and considerably younger than he, shared his interests in the arts and also continued with the grand scale of entertaining, though without the autocratic tendencies of her famous mother-in-law. The Queen and Prince Consort twice visited Holland House to attend the Scottish Fêtes held in the grounds; both Gladstone and Disraeli were among the many visitors as also were William Thackeray and Alexandre Dumas.

The *Illustrated London News* of 14 August 1852 gives a full description of a splendid occasion at Holland House during one of the Scottish Fêtes: 'In the evening was given a superb garden fête. For this purpose the gardens, orangery, conservatory and part of the pleasure grounds were brilliantly illuminated: tiny glass lamps of all hues, and the more fanciful lampions, shedding their sparkling lights in every direction among the trees, and the gay parterres, illumined the floral beauties everywhere. The room set apart for dancing was at the end of the orangery, forming the termination to a long conservatory. We believe that erstwhile these buildings formed a part of the stables of Holland House but a few years since they were altered. . . . Above the room in which the dancing took place and also above the orangery, the roof of the building is perfectly flat, forming a delightful promenade, which on the evening of the fête was lighted by lamps placed in the interstices of the open-worked parapets. . . .'

Describing the garden, the article continued: 'Here are parterres in Italian scrolls and devices, and box and dwarf oak clipped into globes: flower beds in the form of a fox (in allusion to the family name) and the old English "H", the effect of the flowers aided by coloured sand and the outlines of box edging. In a parterre near the house, upon a granite column, is a bronze bust of Napoleon Buonaparte by Canova, the pillar inscribed with a verse from Homer's "Odyssey".'

In 1859 the reign of the Hollands came to an end for in December of that year Lord Holland died childless in Naples; his widow, like her mother-in-law, was disinclined to continue living in the grand mansion and spent only a couple of months of each year in residence, during which she kept up the liberal entertaining inherent in the history of Holland House; this, together with extravagances in other fields, brought about a crisis in her financial affairs.

As a remedy for this awkward predicament, Lady Holland made over the property, in 1873, to the fifth Earl of Ilchester, great-grandson of Stephen Fox, in return for a handsome annuity and a guarantee that she remained in possession of the house during her lifetime, an advantage she was to enjoy for a further sixteen years.

Princess Marie of Liechtenstein, adopted daughter of the fourth Lord and Lady Holland, presents a vivid description of the house and its contents as they were in 1873 and enables one to picture the gracious surroundings in which the Holland family lived.

Originally, the main entrance was from the south, but that had been changed some long time before to the east side of the house and visitors passed through a vast entrance hall decorated with Italian tiles, busts by Nollekens and Chantrey and relics of Charles James Fox, including a case in which were a fowling piece and a brace of pistols, richly ornamented in silver and gold, presented to him by Catherine the Great in 1785.

On the left was what was termed the Smoking Room but, by then, a depository for family documents, and on the right stood the chapel, long since disused, to provide rooms for the servants.

Immediately opposite the front door was a flight of steps to the main hall and grand staircase to the first floor. Elaborately carved ballusters, Tournay tapestries, a fine display of porcelain and a brass font cast by Michele Garelli in 1784, immediately caught the eye.

Beyond the Inner Hall, communicating doors led from one room to the next, the first being the Breakfast Room, originally the Entrance Hall, and facing south. Large enough to hold a grand banquet, the walls were hung with Genoese silk, a velvet brocade and tapestries representing Greek Gods after designs by François Boucher. The panelled ceiling was ornamented with white and gold pendants and on the cornice Earl's coronets alternating with the famous 'H' of the Earls of Holland, bearing witness to the fact that this room dated from the Rich period; Sèvres porcelain, Venetian mirrors in gilt frames and marble busts added to its splendours.

On the west side of the Breakfast Room a door gave access to the China Room of much smaller dimensions; here were displayed dinner, dessert and coffee services, vases and other items of porcelain of Sèvres, Dresden, Berlin and Chelsea manufacture.

As its name implies, the Map Room next door to the China Room, was full of maps and atlases, besides books and portraits; appropriately a portrait of Charles II hung between Nell Gwynn and the Duchess of Portsmouth, and not only in this room, but in many others, several of G. F. Watts' works were to be found, for he was a close friend of the family both in Florence and later in Kensington.

Of the remaining rooms, on the west side overlooking the Dutch garden, the Picture, the Print and the Princess's Rooms, used for visitors, the Print Room contained a representative collection of Italian, German,

Dutch, Flemish, French, Spanish and English schools, including the works of Albert Dürer, Rembrandt, Rubens, Watteau, Hogarth, Lancret and Boucher.

Looking out to the north, were Dr. Allen's room, the Journal Room, for State papers, and the White Parlour used as an ante-room. This last was panelled in white and gold and in it were two large chests in which, it was said, Sir Stephen Fox kept his official papers when Paymaster General.

As on the ground floor, the rooms on the first floor opened into one another; a visitor, on arriving on the landing at the top of the Grand Staircase, would have seen a door leading into the magnificent Gilt Room, above the Breakfast Room, in which the décor was much the same as it had been when Henry Rich prepared it for a sumptuous ball to mark the occasion of the marriage of Prince Charles to Henrietta Maria. For reasons unknown, the ball never took place but, since those days, it had been the scene of many a festive occasion.

The main difference in the original décor of this splendid room was the ceiling, which fell in during the infancy of the third Lord Holland and was replaced with a white one embossed with fleurs-de-lys and crosses.

The wainscotted compartments were separated by bas-relief columns and each contained panels framed in blue and gold, within which were, alternatively, either silver fleurs-de-lys on an azure shield or a gold cross on a red shield, both being surrounded by palm leaves crossing at the top and appearing through an earl's coronet. Other parts of the room were decorated with medallions of Charles I and Queen Henrietta Maria, the arms of Cope and Rich and the united arms of both families.

A door on the west side opened into the yellow Drawing Room, with its walls of yellow and the cornice decorated in blue and gilt. Here were kept a number of relics of famous personalities, among them a pair of Byzantine candlesticks owned by Mary Queen of Scots, the badge of the Jacobites, a medal inscribed with Charles I on one side and Henrietta Maria on the other, a chatelaine of the second Lady Holland, in which was a ring with a miniature portrait of Charles II within, engraved 'C.R.', filled in with enamel and given by the Monarch to the Duchess of Portsmouth, and the gold enamel snuff box owned by Governor Howell, one of the very few who survived the horrors of the Black Hole of Calcutta. Of great historical interest and much prized by the third Lord Holland and his wife, for both were strong Napoleonists, were the mementoes of the Emperor: his Cross of the Légion d'Honneur; a crystal locket, surmounted by an eagle and crown of laurels and with NAPOLEONE inscribed on the back, and containing a snippet of his hair; and, strangely, a sock he was wearing on his death bed. The small box given by him to Lady Holland, a 'témoignage de satisfaction et d'estime', was presented by her to the British Museum.

The whole of the west side was occupied by the Library, previously the Long Gallery, often considered to have been the most majestic room in the house. Such of the walls as were not devoted to books, were covered with Cordova leather; coronets entwined with the letter 'H' appeared frequently on the cornice and the ceiling, comprising seven vaulted compartments, was of oak, decorated with golden stars on a blue background.

The Dining Room, in which Addison died, the Crimson Drawing Room, so called after the colour of the silk that covered the walls (it was also called the Sir Joshua Room, after Reynolds, a frequent visitor), and Lord Holland's Bed and Dressing Rooms, were at the rear of the house facing north; Lady Holland's Apartments, sitting-room, boudoir and dressing-room were immediately above the entrance hall. An outstanding feature of the Dining Room and Crimson Drawing Room were the paintings ranging from Murillo and Velasquez to a very large selection of English artists, such as Reynolds, Kneller, Lely and Watts.

*

In the early part of the century taxation and rising costs were beginning to make themselves felt on large property owners generally, an imposition that was to increase with the years, and the sixth Lord Ilchester was compelled to resort to developing some of the land adjacent to the house in order to defray the cost of maintaining the estate. Since Ilchester's interests lay mainly in the countryside and the literary field (his capability in the latter bringing him renown as a historian, the history of Holland House, published in 1937, being his most notable work), and because his wife did not aspire to be a great hostess, the pace of entertainment slowed down considerably.

The last time on which Holland House was to be seen in all its splendour was the occasion of a grand ball in July 1939. Their Majesties King George and Queen Elizabeth dined with the Ilchesters beforehand; foreign Queens, Princes and Ambassadors were among the guests and the house was decked with flowers in profusion. None of those present could imagine that within eighteen months the magnificent house would be left in ruins, devastated by incendiary bombs on the night of 27–28 September 1940. So, this magnificent Jacobean mansion ceased to be what was described until then as the finest example of the country house in the County of London.

Even so, under the auspices of the Greater London Council, what remains of the house and its splendid garden still play an important part, not only in the life of London, but also of visitors from all parts of the country and abroad.

Some of the original façade has been restored to give a glimpse, however sad, of the glory of its past; a youth hostel built to the design of Sir Hugh Casson and Neville Conder includes the reconstructed east wing. Plays are performed in an open air theatre, the façade providing an excellent back-drop; the grounds have become a public park with newly planted trees and shrubs, while the flower beds present a brilliant display in the spring and summer; facilities also exist for all forms of recreation, cricket, tennis, and the like, while children play happily under their play-leaders in the playgrounds; there is also a well-equipped restaurant.

In effect, Holland House and its grounds are now one of the oases of the capital in which men, women and children can get away from the noise, traffic and general hurly-burly of the London streets, and enjoy a country house environment on their doorsteps.

*

To the north of Holland House the ground rises towards the summit of Campden Hill from which, in Walter Cope's time and until modern Kensington came into being, a superb view was obtained over parts of Surrey and the completely rural scenery towards Harrow, Hampstead and Primrose Hill.

In the early 1600s the hill itself was a barren heath interspersed with gravel pits and mineral springs, but because of the view, its high and dry situation and proximity to two main roads, it was an eminently desirable spot to build a retreat from the City—and not too far from it.

According to tradition the fact that one of the famous houses of Kensington ever came to be built on this hill, was due to a game of skill or chance between Sir Walter Cope and Sir Baptist Hicks, in which the latter was the successful contestant. What the game was history does not record, but part of the stake was that piece of the hill lying between Hornton Street and Kensington Church Street, an area which suited Hicks in every respect.

Hicks, an extremely wealthy silk merchant of Cheapside, had been of financial assistance to James I immediately after his accession and, since that monarch had the habit of granting honours to those who helped to refill his often empty coffers, Hicks advanced rapidly towards a peerage— first a baronetcy, then as Baron Hicks of Ilmington and Viscount Campden of Chipping Campden in 1628, the year before he died aged seventy-eight.

His business was a thriving one demanding his presence all the year round and he wasted little time before taking advantage of his victory to build a country residence on Campden Hill, to which he could commute and which he completed in 1612: compared with Holland House, it was smaller and not so ornate but, as *Mercurius Politicus* of 14 June 1660 recorded, both it and its owner were sufficiently important for Charles II to sup there, with the third Viscount, after a busy day.

'On Friday, 8th June, His Majesty went to Hampton Court about five in the morning, returned about eleven and then touched many that had been troubled with the evil. At three of the clock in the afternoon, his Majesty gave a meeting to the Parliament in the banqueting house and, having heard Mr. Speaker, returned a most gracious answer. His Majesty was pleased to sup this night with The Lord Campden at Kensington.'

Like Holland House, this magnificent building was approached from the High Street through a long avenue of elms; the main features of the immense dining-room were the stuccoed ceiling with the Campden Arms in the centre and the gigantic chimney piece, the pediment of which was supported by six Corinthian pillars in turn supported by two caryatid figures, the whole affording a fine example of the architecture of the period. On the first floor were the State Apartments comprising three large rooms, the walls and ceilings richly decorated; in the garden, an unusual shrub, a caper, flourished in its unnatural surroundings (still living in 1799), and fruited prolifically.

His three sons having died in infancy, Lord Campden found himself in the same position as Sir Walter Cope, with a daughter, Juliana, who lived to be one hundred, as his heir, and by specific remainder, her husband, Edward Lord Noel, succeeded to the titles of Lord Hicks, second Viscount Campden on the death of his father-in-law. Once again in the history of Campden House, the ownership passed to the female line in the person of Juliana, the third Lord Campden's grand-daughter who had married Charles, Earl Burlington, and Campden House remained in their possession until the whole estate was sold in 1708: their son, Richard, acquired his remarkable taste in architecture during his formative years at Campden House.

*

In the year 1691, Princess Anne and her husband Prince George of Denmark were searching for a more salubrious neighbourhood than Hampton Court to bring up their only surviving child out of seventeen, the delicate Prince William Henry, styled Duke of Gloucester, and settled on Campden House which they took on lease from the Burlingtons; at the same time, the charming Little Campden House, in the style of Christopher Wren, was built in the grounds to accommodate the Princess's suite.

Despite his frailty, the little Prince William was determined to be a great soldier like his uncle William III and, discarding his childish toys at a very early age, 'nothing pleased him but drums, arms and stories of war', as his faithful attendant Jenkin Lewis has recorded.

To this end, a private army of ninety boys was raised for him and formed into two companies, one from Kensington, the second from London commanded by one of the Prince's pages; armed with wooden swords and muskets, they wore smart Grenadier caps on their heads and, on the occasion of a visit to Campden House by the King and Queen, the juvenile army was summoned to the garden by beat of drums in order that Their Majesties could see the boys at their martial exercises.

The King was delighted and, at the conclusion of the manoeuvres, a boost to recruiting was given, for not only were the boys regaled with a feast from the Royal kitchens, but the King ordered twenty guineas to be handed to the boy soldiers; a special prize of two guineas was awarded to William Gardener, aged six, who 'beat his drum almost equal to the ablest drummer'. Unfortunately the 'Army' did not confine its activities to the gardens of Campden House and, becoming more ambitious, took to waylaying travellers to and from the City until complaints brought this practice to an end. Presumably disbandment came when the young commander-in-chief died at Hampton Court at the tender age of eleven.

After the sale of the estates by the Burlingtons, the house was occupied by a variety of tenants until about 1751 when it became 'an eminent boarding school for young ladies' for nearly a hundred years. In 1776, it was under the direction of a Mrs. Terry as an expensive and popular seminary to which fashionable ladies sent their daughters. Lady Harbord, writing to Lady Bingham that same year, described it as 'a most healthful and desirable situation', adding that because of her high opinion of Mrs. Terry's establishment she had sent her two daughters there; Lady Bingham, a famous beauty of the day, also placed her daughter in Mrs. Terry's care. But by 1797, whether or not Mrs. Terry was still the headmistress, the character of the school must have greatly changed according to one, Arthur Young, whose daughter, Martha, died of consumption, it was said through bad living conditions. (She was compelled to share a very narrow bed with a deaf girl.)

Thoroughly embittered by her death, he wrote: 'In the country she had health, spirit and strength. . . . The rules for health are detestable—no air but in a measured formal walk and all running and quick motion prohibited. Preposterous! . . . the school deceptive of all sorts, the food etc all contributed. She never had a full belly at breakfast. Detestable this at the expense of £80 a year.'

After its closure in 1847 or 1848, it reverted to use as a private residence, but in 1862 it was burnt to the ground under suspicious circumstances and became the subject of a celebrated court case concerning the insurance. Four years later another house was erected on the site, but this was demolished in 1900, since when Campden House Court has taken its place.

*

In the same decade as Walter Cope disposed of the piece of land on Campden Hill to Baptist Hicks, he also sold some thirty-six acres astride the eastern boundary between Kensington and Westminster to Sir George Coppin, Clerk of the Crown to James I; most of the estate lay in the parish of Westminster, including that area now covered by Kensington Palace and Kensington Gardens, and not until 1899 when, at the express wish of Queen Victoria, the boundary of the Royal Borough was extended eastwards to the Broad Walk, did Kensington Palace become part of Kensington proper.

The house that Sir George Coppin built for himself on the site of Kensington Palace did not remain in the hands of his family for long, since, on his death, his son Thomas sold the property to Sir Heneage Finch in 1620 and for the next seventy years it was in Finch occupation. The 'Finches of the Grove' distinguished themselves both in the legal and political fields, for the first Sir Heneage held the appointments of Recorder of London and Speaker in the reign of Charles I, while his eldest son, also Heneage, later became Attorney General, Lord Chancellor and eventually Earl of Nottingham in 1681.

On the death of the old Heneage, for some reason the estate passed to the second son, John, physician and diplomat who, in turn, sold it to his elder brother in 1661, and the latter, on being raised to the peerage, renamed the house Nottingham House. To enhance the surroundings he built the first ha-ha, so called by the public, according to Faulkner, to express their surprise at finding a sudden and unperceived check to their walk, and planted the first of the many avenues of trees, which were to feature so often in the history of the Gardens.

So dark was the complexion of Daniel, the second Earl, and so sombre his expression, that he was likened by one to 'a chief mourner at a funeral' and, because of these characteristics, he gained the sobriquet of 'Dismal Daniel' or 'Don Dismallo'. It was he who sold the estate to William III for £18,000 in 1689, to begin the history of Kensington Palace, or Kensington House as it was first called, as the residence of four successive reigning monarchs and, for a very short period, of Queen Victoria before she moved to Buckingham Palace.

*

'Windsor Castle is a place to receive monarchs in; Buckingham Palace a place to set fashion in; Kensington Palace to drink tea in,' wrote Leigh Hunt, in *Old Court Suburbs* (1851), but in the time of William III, *tay* was 60s. per pound, a price hardly conducive to drinking the beverage in large quantities.

Because of the King's health, both he and Queen Mary were anxious to move in as quickly as possible and speed was essential in turning the smallish house into a suitable Royal Residence.

William, a small thin man, by nature shy and reserved in public, suffered acutely from asthma accompanied by a hacking cough, but would never give in or allow his physical disabilities to interfere with his duty: a prodigious worker he was often reduced to complete exhaustion, but once in the open and leading his army in the field he was at his best. When not campaigning, the fogs, damp and smells of Whitehall only added to his discomfort so that his nights were frequently sleepless, while the journey to and from Hampton Court was both tedious and inconvenient. Kensington, on the other hand, was much nearer to the hub of government than Hampton Court, though sufficiently far away to allow the King some privacy, and it was hoped that its clean air would alleviate his suffering.

So Sir Christopher Wren was put in charge of the work in July 1689. Four wings were added and the original entrance on the south side transferred to the west; while the project was in hand the Queen watched impatiently from Holland House where she was staying, reporting progress to the King who was at that time busily engaged with the rebellion in Ireland.

It was a rushed job involving set-backs and casualties for, in November, part of the new work collapsed, the falling masonry killing a carpenter, while a plumber fell off a scaffold when at work on the same edifice and died of his injuries. Nevertheless, by Christmas enough had been done to enable William and Mary to take up residence, and John Evelyn, after a visit to Kensington House in February the following year, described it as 'a patched building yet with the Gardens it is a very sweete Villa, having to it the Parks and The straite new way through the park'.

This 'straite new way', a section of which is still extant in Rotten Row or Route du Roi, was very necessary at the time to enable the King, Queen and members of the Court to travel quickly and safely to and from Whitehall when the English climate reduced the normal roads to quagmires. For protection against footpads with whom the area was infested, a series of posts were erected and hung with lanterns, lit when the Court was in residence at Kensington, and soldiers patrolled the road during the hours of darkness.

Unfortunately Wren's troubles were not yet over for one night in November 1691 a part of a new wing was burnt down. During the conflagration the royal couple went into the garden to watch the fire-fighting and the ladies of the Court milling around in their night attire; the odd assortment of parcels hurriedly packed up and lying about in the garden gave the King much amusement, particularly one containing food and wine got together by somebody as if that person expected to have to undergo a siege.

After this episode, the Palace settled down to a normal life and the King was able to lay out the gardens to his liking, which tended towards 'long and straight gravel walks with clipped hedges extended throughout: only varied by giants, animals and monsters in yew and holly'.

However shy and austere William may have been in the company of grown-ups, he was perfectly at home with children and especially with his short-lived nephew, Prince William, into whose military fantasies he entered enthusiastically; another of his young friends, the four-year-old Lord Buckhurst, son of Lord Dorset, the Lord High Chamberlain, had no inhibitions regarding Royalty. One day, rather later than usual, the King was in his closet doing business with one of his secretaries, when there was a knock on the door. 'Who is there?' called the King, to which a small voice cried, 'Lord Buck.' The King rose, and on opening the door there stood a tiny figure looking up at him. 'What does Lord Buck want?' he enquired. 'You to be horse to my coach, I've wanted you a long time,' was the reply. So putting aside his affairs of state with a smile, which the secretary thought him quite incapable of, His Majesty took the string of the toy and dragged it up and down the Long Gallery until his diminutive taskmaster had had enough.

If William was shy, one of his guests, Peter the Great, Czar of Russia, on a State visit to England in 1698, was more so and had a strong dislike of even being seen in public; even when attending at Kensington Palace, which he did often to dine or sup with the King, he was always admitted by the back door. On the occasion of a ball given in honour of Princess Anne's birthday, he hid in a closet from which he could watch the company without being seen himself and when invited to listen to a debate in the House of Lords he adopted exactly the same procedure. On his departure from England, a small parcel wrapped in brown paper was delivered to the Palace which, on being opened, was found to contain a priceless ruby, the Czar's parting gift to William.

In 1694, the Queen was stricken with smallpox and died, to be followed by the King eight years later. While riding at Hampton Court, his horse stumbled and threw him and though at first he seemed to be on the mend, he contracted pneumonia when falling asleep in his chair by an open window and this proved fatal.

*

Five years after his first visit to Kensington Palace, Evelyn paid a second in 1696 and recorded: 'The House is very noble, tho' not greate.' He went on to describe the picture gallery with its superb paintings by Titian, Correggio, Holbein, Van Dyck, Tintoretto and others, for William was a great connoisseur and collector; he also referred to the splendid collection of porcelain, Queen Mary's special pleasure, and finally remarked, 'the Gardens about it very delicious'.

Queen Anne, however, thought differently about the gardens in particular and set about changing the Dutch atmosphere created by William. The topiaries and box hedges were uprooted and instead a more English type of garden took their place. On the northern boundary between the Palace and the Bayswater Road, along the southern side of which extended 'the Gravel Pits', a derelict and untidy plot of about thirty acres was laid out and planted under the direction of the Queen's gardener, the famous Henry Wise. Of these changes John Bowack, in 1705, observed that the gardens 'want not any Advantages of Nature to render them entertaining and are beautified without all the Elegancies of Art (Statues and Fountains excepted). . . . Theres a noble Collection of Foreign Plants and Fine, Neat Greens which makes it pleasant all the Year. . . .' Concerning the new garden, he wrote: 'Her Majesty has been pleas'd to Plant near Thirty Acres more towards the North. . . . Upon this Spot is near 100 Men dayly at Work and so great is the Progress they have made, that in less than Nine Months, the whole is level'd, laid out and Planted and when Finished will be very Fine.' When it was completed Addison also eulogized it with the words: 'It must have been a fine genius for gardening that could have thought of forming such an unsightly hollow into so beautiful an area!' Alas, all that additional garden has long since disappeared, although Queen Anne's most famous contribution to the Palace—The Orangery—still stands as one of the best architectural examples of the period.

The Orangery or Banqueting House, for which purpose it was originally intended, was designed by Hawksmoor but modified by Vanbrugh and is situated on the north side of the Palace. Comprising three rooms—the banqueting room in the centre with two smaller semi-circular rooms at each end—it was the scene of sumptuous supper parties, balls and concerts, on which occasions certain members of the public were admitted to the gardens provided they appeared in full dress.

Another addition made by the Queen, the new Summer House, since known as 'The Alcove', a delightful brick work by Christopher Wren, bearing the Royal Monogram, stood just east of the gateway carrying the arms of William III, which to-day gives entrance to the Palace from the High Street; The Alcove is no longer there but is preserved in a position in the Fountain Gardens marking the beginning of the Serpentine.

*

Both the Queen and her Consort, Prince George of Denmark, were in ill-health when they moved into the Palace on William's death, some said with such haste as was 'scarce decent'. The Queen, due to immodest love of fine fare, was fat, lethargic and spotty and because she suffered severely from gout, her feet were often enclosed in 'nasty bandages'. 'When in good humour,' wrote Macaulay, 'she was meekly stupid and when in bad humour she was sulkily stupid.' Yet, although she dressed untidily, her expression was pleasant, her voice attractive, her heart kind and her friendship warm. A strong supporter of the Protestant Church, a devoted wife and mother, just and charitable, she had many of the qualities to earn her the epithet—'Good Queen Anne'.

Like his brother-in-law, Prince George was afflicted with chronic asthma; like his wife he ate enormously, but was also over-fond of his claret, and of him Lord Stanhope wrote: 'If there were in England any person duller than Her Majesty, that person was Her Majesty's Consort!'

But the marriage was a happy one, the Royal couple spending much of their time at Kensington, particularly during the summer months. Then, between seven and eight o'clock on the morning of 1 August 1714, the Queen breathed her last, her husband having pre-deceased her by six years, leaving future generations much to enjoy from the alterations and additions she made during her twelve years' residence in Kensington Palace.

*

A King who could speak no English so that matters of State were conducted with his Prime Minister in Latin, a language in which neither was in the least qualified: a King who shut up his divorced wife in a castle in Germany before setting out for England bringing with him two mistresses, a large retinue of German courtiers and servants and his two Turkish valets, Mustapha and Mahommed—such a man was George Lewis, George I, son of the Elector of Hanover, who ascended the English throne in the autumn of 1714 at the age of sixty-three.

Of medium height, with a pale face surmounted by a flowing periwig of large ringlets, his expression was amiable and his courage without question; through his fondness for food and drink he had grown fat and was considered both dull and obstinate. But Kensington Palace appealed to him, perhaps because it reminded him of his home in Germany and he began to furbish it in a style which is evident to-day.

At this stage, Christopher Wren was dismissed, the King employing William Benson as architect for the alterations he had in mind, and also the fashionable William Kent to decorate the new State Rooms and the Grand Staircase. What remained of the old Nottingham House disappeared and, in its place, three State Rooms took shape—the Drawing Room, the Privy Chamber and the Cupola Room—and in this last room Kent gave full vent to his decorative fancies with Ionic pilasters on the walls, gilded statues on pedestals and a ceiling ornamented with a painting of the Order of the Star of the Garter. On the walls of the Grand Staircase visitors can see to-day his immense painting of a reception committee, composed of well-known people of the period, welcoming the King's arrival while he, himself, accompanied by a lady, gazes down from the painted ceiling.

Other additions were a Prince of Wales's and a Princess's Court, the latter for the daughters of the Prince of Wales, built on the north side, as was also a magnificent apartment for Melusina von Schulenburg, Duchess of Kendal, one of the King's mistresses,[1] whose influence was considerable when it came to the distribution of patronage.

---

[1] The other mistress, who resided at St. James's Palace, was Baroness Kilmansegg, Countess of Darlington. Both were extremely unpopular with the public, who dubbed the fat one 'The Elephant and Castle' and the tall one 'The Maypole'.

Although Queen Caroline, wife of George II, has most of the credit for the landscaping of Kensington Gardens, George I, with the help of William Kent and Henry Wise, was intimately concerned with the planning of them—some of the avenues of trees, the grass, and the Round Pond or 'Bason' as it was then called, which was finished a year after his death.

As for his family life, whereas in the time of Queen Anne the history of the Palace was a comparatively happy one, the same cannot be said of the period when it was occupied by George I, for he quarrelled with the Prince of Wales and the Princess who, for three years, were denied access to any of the Royal Palaces, and he obtained custody and control of their children.

His end came while on a visit to Germany in 1727, when he was seized with apoplexy and died at Osnabrück in the same room in which he was born. Uninteresting and unamiable he no doubt was, but, both the Palace and its surroundings benefited from his period of residence.

*

By 1736, William III's 'straite new way' seems to have gone to ruin and travel between the Palace and London was a nightmare for, in the winter of that year, Lord Hervey, the best gossip writer of his day, wrote: 'The road between this place (*the Palace*) and London is grown so infamously bad,' and, referring to the isolation in which he found himself, he added, 'all the Londoners tell us there is between them and us a great gulf of mud'.

Yet, since the accession to the throne in 1729 of the small red-faced, prominent-eyed George Augustus—George II—the last monarch to lead his army into battle, which he did in gallant fashion at Dettingen, a great deal had been and was being done to embellish the gardens of the Palace under the direction of Queen Caroline, an enthusiastic and clever land-scape gardener, who left Kensington Gardens much as they are to-day; more avenues of trees were planted, vistas created and summer houses erected, all at no small cost to the King who was unaware he was paying.

For these enterprises and others, the Queen has been accused of filching three hundred acres of Hyde Park, but the charge is without foundation since the area she landscaped with the assistance and advice of Charles Bridgeman, successor to Henry Wise as Royal Gardener, approximated to the original parkland of Nottingham House.

Perhaps her greatest achievement was the making of the Serpentine so-called 'for its being not exactly straight as all ponds and canals were before'. Until she had them joined together there had been only a series

1a. Henry Rich, 1st Earl of
Holland. From the original
painting by Vandyk

1b. Henry Fox, 1st Lord
Holland

2a. Holland House, 1817. Engraved by R. Havell & Sons after a drawing by J. C. Smith

2b. Holland House, following severe damage by incendiary bombs on the night of 27/28 September, 1940

3. The library, Holland House, 1838. *Left to right* 3rd Lord Holland, Dr John Allen and Lady Holland. Mezzotint by W. Reynolds from an original painting by C. R. Leslie

4. Joseph Addison. Engraving by J. Simon

5a. Daniel, 2nd Earl of Nottingham, from whom William III bought Nottingham House, now Kensington Palace. Engraving by J. Houbraken after a painting by Sir Godfrey Kneller

5b. The North Side of the King's House at Kensington, c. 1690. Nottingham House as it was before enlarged by Sir Christopher Wren to become Kensington Palace. Engraving by Sutton Nicholls

6a. Notting Hill House, now Aubrey House. Lithograph by Miss Emma Shepheard from a sketch by Thomas Maisey

6b. The lane leading to Aubrey House, now Aubrey Walk, c. 1817. Drawing by Louisa Goldsmid

7a. St. Mary Abbots Church, 1807, with the stocks and village pump in the foreground. Engraving by Samuel Woodburn

7b. The Dining-room of Campden House. Originally built in 1612, the house was used as a private school for young ladies between 1754–1847. It was destroyed by fire in 1862. Lithograph by C. J. Richardson

8a. Holly Lodge, the house of Lord Macaulay. It was demolished in 1965 and the site is now occupied by a part of Queen Elizabeth College

8b. Cam House (previously Bedford Lodge and Argyll Lodge), Campden Hill, 1951. It was demolished in 1955 for the building of Holland Park School

of separate marshy ponds fed by the Westbourne Brook and, by her action, she produced that long stretch of water which has given so much pleasure to so many over the years. Nearer the Palace itself, Queen Anne's superb building ceased to be a Banqueting House and instead was filled with a fine collection of exotic shrubs and trees—orange, pomegranate, Chinese pine, camellia and oleander to name a few.

An innovation was made when the King authorized the opening of the Gardens on a Saturday, the day the Court usually moved to Richmond, and the 'promenades' began. Only those attired in full dress were admitted. There Society paraded—Duchesses, maids of honour and beauties of the day, dressed in the height of fashion and accompanied by escorts similarly attired. Now and again a cavalcade comprising the King, Queen, their equerries and maids of honour was to be seen strolling along the Broad Walk, Their Majesties acknowledging the bows and curtsies and stopping to chat with some whom they knew.

The unexpected occurred on one of these occasions when a pretty little girl dashed from her surprised and confused governess and, skipping up to the King, exclaimed, 'Comment vous portez-vous, Monsieur le Roi? Vous avez une grande et belle maison, n'est-ce-pas?' She turned out to be Lady Sarah Lennox, daughter of the Duke of Richmond, and later beloved by George III when Prince of Wales. She was out walking in the Gardens with her sister, Louisa, and their French governess, who had promised—if they were good—that they might see the Royal Family. The King was highly delighted to be so accosted and, on learning who the child was, requested that she might be brought to see him frequently: she subsequently much enjoyed watching the Monarch counting out his money as in the nursery rhyme—a Monday morning ritual—and playing games with him in the Royal Apartments.

Fifty years later, when Kings and Queens no longer lived in the Palace, the wearers of silk neck-ties, leather trousers or anything less than top boots were barred from entry as were common soldiers and sailors. As late as 1814, servants in livery and dogs were not allowed in, but by 1844 the Gardens were open to all and sundry from sunrise to sunset, as the contemporary doggerel, found on a seat, indicates:

> Poor Adam and Eve were from Eden turned out
> As a punishment due to their sin.
> But here after eight, if you loiter about
> As a punishment you'll be locked in.

The King's Road, Chelsea, at any time and particularly on Saturday afternoons, recalls the appearance of 'The Macaronies' sauntering up and down the walks in Kensington Gardens in the early 1800s. These young men who belonged to a Club which specialised in importing foreign clothes and foreign dishes—hence their name—sported a small cocked hat, adorned with gold tassels on each side sitting precariously on hair dressed in 'multi-shaped knobs with chignon and curls', and skin-tight coats and trousers, the latter festooned with bunches of ribbon.

*

At about ten o'clock on the night of 20 November 1737, Queen Caroline died after a long, most painful and distressing illness; the story makes sad reading. Far more intelligent than the King, a patron of the arts and ever ready to give financial support to deserving causes, she had had much to put up with in her short-tempered husband and his philanderings.

As in the reign of George I, the relations between the King and Queen and the Prince of Wales were strained to the utmost, so much so that the Queen in her last illness, when talking of dying, exclaimed: 'At least I shall have one comfort in having my eyes eternally closed—I shall never see that monster again.'

Overcome with grief, for there is no doubt George II had a deep affection for his Consort, the King continued to live in Kensington Palace for the next twenty-three years, but on his death from apoplexy his grandson, George III, declined to live there and it was not until Queen Victoria ascended the throne that the Palace again became the Monarch's residence and then only for a very short time.

In the interim seventy-seven years, various members of the Royal Family occupied apartments in the Palace, among them Caroline of Brunswick, Princess of Wales, after her separation from the Prince Regent. Her life, if indiscreet, was a gay one and her eccentricities both in dress and habits were legion. For instance, at one of her birthday parties she received her guests in her dressing gown and it was not unknown for her to stroll across the fields to the Paddington Canal attired in evening dress and accompanied by only one maid of honour. Neither did she hesitate to enter empty houses and enquire about the rent, nor, without disclosing who she was, to start a conversation with strangers on a seat in the Gardens and, after questioning them regarding their opinions on herself, to invite them into the Palace. Refused attendance at the Abbey for the coronation of her husband, George IV, she died in 1821.

Another occupant was Augustus, Duke of Sussex, a younger brother of the Prince Regent, who was partially resident in the Palace for thirty-seven years from 1805. An avaricious reader with a vast library and immensely popular with the people, he married twice, but as both marriages were declared illegal under the Royal Marriage Act of 1772 no heir to the throne could result.

Although for close on thirty years Edward, Duke of Kent, fourth son of George III, lived happily elsewhere with his mistress, Madame de St. Laurent, he was also granted apartments in 1798. Then, in 1817, Princess Charlotte, daughter of George IV, died in childbirth, raising the important issue of the future successor to the Throne since, as yet, none of George III's sons had produced a legitimate heir. The pressure was now on Edward to marry and provide a possible heir should his elder brother William, Duke of Clarence, also marry but fail in this respect (it might reasonably have been expected that he would not fail since he had already had ten natural children by Mrs. Jordan).

However, Edward considered it was his duty to marry, whatever the Duke of Clarence decided, and he discussed the matter freely with Creevey in Brussels in December 1817. Creevey made careful note of everything the Duke had said, passing on the news in a letter to his friend the Earl of Sefton. When thanking Creevey for his letter and its 'most amusing contents', the Earl wrote: 'Nothing could be more à propos than its arrival as it was put into my hand while a surgeon was sounding my bladder with one hand and a finger of the other, to ascertain whether I had a stone or not. I never saw a fellow more astonished than he was at seeing me laugh as soon as the operation was over!'

True to his principles and despite the wrench of ending his relationship with Madame de St. Laurent, who, poor soul, retired to a convent, Edward married the Princess Marie Louisa Victoria of Leiningen in 1818. To begin with the couple lived in Germany, but when it was obvious that a child was on the way, the Duke was insistent that it should be born on English soil, so hastily packing up and driving the coach himself, he brought his wife to England and Kensington Palace. On 24 May 1819, he became the proud father of a daughter, the fifth in the line of succession to the Throne, and a month later she was christened in the Cupola Room by the Archbishop of Canterbury. Her names were Alexandrina Victoria. Within nine months of her birth, her father died of a chill while wintering at Sidmouth, leaving the future Queen of England to be brought up by her impoverished mother, with the help and advice of her brother, Prince Leopold, until he succeeded to the throne of Belgium in 1830. Here, in Kensington Palace, Victoria was to spend the first closely guarded eighteen years of her life as a Princess and just under a month as Queen before moving to Buckingham Palace.

Her break with the Palace as a residence took place on the morning of 13 July and, though glad to be moving for a number of reasons, she recorded in her diary her affection for her birth-place: 'I have gone through painful and disagreeable scenes here 'tis true, but still I am fond of the poor old Palace.' It is largely due to that affection and to her fondness for Kensington and its people that Kensington Palace still stands as a home for Royalty and that Kensington assumed the title of The Royal Borough. Many were the battles she fought to maintain the buildings in proper repair and to preserve it as a Royal possession, and in 1898 Parliament voted £23,000 towards its restoration provided the State Rooms were open to the public as they are to-day.

*

During the last 135 years and two world wars, the Palace has been the home of many members of the Royal Family; twice some of the rooms have accommodated the London Museum, now shortly to move to the City of London. In the First World War King George V allowed part of the Palace to be used for the welfare of Irish soldiers at the Front and certain of the gardens were turned into allotments; for the Peace Parade, the Gardens became a huge camp for the soldiers of the nations taking part. During the Second World War, King George VI gave permission for a portion to be occupied by the Army and fortunately, although like other London buildings the Palace suffered damage from enemy action, it came off comparatively lightly. But the Gardens were again disfigured by the temporary buildings erected for the soldiers involved in the Victory celebrations.

In 1867, the Prince and Princess of Teck moved into apartments in preparation for the arrival of their first child, Princess Victoria Mary— later Queen Mary, but because her parents considered that the surroundings were not beneficial to their daughter's health, the family transferred to White Lodge, Richmond when she was only fourteen months old. Nevertheless, like Queen Victoria, she always maintained her affection for the Palace and Kensington in after years.

Among others of the Royal Family who occupied apartments in the Palace have been Princess Beatrice, youngest daughter of Queen Victoria, and her daughter, Victoria Eugenie, later Queen of Spain; Princess Louise, Duchess of Argyll; Princess Alice, Countess of Athlone; the late Princess Marina, Duchess of Kent; and to-day, the apartments on the south side of Clock Court, once occupied by the Duke of Sussex, are the home of Princess Margaret, Countess of Snowdon.

Thanks to the great personal interest shown by the Royal Family since Queen Victoria's accession and, in later years, to the Ministry of Works, often against strong opposition from various quarters, Kensington Palace, which has played so great a part in the history of England, has been preserved and is still lived in: as a National monument it continues to give pleasure to the general public and to visitors from all over the world.

CHAPTER THREE

DIGNITY AND ELEGANCE

AMONG LONDON'S most picturesque treasures are its Squares and in this respect the Royal Borough is undoubtedly more fortunate than most. Kensington, Edwardes, Campden Hill, Brompton, Alexander, Thurloe—one could go on almost indefinitely—but unlike Chelsea, for example, where the Squares open on to the main thoroughfares, some are hidden away and one has to look for them.

Kensington Square, the oldest of them, lying on the south side of the High Street almost opposite the modern Royal Garden Hotel, comes into this category. For the pedestrian the approach is easy but let the motorist who may be unfamiliar with the neighbourhood beware the abundant 'No Entry' and 'One Way' signs for, once inside, the most convenient way out is as difficult to find as the way in.

Built in the early part of the reign of James II, it must have been for many a year the most handsome of Squares but, owing to rebuilding, the acquisition of some properties for commercial use or for purposes other than residential and because of its usefulness as a car park due to its proximity to the shops of the High Street, its elegance has, to some extent, been eroded; in fact two houses only, Nos. 11 and 12, originally one house and said to have been occupied by the maids of honour in William III's time, stand with their salient features little altered from the date they were first built in 1685. On the east side one solitary house remains in private hands.

The earliest record of any building in this vicinity concerns Thomas Young, one of Christopher Wren's workmen who, in the reign of Charles II, obtained permission to build in the fields south of the present High Street (Young Street, one of the entrances to the Square, is named after him). But no mention is made in any document of 'King's Square', the original name before 1686, and not until King William brought his Court to Kensington House in 1689, did the Square really rise to prominence and the houses become eagerly sought after by 'persons of quality, ambassadors, gentry and clergy'.

So long as the Monarch resided with his Court in Kensington Palace, the scramble for accommodation in the Square was so fierce that at one period in its history, diplomacy, the Church and medicine, in the shape of an ambassador, a bishop and a physician, were found to have rooms in the same house. Then, on the death of George II in 1760 and the transfer of the Court to St. James's, its popularity with the Court ceased to be the same.

Because of his indifferent health, King William was, no doubt, anxious to have medical advice close at hand for, in 1697, we find Sir Richard Blackmore, his physician, residing on the south-west corner of the Square; a near neighbour was Bishop Mawson, consecutively Bishop of Chichester and Ely, and described in a contemporary letter as 'a better sort of man than most of the mitred order'. Another prominent ecclesiastic was Doctor Thomas Herring, Archbishop of Canterbury, between 1747–1757, who lived in the south-east corner, as did Talleyrand, in 1793; the latter's memory as Ambassador to the Court of St. James in 1830–4 is preserved by the special hand-rail affixed to the staircase of the Travellers Club to assist his lameness when ascending the stairs.

William Thackeray lived for some time in the area and it would not be unreasonable to expect to find his house in Thackeray Street, leading south-east out of the Square, but the search will be in vain because he lived in Young Street, in the house carrying two prominent bows on the west side of that road: it was here that he wrote *Vanity Fair*, *Pendennis* and *Henry Esmond*, before moving to 36 Onslow Square, where he completed *The Virginians* and *The Four Georges*. But affection for the Young Street neighbourhood called him back to build himself a house on Palace Green, No. 2, into which he moved in 1862. He died in the following year and was buried in Kensal Cemetery.

The plaques attached to four houses bear witness to some of the distinguished people who lived in the Square during the nineteenth and twentieth centuries. At No. 18 resided the philosopher John Stuart Mill (1806–73); at No. 40, Sir John Simon (1816–1904), to whom the country owes so much as the pioneer of Public Health. The arts are also represented at Nos. 17 and 33 for Hubert Parry, the musician, lived in the former and Mrs. Patrick Campbell, the actress (1865–1940), in the latter.

The garden which forms the centre of the Square is a pleasant amenity and since smoking is now common practice and no one to-day wants to show off his horse's paces to prospective buyers, the original rules forbidding such goings-on are no longer necessary.

Close by in Wrights Lane which, in 1858, according to Leigh Hunt, led round a pleasant sequestered corner into the fields, and built about the same time as the Square, once stood Scarsdale House, later the site of Pontings Store. It is thought to have been erected by the second Earl of Scarsdale, related by marriage to the Rich family of Holland House; his father, the first Earl, a staunch and intensely loyal subject of Charles I, is recorded as having 'become so much mortified by the execution of Charles I, that he clothed himself in sack-cloth, had his grave dug and lay in it every Friday morning exercising himself in pious meditation and prayer'.

Another big house, only a short distance from the Square on the east side, opposite the gates of Kensington Palace, was Colby House, built in the early 1700s by a Commissioner in the Victualling Office, Sir Thomas Colby, Bart. Attached was a large garden and, inside, the house was furbished in a lavish manner with a most elegant grand staircase and walls displaying a number of painted goddesses and a full length figure of Justice, while the ceiling in the hall depicting landscapes and the four seasons was a replica of one found at Herculaneum.

Although reputedly of a miserly disposition, besides spending large sums on this decoration, he did not hesitate to adorn the walls with fine examples of artists of the Italian and Dutch schools as well, even so his parsimony seems to have brought about his premature death.

One night, having taken a draught to produce a sweat, he went to bed, but woke up to remember that he had left the key of the wine-cellar on the parlour table and, the fearful thought passing through his mind that the servants would deprive him of a bottle of his excellent port, nothing would do but that he retrieve the key. So, still sweating profusely, he felt his way down the stairs, found the key and returned to bed. But the cold night air was too much for his heated condition and he died, presumably of pneumonia, and having made no will his vast fortune of over £200,000 was divided between five or six day labourers, his nearest relatives.

*

A century was to pass before the development of the north side of the High Street as a residential area began with the building of Lower Phillimore Place and Hornton Street by William Phillimore between 1787 and 1790.

Westwards beyond the Earls Court Road there were no houses and the road to Hammersmith was flanked by hedges and fields, with a toll gate close to the entrance to Holland House to control the traffic into Kensington from the west. Then, following the popularity of Phillimore Place, the houses of which were snapped up rapidly, thoughts turned towards the further development of the south side of the road. Hence Edwardes Square, so called after the family name of Lord Kensington, the owner of the land, began to emerge just west of the Earls Court Road opposite the gateway to Holland House.

Concerning its original purpose, many suggestions have been put forward. One was that it was built by a Frenchman for the officers of Napoleon's Army in preparation for its successful invasion of England; another that it was to house *émigrés* from the Revolution; and a third that the price of the houses would not be beyond the purses of the widows of Waterloo. But apart from the fact that building was started by a Frenchman, Louis Léon Changeur—but not before 1811 when the threat of an invasion had passed—and that many of the early occupants had foreign names, none of these theories holds water and the development could only have been for profit.

Changeur, a builder, dealer and chapman[1] of Hammersmith, a man in his thirties, whose English was indifferent, obtained the right by a signed agreement with Lord Kensington to build on eleven acres south of the main road, but as he went bankrupt in 1812 he quickly faded out and, at one time, Daniel Sutton, who forsook his carpet manufacturing to become a property dealer, bought up half the houses of the Square.

The first to be erected were the twenty-five imposing houses of Earls Terrace which screens the Square from the busy High Street; a carriage way was also made with a porter's lodge at the entrance and exit and lanthorns surmounted the piers of the gateways. Both the lodges and the empty lanthorns are still evident and in good repair.

As for the Square itself, the eastern side was the first to be built and given the name of Kensington Place East; this was followed by the western side—Kensington Place West—and, finally, stables and mews were sited on the southern side, the whole being completed in 1819. At the same time the Horticultural Society laid out its first experimental garden immediately behind the then Kensington Place West.

Although the houses are considerably smaller than those of Kensington Square, the garden, laid out in 1820, covers a much larger area and from its earliest beginnings stringent rules and regulations were set out for its upkeep and for the general orderliness of the Square. The terms of an Act of Parliament passed in July 1819 dealt with such subjects as the paving, lighting, watering and planting, and twenty-two Trustees, selected from the residents, were appointed to implement the Act.

'Do-it-yourself' was the order of the day, for the Trustees had to put

---

[1] An itinerant dealer.

up lamp-posts and provide lamps; the upkeep of railings, paths, lodges, etc., the sinking of wells and the disposal of rubbish were also their responsibility; able-bodied watchmen by night and inspectors by day had to be enlisted, instructions given for their arming and posting and payment made; in the event of the arrest by the watchmen of vagabonds, malefactors and rogues, the vandals were to be taken speedily to the watch-house of the Parish of St. Mary Abbots.

In their turn, the Trustees issued a set of rules to comply with the Act of Parliament. Daily, before nine o'clock in the morning, all tenants had to cleanse the footway in front of their houses and in default thereof pay a fine of five shillings; no beating of carpets or dumping of rubbish outside the house (it is a pity that this rule does not still obtain throughout the Borough) was permitted, nor could a horse be broken or exercised in the garden, neither could it or any other beast be led on the pathway, nor swine allowed to roam about; the obstruction of pathways by goods or wares was strictly forbidden; and, finally, any person offending the aforesaid by-laws was liable to a fine of up to £5 or, in default of payment, hard labour not exceeding three months! There was also a clause permitting the Trustees to exclude offensive residents from the garden but 'generously' exempting those excluded from paying the garden rent during their period of banishment.

Among the first residents with foreign names were William à Beckett, the lawyer who drew up the constitution of the Square, Augustino Aglio, the artist and lithographer, Foscolo, Italian poet and dandy, Foreaux, a clerk in the War Office, and de Franco, a wine merchant. The district was also popular with naval officers on half pay, possibly because of its proximity to the road to Portsmouth; Sampson Coysganne, former purser of Nelson's flagship, H.M.S. *Foudroyant*, and Joseph Bazalgette, lamed by wounds received in fighting the French, were two naval officers to frequent the area in the early days. At about the same time, Mrs. Elizabeth Inchbald, actress, novelist and dramatist, occupied No. 4 Earls Terrace.

Of the later residents, Leigh Hunt lived in No. 32 Edwardes Square for eleven years from 1840, Sir Henry Newbolt, the poet, in No. 23 Earls Terrace, and George du Maurier at No. 12; G. K. Chesterton's first home after his marriage in 1901 was No. 1 the Square, but the plaque commemorating him is at 11 Warwick Gardens where he lived for some years.

From all accounts the residents enjoyed a life of peace and quiet until 1908, two years before the leases of the houses were due to fall. Then the hard-fought 'Battle for Edwardes Square' began, a contest whose issue was in doubt for several months.

In 1908, a firm, Allen Bros., bought the freehold of Earls Terrace and the Square garden with the intention of pulling down the former and rebuilding both on its site and on the site of the garden, with the result that most of the houses in the Terrace were vacated by March 1910, while those in the Square began to empty. On 21 May the fight was on, when Allen Bros closed the gates into the garden and also the carriage way of the Terrace; immediately the residents and the Borough Council went into action.

The Chairman of the Garden Committee, who happened to be away at that moment, telegraphed: 'Keep possession of remaining gate; take gate off hinges if necessary; employ watchmen day and night to guard', and the Council, disputing Allen Bros' right to erect them, tore down each night the barricades put up by the firm by day.

Events then moved swiftly. An injunction was applied for to restrain the Company from closing the garden gates; on 26 July the case was heard in the Courts and, the decision having been given in favour of the Garden Committee, the barricades were removed and the garden reopened to the residents. However, the Company was not prepared to surrender lightly and appealed against the judgement in November; when this was dismissed, a further appeal was made to the House of Lords, which was equally unsuccessful, final judgement being given on 22 January 1912.

Celebration night was Edwardes Square's greatest hour. Fifty cartloads of timber were taken into the garden and well saturated with oil to make a forty-foot-high bonfire. At 9 p.m., when all the windows were lit, some with fairy lamps, it was set ablaze to the beating of gongs and cheers of the residents, who later processed round the Square with a pipe band at their head.

To-day, the Square retains an air of peace and order, unlike the war days when the garden was a barrage balloon site. In the summer months the small front gardens of the houses on the east and west sides are full of colour, and fortunately the Victorian lamp-posts have not as yet been replaced. The Square garden, by atmosphere and appearance, might well be situated around some large mansion in a rural county. Beautifully kept with closely mown lawns, brilliant flower beds, stately trees and a large variety of shrubs, it also has two tennis courts and a play area for children. On the south side is 'The Temple', or gardener's lodge, designed in the form of a Grecian Temple with Doric columns on both north and south façades; a relic of the past is the hand pump against the southern wall.

*

'Do you suffer from acidity, heartburn or any form of phthises? If so, come to Campden Hill and take the waters.' This might well have been the advertisement for that part of the Hill covered by Aubrey House, Aubrey Walk and Campden Hill Square, for an analysis of the mineral springs and wells in that area taken in 1711 recorded that 'the water was computed to be most appropriate to take off the Acidity of the Juices and Blood, and to Incarnate and suit in Heartburns and some sort of Phthises and may agree with the Cold and Phlegmatick best'.

For the last 150 years Campden Hill Square, previously Hanson's and then Notting Hill Square, has stood on this site, the first seven houses going up in 1827 after Mr. Hanson had purchased the property four years previously; one hundred years later the tenants numbered forty, mostly professional men, retired officers, clergymen and single ladies.

On a warm Sunday afternoon, the Square has a distinct atmosphere of tranquillity and J. M. W. Turner, the famous painter, must have found it so since, perhaps during his early years at Hammersmith or possibly in later life when he could escape from Queen Anne Street to his hide-out in Chelsea, he used to sit under a tree on the south side of the Square garden to paint the sunsets. The plaque recording the great artist's visits was hung on the tree but when that succumbed during a storm in 1909, the plaque was transferred to another nearby. Originally, a resident was appointed as 'Agent or surveyor of the owner of the lawn or area in the centre of the Square', but for more than a century a garden committee has been in charge and has kept a full record of its activities.[1]

To the north the Square dips deeply to the busy Holland Park Avenue, or Via Trinobantia and later Via Strata of Roman times, over which the legions marched to and from Londinium. Evidence that some habitation may also have existed then is the discovery of Roman graves just north of Campden Hill. It is hard to imagine this road to have been impassable at times because of the streams that raced across it in bad weather, and that in 1788 a gentleman in his carriage had to be rescued with much difficulty when the column of water was so high and strong that 'it bore up both it and the horses'.

Backing on the houses on the south side is Aubrey Walk leading to one of Kensington's jewels—Aubrey House or Notting Hill House as it was known until the middle of the nineteenth-century. Although doubts

[1] A unique custom was instituted in 1926, one peculiar to this Square alone, in the display of lighted candles by each householder in every window of his house on Christmas Eve, and new arrivals are made aware of their responsibilities on taking up residence.

exist as to when it was actually built, it would seem that it was probably about 1720, with wings added in the 1750s before Lady Mary Cope, youngest daughter of the second Earl of Argyll, bought the lease of it in 1767. It is from her journals that one obtains a fascinating picture of the village of Kensington and its environs in the early years of George III's reign.

That the house was then in the depths of the country is shown by Lady Mary's account of the wanderings of 'Miss Pelham', her black and white cow (named after one of her friends), which 'took a frisk this morning, got out of my grounds and went very nearly as far as London before I heard of her. I believe she thinks my Place too retired, for she was found among a great herd of cattle.' She also recorded the occasion when, to her annoyance, the hunt streamed across her garden to disappear into the grounds of Holland House, the boundaries of which marched with her property.

Following Lady Mary's departure in 1788, the house was let on two occasions as a school, until it was bought in 1873 by William Cleverly Alexander, the banker, who died in 1916, since when it remained in the family until 1972 when the last Miss Alexander died.

A connoisseur of high repute and a discriminating collector, William Alexander built up a priceless collection of paintings, furniture and ceramics. The portraits, landscapes and seascapes and religious subjects represent the works of many famous artists of the Dutch, Flemish, Italian and English Schools from Anthonis Mor in the sixteenth century to Whistler in the nineteenth, while much of the Chinese and Japanese porcelain can now be seen in the Victoria and Albert Museum. Fortunately, what must be among the choicest private collections in the country is not to be dispersed but is to become the property of the nation.

*

Beyond the southern wall of the Aubrey House garden and as far as the cul-de-sac, Campden Hill, a number of mansions with extensive grounds were built between 1812–20 as a further development of the Phillimore Estate, begun some twenty-five years before by the erection of the houses of Phillimore Place in the High Street between the old Public Library adjacent to the Town Hall and Holland Walk.

Whereas the large residences were occupied by peers of the realm, William Phillimore had developed Phillimore Place to meet the great demand for houses among those lower down the social scale, and by 1801 no less than sixty-two houses made up Lower and Upper Phillimore

Place. Elegant though they were, they did not meet with the approval of George III who, when passing by in his coach, is purported to have exclaimed, 'Dishclout Row',[1] and to have pulled down the blinds. At No. 6 lived the great-grandfather of G. K. Chesterton, Charles Chesterton, agent to the Phillimore Estates in Kensington and founder of the firm Chesterton & Son who still practise in the same capacity. Further west No. 29 and later No. 24 were occupied by the celebrated artist, David Wilkie (1785–1841), who first came into prominence with his picture, 'The Village Politicians', exhibited successfully in the Royal Academy in 1806 and sold to Lord Mansfield for the absurd price of thirty guineas. On the death of Sir Thomas Lawrence in 1830 he was appointed Painter in Ordinary to the King.

Among his many works that hang in the National Galleries of London and Scotland, in Windsor Castle and in private collections, is 'Chelsea Pensioners receiving the Gazette of the Battle of Waterloo', on display in Apsley House, commissioned by the Duke of Wellington in 1816, and for which Wilkie was paid £1,200 guineas counted out in bank notes. The Duke, accompanied by the Duke and Duchess of Bedford, General Lord Lynedoch, his old friend of Peninsular days, and Lady Argyll visited Wilkie by appointment to discuss the painting, and Wilkie made arrangements for his mother and sister to watch the arrival of the national hero from the parlour windows of No. 29. In a letter to Benjamin Haydon, the artist and his lifelong friend, Wilkie wrote of his reaction to that afternoon: 'The sensation of this event quite unhinged us for the rest of the day. Nothing was talked of but the Duke of Wellington and the chair he happened to sit upon has been carefully selected out and has been decorated with ribbon and there is talk of having an inscription upon it, descriptive of the honour it had received.'

On 1 June 1841, when returning from a visit to the Near East and shortly after the ship left Malta, David Wilkie died and was buried at sea within sight of the Rock of Gibraltar.

*

The first stately home of Campden Hill to be built, in 1812, was Bute House, occupied by the Marquis of Bute between 1830 and 1842;[2] its

---

[1] His term 'Dishclout' referred to the drapery ornamentations decorating the façades.

[2] Demolished and rebuilt in 1914. The census of 1851 records that of the sixty-two persons living in Bute House, Thornwood Lodge, Holly Lodge and Bedford Lodge, forty-two were servants, mostly from the West Country, East Anglia and Kent. Four years later, when the Duke of Argyll lived in Bedford Lodge, twenty-seven servants were employed for a family of eight.

name was later changed to Blundell House, or No. 2 Campden Hill as it is to-day. The remainder of the houses, Thornwood Lodge, Holly Lodge and Argyll Lodge, have disappeared and Queen Elizabeth College has been built on their sites.

It was in Holly Lodge that Lord Macaulay spent the last three years of his life (1856–9) after moving from his chambers in Albany. Here he could take a delight in his large garden, which extended as far as Duchess of Bedford Walk, or spend hours working in his spacious library, from the windows of which he was able to gaze on the lilacs, laburnums, rhododendrons and the rich green lawns which were his special pride and joy. Dandelions, however, were anathema to him and in a letter to his favourite young niece, he wrote: 'I have no friends near me, but my books and my flowers, and no enemies but these execrable dandelions. I thought I was rid of the villains; but the day before yesterday, when I got up and looked out of my window, I could see five or six of their great, impudent, flaring yellow faces turned up at me. . . . How I enjoyed their destruction! Is it Christianlike to hate a dandelion so savagely?'

A side of his character not always recognized was his deep love for children and their company and his ability to enter into their realm of imagination. Much of his correspondence must have been devoted to them and he never tired of playing their childish games—cops and robbers, lions and tigers and the like—with newspaper dens erected behind the sofa; nor did he hesitate to expend valuable time listening to their troubles, to entertain them with toys and treats, and to watch their careers with interest and advice.

But his generosity and kindness were not confined only to the young. The £20,000 he received in royalties for his *History of England* had relieved him of any financial anxieties he may have had and his purse was ever open to those who he felt were in need. The applications for help were constant and such was his consideration for those in trouble that he found difficulty in refusing them. Twenty-five pounds to a clergyman, to a lady in distress £130 over a period of a few months, and to an impecunious author, who begged a few guineas, the gift of £100. Besides his gifts of money to the needy, few things gave him more pleasure than to entertain in his own house. His guests ranged from learned Fellows of Trinity College, Cambridge at a substantial dinner, to schoolboys for a less elaborate but no less substantial meal. On the Wednesday after Christmas 1859, he died peacefully in his library with the latest copy of the *Cornhill Magazine* open beside him, and was buried in Westminster Abbey close to the statue of Addison in Poets' Corner. A plaque denoting

Macaulay's occupation of Holly Lodge, the first ever to be approved by the London County Council, can be seen on the wall of that part of Queen Elizabeth College on which the house once stood.

*

Because of its general rural character and its quiet surroundings, such was the attraction of Campden Hill that another large house—Bedford Lodge— was erected in 1815, between Holly Lodge and Holland Walk, and became the residence of the Duke of Bedford three years later: here he lived until his death in 1839, after which his widow continued to occupy it for a further fifteen years.

The Duchess,[1] famous for her entertaining, did much to beautify the property by adding an immense drawing room enhanced by superb white gold panelling brought from a French château, and by laying out the formal garden with the assistance of Sir Edward Landseer, the popular Victorian artist.

The eighth Duke of Argyll, the next occupant, renamed the house 'Argyll Lodge' and thus it remained for fifty years until the first Lord Phillimore took up residence in 1901 and altered the name to Cam House, after Cam in Gloucestershire where his ancestors once lived. The Duke, a prominent member of the Government as Lord Privy Seal and later Postmaster General, was an enthusiastic ornithologist and it was largely due to the variety of birds he saw in the garden when inspecting the property that he decided to buy it.[2]

The last private owner of Cam House was Mrs. St. George, a wealthy American lady, who, like the Duchess of Bedford before her, reconstructed the house and garden to her own design in 1931, employing three hundred men continuously for nine months. Giant new entrance gates, lit with electricity instead of gas, the bulbs set in the tails of decorative fish, replaced the old; an iron studded door from the demolished Newgate prison was installed at the entrance to Holland Walk and figures of St. George and the dragon figured on the exterior of the house. The interior, too, was furnished in lavish style with superb furniture and tapestries. The walls of the drawing room were decorated with fifteenth-century painted leather panels depicting scenes from the Old Testament, while the Gothic chimney piece of the same period displayed St. George slaying the dragon. Since Sir William Orpen, the Academician, was a

[1] Her name is remembered in 'The Duchess of Bedford Walk' dominated by the Campden House Gate block of flats, which stands on part of the Duchess's garden.

[2] See page 64.

relation of her husband's, it is not surprising that his works were on view in many of the rooms.

The garden, too, underwent a complete re-design. A fountain filled with coloured lights was constructed on the lawn and a temple erected in the middle of the gardens. A cottage was also built for Mrs. St. George's daughter and, to make room for all these additions, instead of cutting down the trees, the larger ones were uprooted and replanted in the grounds of Holland House.

Then, just before the outbreak of the Second World War, Mrs. St. George died and Cam House, on which so much care and money had been spent, came to a sad end when it was requisitioned. Neglected and severely damaged over the years, it fell into such disrepair as to be declared a dangerous building and was pulled down in 1955.

*

Next door to Aubrey House on the east side stood Moray Lodge, which was built in 1817 and was to become the headquarters of the 'Moray Minstrels' when Arthur J. Lewis, the founder of the Arts Club, moved in during 1862. A wealthy bachelor with a profound interest in the arts, Lewis found in Moray Lodge the surroundings and atmosphere he required to entertain his friends, Saturday being the special day when he regaled them with oysters and beer, while they enjoyed billiards and croquet or played music and sang. The company was an assorted one, and many famous men in all walks of life were pleased 'to go into Bohemia for a night', as Holman Hunt puts it, among them William Thackeray, Charles Dickens, Anthony Trollope, John Millais, James Leighton, Arthur Sullivan, George du Maurier and Tattersall, the horse dealer, besides other personalities of the day. Theatricals were encouraged and it was at Moray Lodge that *Box and Cox* was first produced with George du Maurier as 'Bouncer'.

In 1867, Arthur Lewis married Miss Kate Terry, the actress, by whom he had four daughters, the eldest being Kate Terry Lewis, who later married Frank Gielgud in 1892. Except for a short interval the Lewises continued to live in Moray Lodge until it was sold in 1899. Nevertheless, it was to figure prominently in the news three years later during the ceremonies for the coronation of King Edward VII, solving a problem that appeared to be insoluble and averting a crisis.

With the arrival of so many crowned heads, princes and Heads of State from all over the world, accommodation in London was at a premium and the Lord Chamberlain's office was hard put to it to satisfy the needs of so many distinguished people. This was particularly difficult in the case of the Maharajah of Jaipur who arrived with a retinue of two hundred, all of whom had to be found a place near Buckingham Palace, a proximity to which the Indian Princes attached much importance.

To Mr. Percy Armytage fell the responsibility of finding a house big enough for this large party, and in his book *By the Clock of St. James'*, he describes the many difficulties he had to face. First, a cow—and it was vital that it should be a white shorthorn—had to be produced to provide milk for His Royal Highness; second, because he was a strict Hindu, the Maharajah was not allowed to drink water conveyed through an iron pipe; and thirdly, the area had to be sufficiently large to create temporary accommodation for the large number of staff and servants. By unexpected good fortune Armytage's problems were overcome when he discovered that Moray Lodge was vacant at that moment, that there was a well in the garden, grazing for the cow in the paddock and sufficient room for the temporary buildings. The situation was thus saved and everybody much relieved. Although Moray Lodge continued in private ownership until 1940, like so many big houses it was then requisitioned and the tennis court used for a barrage balloon site. After serving as a hostel, a hospital for Civil Servants and as accommodation for visiting colonial students, the L.C.C. demolished it in 1955.

*

Close by and built in the same year as Moray Lodge, was Thorpe Lodge,[1] as it came to be known, bought in 1904 by Captain Montagu Norman, better remembered as Governor of the Bank of England for twenty-four years (1920–44), and as Lord Norman of St. Clerc after his retirement. His well-known figure with its pointed beard and broad-brimmed hat was often to be encountered on Campden Hill for almost half a century.

Since no money had been spent on the upkeep for many years, the property was in a deplorable condition and Montagu Norman exercised his remarkable artistic capabilities to the full in reinstating the house and garden. An expert in timber, he made considerable use of a wide assortment of wood from all over the world, some of which he had collected during his travels, while the outstanding feature in the Music Room was a fine chimney piece, once in the possession of the Medici family and brought from Florence. To rehabilitate the garden a large number of

[1] H. T. Wells. R.A. (1828–93), the painter of the well-known picture of the Archbishop of Canterbury and the Lord Chamberlain informing Queen Victoria of her accession to the Throne in 1837, occupied the house in 1885.

trees and shrubs, such as tulip, bay, magnolia and wistaria, were planted and special attention was paid to the laying out of the lawns, the overall effect being most attractive.

One of Norman's characteristics was his abhorrence of publicity and the story is told that when the Press besieged the reception after his wedding in 1933, he and his wife escaped their attentions by scaling the garden wall, racing across the gardens of Moray Lodge and disappearing down Holland Walk to their waiting car in Phillimore Gardens.

Though threatened with demolition by the London County Council in 1948 in order to make room for multi-storied flats, Thorpe Lodge did not go the same way as some of the other houses on Campden Hill, due to sturdy opposition to the scheme by the local residents. Instead, agreement was reached with the Council that Holland Park School should be built and the house and garden preserved as part of it, so that today it houses the library of the school, opened in 1958.

One other house on the hill deserves mention and that is Elm Lodge, adjacent to Thorpe Lodge, the house of Sir James McGrigor (1770–1858), the founder of the Royal Army Medical Corps, whose memory is retained by two large statues, one outside the Corps' Officers Mess on Millbank, the other at Marischal College, Aberdeen, and also by a stained glass window in St. Mary's Church, Kensington.

After long campaigning with the Duke of Wellington as a surgeon in the Army, he could have set up in practice in London, but instead agreed to become the Director General of the Army Medical Department. He held the appointment thirty-eight years and entirely reorganized the medical services to the lasting benefit of all who have served in the Army since.

*

The hot and dusty traveller of the eighteenth and nineteenth centuries on his way from London to Kensington would always find a convenient stop to quench his thirst at The Bell and Horns, an inn or public house standing on the western corner of the junction of the Brompton and Cromwell Roads, at which point the former turns south-west to join the Fulham Road. It was certainly there in 1745 and, though much altered from time to time, its stucco façade was standing in 1914, until it was pulled down for the erection of the Rembrandt Hotel and other buildings in the vicinity then under construction.

Beyond the Bell and Horns on the west lay Harrison's nursery,[1] while

[1] See page 56.

as late as the middle of the nineteenth century, the Brompton Road was so narrow 'that you might easily jump across it with the elms, limes, poplars and aspen boughs forming a green vista'.

To-day all that area, west and south-west as far as Pelham Street, is occupied by the dignified, elegant houses of Alexander and Thurloe Squares, so called after the Thurloe and Alexander families, of whom the latter were responsible for the construction.

The story of the Thurloe estates begins in the time of Cromwell, when John Thurloe, secretary and intimate friend of the Protector, and highly efficient chief of the Intelligence Department in 1655, was granted by his master, although there is no written proof, a parcel of land in Brompton in recognition of and in gratitude for his devoted service.

Whether the story is true or not, there can be no doubt that John Thurloe knew his Brompton well, for he was also a friend of the Protector's fourth son, Henry, who may have resided for a time in Hale House which, in later years, became Cromwell House and from which the Cromwell Road, driven through the site of the house in 1852–3, derives its name.

But it was with his grandson, John Thurloe Brace, the son of one of William Thurloe's daughters, that the family's real connection with Brompton began in 1713, when he married a widow, Anna Browne, who made over to him 'all that messuage or tenement situate in Brompton and Kensington'. On their deaths the property passed to their son, Harris Thurloe Brace, who died a bachelor in 1799 and in turn left it to his godson and step-nephew, John Alexander, the original developer of the Thurloe Estate.

Because in 1808 that part of Brompton was countryside and renowned for its clean air and fertility, emphasized by the number of nurseries that had flourished there for one hundred years or more, it was obviously a place to attract prospective house buyers and, with the intention of developing the area, John Alexander acquired from Lord Kensington the triangle made by the junction of the Fulham and Old Brompton Roads. But he had to wait until 1822, when the leases of the nurseries were about to fall due, before he could employ George Basevi as his surveyor and architect.

George Basevi (1794–1845), cousin of Benjamin Disraeli, was probably Sir John Soane's most brilliant pupil and one of the leading architects of the day. Among his many works, he designed and supervised the building of a number of the great houses in Belgrave Square, collaborated with Sidney Smirke in the erection of the old Conservative Club in St. James's, laid out the delightful Pelham Crescent and other properties of the Smith's Charity Estates[1] and was also the architect of the Fitz-William Museum, Cambridge, begun in 1837. His untimely end came in October 1845 when, while supervising work on Ely Cathedral, he fell to his death from the scaffolding.

The houses of Alexander Square, which in fact is not a Square at all but comprises two terraces with a private carriage way in front and, beyond, narrow gardens separating the property from the Brompton Road, was completed between 1827-30 by James Bonnin, the builder who also worked with Basevi in the development of the Smith's Charity Estate; those in South Street (now South Terrace) were not finished until 1839 by which time John Alexander had died, leaving his son, Henry Browne Alexander, to continue with the building of Thurloe Square, the houses of which are somewhat larger than Basevi's original and date from 1843.[2]

But, Henry Browne Alexander was not content merely with the land he owned by inheritance, for in 1838 he purchased further plots, adjoining the Cromwell Road opposite the Natural History Museum, together with more land west of Queen's Gate as far as the Gloucester Road. In 1859 the monster houses in that area began to go up to meet 'the extraordinary demand for first class houses in this singularly favoured spot'.

At first well suited for bringing up the large families of the mid-Victorian era, as times passed and families of ten and twelve were no longer popular, so it became more difficult to find desirable tenants for such large houses. Nevertheless the freeholders were determined to maintain an air of respectability even if the houses were to be used for multiple occupation. Thus when, in 1906, a lady applied to turn her house in Queen's Gate Gardens into a boarding establishment, the lease was reluctantly granted with the provisos that no cabs be called by voice or whistle and that all windows be so curtained as to make it impossible to see anybody seated inside.

[1] Henry Smith, a salter by trade and an Alderman of the City of London who, in his early youth, was whipped out of Mitcham for begging, was a man of some wealth. In 1628, he made over practically the whole of his estate to 'Smith's Charity' to relieve the sufferings of Christians held prisoner by the North African pirates and as a result, approximately eight acres of farmland south of the present Cromwell Road opposite the Natural History Museum, were purchased by the trustees. A century later, when no application for funds had been made for many years, an Act of Parliament enabled the trustees to use the estate for the benefit of the parishes of Kensington, Chelsea and St. Margaret's, Westminster.

[2] 'The Hoop and Toy', once a public house and now a restaurant, standing at the western extremity of Thurloe Place, goes back to the late fifteenth century when an elm tree grew through the roof of the stables and 250 years later steps led up to a seat erected in one of the trees in the garden. But these curiosities have long since disappeared: the premises were rebuilt in 1926 and have altered considerably since.

Of course, the installation of the South Kensington and Gloucester Road stations of the Metropolitan Railway in 1860 brought some disruption to private houses and part of the Alexander estate went by compulsory purchase, but not to such an extent as to cause severe alteration to the splendid Alexander and Thurloe Squares, though residents of the latter took the strongest exception to the South Kensington Station in particular and to the railway line in general.

But it is not only for the squares and great houses they built that the name of the Alexander family will be remembered, it is also for the munificence of Henry Browne Alexander's son and heir, William Henry. Distinguished for his wealth and liberality, in 1899 he presented the nation with a permanent home for the National Portrait Galley adjacent to Trafalgar Square.

*

Concurrently with the emergence of Alexander Square, houses began to appear on the opposite side of the road in what was to become Brompton Square. The developer was William Farlar, a citizen of Brompton who, it is thought, also employed Bonnin as his builder.

In its early days, it is said not to have enjoyed a very high reputation and though it was much favoured by the stage, W. J. Loftie, in 1880, wrote somewhat disparagingly of the Square, 'It does not look inviting and has, so far as I can gather, entertained no inhabitants of any great distinction except Shirley Brooks, Editor of *Punch* (No. 22).'[1]

When first constructed between 1822–30, it comprised just the two sides with a garden between them, the northern end, leading into open fields, being left open until the semi-circle of houses, built at a later date, partly sealed off that end.

From 1826 and until the horse and carriage gave way to other methods of transport, the jingling of harness, the rattling of wheels and clip of hooves on the cobblestones must have often woken from their slumbers those occupants of houses at the north-eastern corner of the Square, for the delightful next-door cul-de-sac of Rutland Mews was once the stables and quarters for coachmen in the service of the gentry of the Square.

Although the area was badly bombed in the war, some of the houses were untouched, as also were relics of the past, for example posts to which the horses were tethered for grooming and, in one drawing-room, the alcoves for hanging the harness. Normally one of the most sequestered

[1] Henry Luttrell (1765–1851) lived at No. 4., Stephane Mallarmé, the poet at No. 6 in 1863, and Francis Place, political reformer, at No. 21 between 1833 and 1851.

spots in London, the tranquillity of the Mews has been interrupted on occasions by film directors, cameras and persons in strange costumes assembled for the shooting of scenes from three well-known and very different films: *Round the World in 80 Days*, *Genevieve* and *The Killing of Sister George*.

To-day the Square offers an uneven and somewhat untidy appearance, since some of the façades have been altered and indiscriminate additions made to many of the elevations. But such comments do not apply to several of the interiors which must rank with some of the most beautiful in London.

CHAPTER FOUR

FRUIT, FLOWERS AND FROLICS

A T THE time of William IV's accession in 1830, Kensington was still separated from London. Then and since the latter half of the seventeenth century, whether, according to one's means, one walked, rode a horse or sat back in a carriage from London along the Kensington, Brompton or Fulham Roads during the spring and summer months, the air would be fragrant with the scent of flowers or fruit blossom from the market and nursery gardens that ranged as far as and beyond the boundary between Kensington and its neighbours Fulham and Hammersmith. On the way one would meet carts loaded with vegetable produce, and women carrying flat baskets of strawberries on their heads, proceeding towards the capital.

For nearly two centuries Kensington was the garden centre of England for, besides supplying the City of London with fruit, vegetables and flowers, many of the great parks and gardens throughout England were designed by the nursery owners and planted by them with trees, shrubs and plants grown in their own nurseries.[1]

Among the many who made this famous horticultural enclave, the most prominent names must be those of George London (d. 1714), Henry Wise (1656–1738) and William Curtis (1746–98), all of whom offered so much, both in the practical and scientific sense, and whose contributions to horticulture at its best are still to be seen to-day.

By far the largest was the Brompton Park nursery lying on the south side of the Kensington Road between Queen's Gate and Gloucester Road and stretching as far as the Brompton Road. Originally opened in 1681, when the celebrated partnership of George London and Henry Wise[2] came into being, in 1694 it covered over one hundred acres of trees, evergreens and shrubs, potagères, melonières and culinary gardens,

[1] In 1820 there were 400 acres of farm land and market gardens in Kensington, chiefly in Earls Court, the largest being that of Mr. Hutchins (213 acres).

[2] The portrait of Henry Wise, gardener to Queen Anne, by Sir Godfrey Kneller, hangs in the Royal Palace at Kew.

seeds, roots, bulbs, slips for the flower garden and a half-mile-long wall for the cultivation of vines of all kinds. By 1705 Bowack could describe it as 'a nursery so much famed all over the Kingdom for nursery plants and fine greens of all sorts which supply most of the nobility and gentry of England'. From the mercenary angle, he added that if the plants of the nursery were valued at one penny each, the total would be in the region of £40,000, a prodigious sum for those days.

Business was brisk and the London–Wise partnership a highly successful one, for Wise was also a practical gardener and ready to use a spade himself. In the early days, while he and his assistants tended the garden, London covered fifty or sixty miles in a day on horseback, visiting, taking orders from or giving advice to the gentry on their country estates, and was away for as long as a month at a time.

Longleat, Blenheim, Chatsworth and Castle Howard are some of the glorious gardens laid out by these two experts, the last three being the responsibility of Wise himself. Evidence of the extent to which the Brompton Park nursery could supply at any one time is a consignment to Blenheim of 18,000 yellow crocus, 4,600 tulips, 5,100 hyacinth and 100 damask roses.

After Wise's marriage to Patience Banks, it became necessary to find larger accommodation for their growing family, and to this end, he moved to Brompton Park House, a mansion of twenty rooms situated at the south corner of the nursery, around which the South Kensington or Victoria and Albert Museum was erected. For his retirement he also bought the Priory Estate on the outskirts of Warwick, to which he moved in 1727 and, having laid out the charming garden, he died there in 1733. On a stone slab in the floor at the west end of the beautiful Collegiate Church of St. Mary's, Warwick, the names of Henry and Patience are just legible. Sixty years later the Brompton Park nursery, by then reduced in size, was in the hands of Messrs. Gray & Co who turned it over to forest and fruit trees which they continued to supply to the gardens and parks throughout the country.[1]

Two other nurseries in the same area were those of Robert Furber, immediately adjacent to Brompton Park on the west, and Mr. Kirk's in Brompton Park Lane on what was once part of the Cromwell House estate. While the former is noted not only for his skill as a nurseryman but also for his superbly illustrated *Twelve Months of Flowers* (1730) and his catalogue of fruits (1732), the latter largely concentrated on fruits of all kinds, for it is said that one hundred different varieties of apple grew in

[1] The nursery was still there in 1850.

the garden and, in the summer, swelling bunches of luscious muscadine grapes hung on a nine-hundred-foot-long wall.

Opposite Wise's house, across the Cromwell Road, lay Samuel Harrison's nursery of twenty-seven acres which, until the owner, Henry Browne Alexander, acquired it to build Thurloe Square, had been in the Harrison family (they were tenants) for over 130 years. Bad debts seem to have caught up with the unfortunate Samuel who went bankrupt in 1831 and he was forced out of business. Nevertheless, where the houses of Thurloe Square and South Kensington Station now stand, Harrison's orchard and tree nursery once bordered the south side of the road to Brompton Village.

Within a stone's throw of Harrison's property, on the site of the Brompton Hospital[1] and from Sydney Place to Selwood Terrace, a series of nurseries occupied the north side of the Fulham Road: insignificant in size as compared with Brompton Park they were none the less as important from the scientific aspect.

Coming from the direction of London the first, comprising six acres, was that of Thomas Gibbs, seedsman and nurseryman to the Board of Agriculture, whose shop stood at the corner of Half Moon Street, Piccadilly, and whose name still appears in the rate books of 1841. A horticultural and agricultural experimental nursery, it was divided into small plots containing every vegetable known to farming and a section was devoted to growing wheat, barley, roots for cattle and a variety of grasses to determine the best for different types of meadow, grassland and crop rotation. But if one was looking for lettuces in large quantities one went further down the road to Mr. Rubergall's nursery on the corner of Selwood Terrace[2] where Rubergall, a Frenchman, had acquired five acres on which, it is claimed, he was the first to grow salads on a commercial scale in England. Opposite, on the other corner of Salad Lane, William Curtis (1746–99), celebrated botanist, entomologist and ornithologist, established his famous botanical garden in 1789.

Born in Alton in Hampshire, William, the son of a Quaker tanner, was destined to become an apothecary and was apprenticed to his apothecary grandfather in the same village. However, John Legge, the ostler at The Crown Inn, fired William with so much enthusiasm for his own wide botanical knowledge that it was decided to send William to London to

---

[1] In 1846 the Foundation Stone was laid by the Prince Consort who arrived on horseback for the ceremony—and the Hospital was officially opened in 1848.

[2] So called after Mr. Selwood, the previous owner of the nursery, but in Rubergall's time it was known as 'Salad Lane'.

concentrate on his studies rather than on herbarising excursions with Legge.

So to London he went, to Mr. Thomas Talwyn, an apothecary of 51 Gracechurch Street,[1] from whom he eventually inherited the business. But Curtis was an apothecary by necessity and not from choice. Botany was his great love and this he combined with the study of entomology and ornithology, his first publication of 1771 being the *Instructions for collecting and preserving insects*.

To realize his dreams, his first venture was a very small rented garden at the bottom of Bermondsey Street[2] for the cultivation of British plants, but when this overflowed he moved to a larger plot in Lambeth Marsh where he assembled 'the largest collection of British plants ever brought together in one place'. But money was scarce and to enable him to carry on his work, he advertised among his friends for subscriptions, opening the garden to members every day except Sunday. Those who subscribed one guinea were allowed to introduce one guest, while those who invested two guineas were permitted two guests and to buy such roots or seeds that Curtis could spare.

Because pollution and building around the garden had a bad effect on the rarer plants, Curtis had to move and, finding exactly what he wanted in the Fulham Road, he transferred his precious specimens. He also built himself a house in Pond Place on Chelsea Common opposite Pelham Crescent, a lonely area since building did not begin in that part of Chelsea until fourteen years after his death in 1799 at the age of fifty-three.

Curtis, in fact, bought two plots of land, three and a half acres for his botanical garden west of Salad Lane and seven acres on the site of Brompton Hospital and behind it for experimental purposes.

On the imposing doorway giving access to the former was inscribed 'Botanical Garden. Open to subscribers' and once inside visitors walked along a gravel pathway on each side of which were parterres exhibiting his large collection of specimens—foreign trees and plants (Alpine and rock), foreign hardies, British herbaceous, bulbs, roots, grasses, aquatics and medicinal herbs. In addition there was a greenhouse for the more delicate exhibits, a library, an aviary and the gardener's cottage.

[1] A plaque was affixed to the site by the Corporation of London to commemorate William Curtis having lived there.
[2] Here he conceived the idea of publishing his great work *Flora Londininsis*. Because sales of it were slow, in 1787 he started *The Botanical Magazine*, one of the most popular periodicals of the day.

On one of the walls of the Lindley Library of the Royal Horticultural Society in Vincent Square hangs a portrait of Curtis by Joseph Wright of Derby in which he is shown as thickly built with an open, full and ruddy face; there is also a delightful miniature of him by Angelica Kauffman in the possession of the Curtis family.

Up to the date of his death, he was immersed in publications on botany and entomology and in a voluminous correspondence with enthusiasts country-wide. Among his more intimate friends and supporters he could count Sir Joseph Banks who travelled around the world with Captain Cook, was President of the Royal Society, Royal adviser to the gardens at Kew and one of the outstanding members of the Council of The Royal Horticultural Society. Renowned in the world of horticulture as he was in the eighteenth-century, Curtis's name is still well remembered to-day because what he began as an individual, The Royal Horticultural Society, has continued as a body.

A year before his death, he took William Salisbury as a partner and he, after Curtis died, removed the business to a vacant plot of land in the vicinity of the present Sloane Street and Cadogan Place.

*

Because the Londoner of the eighteenth century had no cinemas, discothèques and other modern entertainments to amuse him, he often spent his leisure hours on Sundays and summer evenings in the Pleasure Gardens outside the City, one of the first on the list being 'The Florida Gardens of Kensington', adjoining the Hale House Estate.

Situated on the east side of Hogmore Lane (now Gloucester Road), opposite the present Underground Station, the garden had its centre in Stanhope Gardens and was flourishing as early as 1762. Within a pleasant country walk of Hyde Park, Chelsea and Kensington, by 1776 it had gained great popularity with the fashionable gentry of Kensington and the West End and, it is said, with ladies whose character was not entirely beyond reproach. One contemporary remarked that 'its retired situation was well adapted for gallantry and intrigue'! For these reasons alone Protector Cromwell would not have approved of the pewter or brass entrance plaques' poor imitation of his pattern-shilling, some of which carried his effigy as well.

In 1781, Rudolph Heim, a German florist and gardener, bought the lease, using part of the garden to grow flowers, strawberries and cherries, the last named being of the Grafton variety, which he was the first to introduce into England and with such success that his advertisement

boasted that the fruit measured no less than four inches in circum-
ference.

Encouraged by the number of visitors, Heim set about improving the
attractions of his Pleasure Garden by serving refreshments—tea, coffee,
syllabubs and hot rolls—in the secluded arbours; making topiaries of
birds and animals and laying down a bowling green; arranging equestrian
displays, balloon ascents and firework displays; and by engaging an
orchestra subscribed for by the nobility and gentry. And he did a great
deal more as is evident from his advertisement in the Press of 1789.

'R. Heim most respectfully acquaints his Friends and the Public in
general, that his gardens are now opened with great improvements and
elegant addition of a new Long Room which comprises 110 feet in length
suitable for a company of 500 people on any occasion, with five other
rooms over the new erection to entertain smaller parties. A cold larder
will be kept in summer and a man cook to dress dinners at the shortest
notice. Stocks of excellent Wines and Liquors of all kinds are laid in for
the summer.

'R. Heim's entire wish is to give the utmost satisfaction to his Friends
and the Public in general and hopes as soon as possible to provide them
with ice creams.

'N.B. Tea at 6d each with the best of attendance.'

Besides indulging in the Swiss and German cooking, in 'gallantry and
intrigue' or in watching firework displays and other frolics, visitors to the
garden could gather flowers and fruit for a small consideration. Heim
seemed to have struck gold. But whether it was that he was over-ambitious
or that the public lost interest, or because his garden incurred an unsavoury
reputation, he became bankrupt in 1790 and disappeared from the
scene.

Following Heim's departure, the lease was bought by the widowed
Duchess of Gloucester, illegitimate daughter of Sir Edward Walpole,
whose marriage to William Henry, a younger brother of George III, was
one of the causes of the Royal Marriage Act. Here she built Orford Lodge
and lived in it until her death in 1807, after which the property passed
to her daughter, Princess Sophia, who, in turn, sold it to George Canning,
Prime Minister in 1827 and father of the famous Governor-General of
India, 'Clemency' Canning.

To commemorate the Duchess's residence there, Canning renamed the
house Gloucester Lodge and Hogmore Lane was changed to Gloucester
Road.

*

On the wall of Messrs. Hatchard, the booksellers, of 187 Piccadilly, is a tablet stating that the Horticultural Society held its inaugural meeting in a room in the house of Mr. Hatchard on 17 March 1804. Founded by John Wedgwood, son of the well-known Josiah Wedgwood, with the support of William Forsyth, gardener to George III at Kensington Palace and after whom the shrub Forsythia is named, the Society's activities were at first confined to discussions, reading of papers and the publication of 'The Transactions' corresponding to the Society's present-day *Journal*; the fellows, who paid a three-guinea entrance fee and two-guinea subscription, also held an annual dinner.[1] But it soon became obvious that the Society needed something more than a mere meeting place, in other words a garden of its own to grow and exhibit the specimens of its choice.

So, in 1818, one and a half acres were bought immediately west of Edwardes Square.[2] Glass houses and frames were installed, and the Society's plants, boarded out in nearby nurseries, including valuable Chinese specimens housed in the Physic Garden, Chelsea, were brought to Kensington. Simultaneously, a new House of the Society, from which visitors could obtain tickets to view the garden, opened at 21 Regent Street, on the site of the Paramount Cinema, and a further stimulus was added when the Prince Regent agreed to become the President.

The future indeed looked rosy, but within two years the Kensington garden became so overcrowded that it was necessary to find a larger one. After a lengthy search, it was moved to Chiswick where it remained until 1859, by which time the Society had run into a crisis of such proportions, basically financial, that its closure was imminent. Immediate and stringent steps were called for if it was to survive. The garden was given up, as was the house in Regent Street, for a smaller establishment but, disastrously, the splendid library with 1,500 original drawings was sold at Sotheby's for just on £1,000 and, consequently, all the old records were lost.

But help was at hand, for the Prince Consort had by this time become the Society's President and, with his Royal support, the Commissioners of the Great Exhibition of 1851 agreed to lease to the Society twenty-two acres of their land behind the not yet built Albert Hall, and a Council was held at Buckingham Palace in June 1859 to determine the terms of the lease.

Two important factors emerged from the meeting. First, the Com-

---

[1] Ladies were not permitted to attend but were 'kindly' allowed to view the dessert beforehand; this was supplied by the members who vied with one another to produce the finest fruit, pineapples being the most popular.
[2] See p. 39.

missioners agreed to spend £50,000 on surrounding the ground with Italian Arcades[1] open to the public and to execute extensive ground works, provided the Society spent a similar sum on laying out the garden and on erecting a suitable winter garden. Secondly, they agreed to a thirty-one-year lease with a rent in accordance with the revenue.

To meet its obligations, the Society's Council decided to raise the money quickly by issuing Life Memberships and Debentures and here the Royal Family led the way, twelve of its members becoming Life Members, while Queen Victoria subscribed £1,000 and the Prince Consort £500. So great was the response that the required sum was found by the end of the year. An added impetus to the Society's status followed in 1861 when it was decreed that 'by the Will and pleasure of Her Majesty, the Society shall henceforth be called "The Royal Horticultural Society".'

There was, however, some restriction in laying out the garden for nothing could be done without the personal inspection and approval of the Prince Consort, who frequently visited the site and, on one occasion, even ordered an alteration to be paid for out of his own pocket.

The design was formal and Italian in character; a plethora of statues, fountains and bandstands were erected, the main feature being a great cascade flowing into a large rectangular basin, the water being pumped from the largest artesian well in London.

Although not quite finished, the gardens were officially opened on 5 June 1861 by the Prince Consort, in the presence of a large gathering including eight other members of the Royal Family and a distinguished company, among them Lord Palmerston, Disraeli and Gladstone. To mark the occasion, a Wellingtonia was planted and the Prince Consort, on receiving a spade from a bystander, threw some shovelfuls of earth over the roots on behalf of himself and the Princesses, the Princes being allowed to act for themselves.

In his speech, he made his views abundantly clear when he described the garden as 'a valuable attempt . . . to reunite the science and art of gardening to the sister arts of Architecture, Sculpture and Painting', and added, 'Unrivalled opportunities are here offered for the display of works of Art and for the erection of monuments as tributes to great men.' It is hardly surprising, therefore, that many members of the Society were of the opinion that his conception of the purpose and appearance of a Horticultural Society's garden had little in common with theirs.

[1] At one period they constituted part of the eastern and western galleries of the Imperial Institute.

In 1862, the Prince Consort died and the Great Exhibition of that year was staged in the grounds of the Royal Horticultural Society. New buildings were erected at the southern end, horticultural shows were held throughout the year and bands played during the summer months. The result was that with the vast numbers of visitors, revenue increased enormously, although a large proportion of the money was spent on more statuary which led to discontent among the members who disapproved of the figures, as well as the skating rinks and tennis courts.

Worse was to come when it was discovered that the cost of finishing the garden was more than expected and that the Council was unable to meet its commitments to the Commissioners. A lawsuit followed with judgement and costs against the Society and, in 1882, the Commissioners terminated the lease. Happily, the Royal Horticultural Society has gone from strength to strength since those days, but a hundred years were to pass before Kensington renewed its connection with it when the Borough amalgamated with Chelsea, within whose boundaries the Society's Annual Show is staged in the grounds of the Royal Hospital, Chelsea.

*

Stepping out of the lift at the seventh floor of what used to be Derry and Toms and is now Biba's, one hundred feet above the roar of the traffic in the High Street, one is amazed to find oneself suddenly removed, as if by a rub of Aladdin's Lamp, from the bustling crowds of the department store below, to a tranquil scene somewhere in Spain—a miniature Alhambra of waving palm trees, cascading fountains, running water and a blaze of flowers against a background of a minaret overlooking a Moorish building roofed with appropriate red tiles and decorated with an ornamented wrought iron balcony.

This is the Spanish and Fountain Garden, only part of the one and a half acres which make up this unique roof garden, famous and admired throughout the world; though it was laid out only forty years ago and opened by the Earl of Athlone in 1938, it gives the appearance of having matured over many years.

Considering that for the most part the depth of soil does not exceed two and a half feet, it is extraordinary to find chestnut, elm and lime trees growing to a height of thirty feet and standing up to the gales which sweep the roof tops from time to time. The same remark applies to the flowering cherries, apple and fig trees and a delightful mulberry brought from an old country property. Vines which fruit annually, cotoneaster, pyracanthus, clematis, honeysuckle and other climbers adorn the walls and columns and a nursery capable of housing five hundred geraniums and six thousand bedding plants provides the flowers for the spring and summer.

The birds were quick to find this safe haven. Mallard nest each year in the undergrowth, the ducklings streaking across the streams and pools after food; greenfinches flit in and out of the trees, hedge-sparrows hop about unconcernedly on the fringe of the shrubs and blackbirds fly fearlessly among the people strolling along the stone flagged paths. To add interest, a large aviary containing exotic species from warmer climes extends the whole length of the west wall of the Spanish Garden.

As Mr. Lodge, the erstwhile gardener, remarked, 'it is gardening with a difference', because of the shallow depth of soil. Because of this and the various fountains and streams which run through the garden, water, thousands of gallons of it, is needed to keep the latter flowing and the five hundred varieties of trees, shrubs, plants and lawns in healthy condition. Luckily the supply is inexhaustible since it is pumped from artesian wells four hundred feet below ground level.

Adjoining the Spanish Garden and approached through a stone colonnaded walk is the Tudor Garden with colourful herbaceous beds, mellowed brick walls and stone archways brought from stately homes long since demolished.

Though in no way a 'Florida Garden' there is a restaurant from the full-length windows of which one looks out on a well-kept lawn and a stream with occasional rock pools bordered with shrubs. Sometimes on the grass and sometimes in the pools, four Alice-in-Wonderland croquet mallets, stately flamingoes, stalk around and add further colour. Recently, during one of the periodical gales, there was an altercation between two of the birds in the course of which one spread its wings as it attacked, but the wind was so strong that it broke one wing. Hastily despatched to the Zoological Gardens Hospital, the wing was set and after being fixed with plaster the casualty was returned to the roof garden. Now past grievances were forgotten and the four birds spent the rest of the day picking off the plaster so that the patient had to return to hospital to be kept under close observation.

Besides the occasional glimpse of Kensington through a number of circular peepholes in the high walls enclosing the garden, there are two observation platforms on the south side which afford a magnificent panoramic view over London and out towards Sheen and Richmond.

Although there has been a change of ownership of this well-known

store, it is good to know that the fascinating garden is to be maintained in
its present state.

*

It is a thousand pities that only since the early years of this century has
a real interest been taken in, and only recently have records been kept of,
those delightful creatures that contribute so much to the interest and
enjoyment of the gardens, expanses of water and open spaces of London—
the birds; and if the bird life of the Borough to-day is any criterion, then
in the days when Kensington was largely rural, the variety must have
been immeasurably wider.

We know, for instance, that nightingales were common in Kensington
Gardens, on Campden Hill[1] and in Holland Park in 1875 and, because
the nights were full of their song, the road past Holly Lodge was locally
known as Nightingale Lane; at the same period the cuckoo was frequently
heard in Holland Park in the spring and occasionally on Campden Hill.

Lord Ilchester, in his *Chronicles of Holland House*, tells of the pheasants
that roamed the surrounding woodlands; and in 1875, George Godwin,
architect of The Boltons and editor of *The Builder*, wrote: 'We remember
an old friend who used to say the adjacent field (to Thistle Grove) was
never without a hare and that he had out of the window counted six brace
of partridge rise from The Boltons.'

The Duke of Argyll, too, after his first visit to Bedford Lodge in 1853
recorded in his autobiography: 'To my amazement I saw some nuthatches
moving over the trees as if they were in some deep English woodland.
Flycatchers and warblers were visible to my accustomed eye. . . . Under
such stimulus from birds it seemed quite a subordinate consideration that
the lawn would be perfect for the children and perfect, too, for breakfast
parties as in the Duchess of Bedford's time. I returned to Town and
instructed my agent at once to purchase Bedford Lodge.'

But although pollution, noise and the spread of building, which has
destroyed much of their natural food, has caused some species, common
in bygone days, to leave their old haunts, many others have adjusted
themselves to man's interference with nature and thrive in a proximity to
human habitation provided they are not unduly disturbed or their nests
robbed.

Kensington Gardens with its ornamental water, the woods and gardens
of Holland Park and the Squares and private gardens afford suitable

[1] The last record of a nightingale on Campden Hill was in 1948 when it made a
prolonged stay.

surroundings for the birds. Furthermore, since these refuges are on the line of migration from north to south and vice-versa, the opportunity to see rarer species often occurs.

Now, thanks to the enthusiastic efforts of a small band of bird watchers, the London Natural History Society and Her Majesty's Stationery Office in its pamphlet *Bird Life in the Royal Parks*, have published comprehensive lists, covering the last thirty years, of birds which abound in the Borough and when and where they are likely to be seen.

In Holland Park, for example, discounting such common birds as the sparrow, blackbird and pigeon, sixteen species are known to have bred since 1920, among the larger, the sparrow hawk, tawny owl, the colourful great spotted woodpecker and jay; of the smaller birds which often nest there are the tit, nuthatch, whitethroat, black cap and goldfinch. Visitors from time to time have seen the kestrel, the dainty long-tailed tit, the elusive tree-creeper, the perky redstart, the goldcrest (the second smallest of England's birds), the hawfinch, the orchard-robbing bullfinch, the brambling, and surprisingly a woodcock, and even a ring ouzel not far from the Park Offices.

Kensington Gardens can boast of roughly the same varieties, but in addition have a wide selection of water birds, some of which, such as the Canada goose, tufted duck and pochard, have bred annually; of the visitors the more exciting have been the grebes, crested and little, and in addition to the extremely unusual sight of three graceful black and white avocets flying over the water, a small flock of crossbills, the cocks resplendent in their pink plumage, were seen in 1966, the first for fifty-seven years. In 1972 a lone partridge was noted in Kensington Gardens.

Fortunately, the attitude of the general public towards birds has changed for the better and this, together with the steps taken by the local authority to preserve and encourage them to stay in the neighbourhood, has led to an increasing tameness in the bird population of Kensington as a whole and particularly among the wood pigeons, jays and tits. In Holland Park tits and nuthatches will sometimes take food from the hand and the former, with jays and starlings, find an endless supply of delicacies in the litter bins. Perhaps nightingales may sing again in the Borough and the cuckoo herald the arrival of spring and summer.

CHAPTER FIVE

ARTISTS, SCULPTORS AND ARCHITECTS

ALTHOUGH CHELSEA is often acclaimed as the centre of English Art from the middle of the nineteenth to the early twentieth century, it would be impossible to find in this country a greater congregation of the renowned artists, sculptors and architects of that period than in Kensington, especially in and around Melbury Road, which runs from the High Street, past the entrance to Holland Park and on to its junction with Addison Road.

And it is not only the men who lived and worked in Kensington who were famous in their different ways, it is also some of the houses they built to their own design. Of these, Lord Leighton's house in Holland Park Road and that of William Burges, The Tower House, in Melbury Road, are unique in Victorian architecture.

The simplicity of the exterior of Leighton House, and the modern environment in which it stands, are in great contrast to the interior with its extraordinary Middle Eastern effect on the ground floor: it is just as if one had entered the palace of some wealthy potentate of Cairo or Damascus.

But first a portrait of the man who lived there—painter, sculptor, diplomat, able administrator and Colonel of Volunteers, a man who stood head and shoulders above his contemporaries and who, in his own lifetime, gained the high regard of Royalty, his fellow artists and the general public.

Born in 1830, the son of a Scarborough doctor, Frederic Leighton was destined to follow his father's profession, but having shown his parents at a very early age that art was his bent, and with their happy acquiescence, he was permitted to study in Berlin, Brussels, Paris and Rome, where he made himself fluent in German, French and Italian, accomplishments which were to stand him in good stead when he rose to international fame.

In 1855, at the age of twenty-five, he put his foot on the first rung of the ladder which was to take him to great distinction when he exhibited in the Royal Academy his 'Cimabue's Madonna', a painting much favoured by Queen Victoria, who bought it to hang in the Buckingham Palace Collection.

He had now made his mark and, following regular exhibitions in the Academy, he was promoted Royal Academician nine years later, and in 1878 became President, an appointment he held until his death in 1896. Concurrently, other honours were bestowed on him for he was knighted at the age of forty-eight, created a baronet in 1886 and, a few days before he died, his elevation to the Peerage was announced in the New Year's Honours List. He thus became the only painter ever to be so exalted. In addition, the memberships of Academies in Austria, Belgium, Italy and Holland were conferred upon him, while, at home, he was exceptionally honoured by the award of the Gold Medal of the Royal Institute of British Architects.

As President of the Royal Academy he was a brilliant success. Conscientious to a degree and determined to reform where he thought it desirable, through his diplomatic approach, his ability and personal example, he dominated the scene and raised the reputation of the Academy, both at home and abroad, to a height it had not attained before, at the same time exercising considerable influence in the international field of art.[1]

Although Leighton cannot be classed among the greatest of British artists, his drawings, particularly of drapery, are of fine quality. Many of these, together with some of his paintings, 'The Bath of Psyche', 'Clytemnestra', etc., are to be found in Leighton House to-day. As a sculptor, he executed some splendid works in bronze, an example being 'An athlete wrestling with a python', which was bought under the Chantrey Bequest, exhibited in Paris and won both a gold medal and a diploma.

Well-built and handsome, with a pointed beard and kindly eyes, Leighton remained a bachelor all his life and, busy man though he was, could always find time to encourage and help the rising generation of artists. One of his characteristics was punctuality and the story is told of how he arrived home from a tour abroad precisely to coincide with the entry of one of his models whom he had engaged some long time before. Such was his enthusiasm for the promotion of art that, by his special wish, the contents of Leighton House[2] were sold at Christie's on his

[1] An example was his appointment as President of the International Jury on paintings for the Paris Exhibition of 1878.

[2] Thanks to the co-operation of the Trustees and Directors of the Tate Gallery, the Victoria and Albert Museum and the York Gallery many of his possessions are once more on display in the house.

death and the proceeds devoted to the Royal Academy and art and artists in general.

Evidence of the respect and affection in which he was held by those in many walks of life, was the grand-scale funeral accorded to him. After lying in state at Burlington House, his body was escorted to its burial in St. Paul's by men of the Artist Volunteers of which he had been Colonel; representatives of the Royal Family, the German Emperor and King of the Belgians, together with Members of Parliament and officials of Art bodies, were among the mourners.

*

Leighton House itself, that combination of the East and Victoriana, child of Leighton's imagination stimulated by the enthusiasm for Middle Eastern Art aroused in him during his travels in that part of the world, comprises two floors with the main windows looking out on the garden, beyond which runs Melbury Road. It was begun in 1866 under the supervision of the artist's friend and architect, George Aitchison.[1] Apart from the addition of two storeys on the east side, structurally and ornamentally it has changed little, though only one original item of furniture remains—a chair made for Leighton in the Royal Workshops at Sandringham, the cover of which was worked by Queen Alexandra—but Harry How, writing in the *Strand Magazine* of August 1892, records his visit to Lord Leighton and provides a picture of the contents[2] of the house as they then were.

On the left of the small entrance hall is what was the library cum study, on the walls of which hung splendid heads by Alphonse Legros and a series of etchings. A feature of the hall is the massive black doors, their jams and lintels displaying gilded roses, as do the staircase and remaining doors in the house. Beyond is the inner hall with a black and white mosaic floor; walls of the first flight of the stone staircase are lined with Persian tiles and followed, on the second flight, by brilliant blue William De Morgan[3] tiles forming a surround for a large Eyoubi plaque from Constantinople; from the stairs one looks down into the hall furnished in Leighton's lifetime with examples of Eastern furniture, marble urns and a

[1] President of the Royal Institute of British Architects, 1896-9.

[2] To give an idea of how the house might have appeared, furniture of the period has been lent by the Victoria and Albert Museum, and placed in the drawing-room and bedroom.

[3] The superb ceramic artist and designer, who specialized in the Persian fashion, fictional beasts and exotic flowers. Much influenced by William Morris, his works comprise tiles, vases, bowls, etc, mainly in shades of blue, green and red.

stuffed peacock which figured in one of Leighton's paintings. Ahead, a door leads to the dining-room and immediately left a corridor, known as the Hall of Narcissus from a statue that stood in its centre, forms an ante-chamber for the famous Arab Hall; a door in the north wall gives access to the drawing-room.

White stone pillars flank the approach to the corridor and, within, the walls are again lined with De Morgan tiles, a perfect background for the display of a selection of sixteenth-century Damascus tiles; a recessed cabinet containing more of De Morgan's works stands against the south wall; at the far end, four tall columns of Cassata marble, the capitals designed by Randolph Caldecott, guard the entry to a fabulous replica of Oriental architecture, the work of George Aitchison, based on his drawings while visiting Andalucia. Here, the tiles are of the thirteenth, sixteenth and seventeeth centuries, collected from Rhodes, Damascus and Cairo, either by Leighton himself or by his two friends, Sir C. Purdon Clarke[1] and Sir Richard Burton.

Directly facing one and sunk into the floor is a shallow pool with a small fountain splashing into a single block of black marble[2], and beyond it, a wooden alcove containing two star-shaped, dark brown thirteenth-century tiles, the one time human faces having been removed at some unknown date; below them, the four colourful tiles, displaying figures, are also believed to be of Persian origin.

Inlaid plaques, enamelled on pottery, are everywhere. The series on the north wall depict beautiful hyacinth flowers, another, on the south wall, orchids, tulips, carnations and roses, while yet more show varieties of birds, each with an incision in the throat to conform with Mohammed's pronouncement that no living object was to be represented; inserted above the plaques are tiles carrying texts from the Koran.

Surmounting the walls is a rich brown, blue, silver and gold frieze illustrating the legend of Persia and the rising sun, designed by Walter Crane (1845–1915)[3] and high up on the eastern wall is a *zenana* from which the ladies of the harem could look down and see without being

[1] An illustration of Leighton's remarkable memory concerns some tiles in Damascus which had taken his fancy and which he was determined to have. His instructions to Clarke, who went to buy them, were meticulous and to the effect: 'Go down X street, take the third turning on the left, the second on the right and in a back room of the fourth house on the left, you will find them.'

[2] The original, made of white marble, leaked and was transferred to the garden. The black marble is not so obvious and visitors, intent on looking up at the dome, have been known to take an unexpected plunge!

[3] Celebrated illustrator of children's books, whose house was 13 Holland Street. He painted 'The Renaissance of Venus', now in possession of the Tate Gallery.

seen; below it a verse from the Koran is inscribed on a sixteen-foot length of tiles. The screens in the *zenana*, as on the windows, are musharabiyeh work from Cairo.

From the dome, originally gilded and still displaying the small stained glass windows brought from Damascus, some of which were broken in transit and have since been replaced with English copies, hangs a copper chandelier by George Aitchison, while the alabaster capitals of the supporting marble columns were carved by Sir Edgar Boehm[1] with exotic birds designed by Caldecott. Here, the oriental setting, begun in 1877 and finished in two years, comes to an end and Victoriana, in the shape of the drawing-room, begins.

The walls of this elegant room were originally nut brown with a pure white ceiling in which was set a study by Delacroix from the Palais Royal in Paris; ceramics of many kinds decorated the walls and, in true Victorian fashion, the tables were cluttered with curios and ornaments of every description.

The marble fireplace is a peculiar feature in that it is sited immediately below the windows looking out on the garden, but can be shuttered as required by a sliding mirror. During Leighton's occupation, four panels by Corot, 'Morning', 'Noon', 'Evening' and 'Night', originally executed for Decamp's house, hung two on either side; other pictures included a fifth Corot and two by John Constable, one being his original sketch for 'The Hay Wain', which Leighton claimed had revolutionized the French school of painting.

A door in the east wall gives access to the now unfurnished dining-room, the décor of which was basically Indian red adorned with a large selection of Rhodean and Damascus plates, as was the dresser on its southern wall; flanking the enormous oaken fireplace stood two Arabian chairs, their backs and arms inset with mirrors and, above, hung a work by Natale Schiavoni.

Leading directly from the top of the staircase is a fair-sized landing roofed with a glass dome and used as a studio by Leighton before he built the adjoining Great Studio; on the far side is the *zenana* through which one can look down into the Arab Hall and on the left, in a small extension to-day called the music room and filled with works of art, the artist kept the pictures given to him by his friends in exchange for some of his own. Among the pictures and sculptures now to be found here are Leighton's original sketch of 'Needless Alarm' presented by him to John Millais who, in turn, gave him his painting 'Shelling Peas'; a portrait of

* Sculptor in Ordinary to Queen Victoria.

Paolo Paruta, the Venetian historian, by Tintoretto; a head by Bassano, and another Schiavoni. Strangely, Leighton's bedroom, entered from the landing, is the only bedroom in the house and although the original furniture has gone, it has been replaced with pieces approximating as far as possible to what used to be there.

The Great and Winter Studios[1] occupy practically the whole length of the house facing the garden; the former, a gigantic room, sixty feet long, twenty-five feet wide and seventeen feet high, has a cast of a section of the Parthenon frieze as part of its southern wall.

When How was shown around by Leighton, the walls of the Great Studio were covered with sketches of scenes from Italy, Egypt, the Holy Land, Greece and Spain, drawn by the artist during his travels, together with views of the English, Welsh and Highland countryside. In the recess by the huge window stood studies and plaster casts for many of Leighton's paintings and sculptures such as 'The Garden of the Hesperides'[2] and 'The Sluggard'. To the left as one enters is an apse and a tall narrow doorway through which the large canvasses were lowered to the garden below for carriage to the Royal Academy and elsewhere.

Until a bomb destroyed it in 1940, a corridor hidden by a plush curtain and lined with bookshelves, gave access to the Winter Studio, containing the 'props' used by Leighton and a quantity of oriental jars to hold his brushes.

Finally there is the garden, a peaceful oasis, surrounded on three sides by tall trees, in which two of Leighton's sculptures 'An athlete wrestling with a python' and 'The Sluggard' and Sir Thomas Brock's 'A moment of peril' are on view.

On one occasion, it was the scene of much no doubt amusing activity, when G. F. Watts, Leighton's friend and close neighbour at No. 6 Melbury Road, was working on his mammoth sculpture 'Physical Energy'.[3] Needing a better light than his studio could give him, he sought Leighton's assistance and the two distinguished men, with the help of some rails, could be seen, pushing and pulling the unfinished sculpture into the Leighton garden.

Since Leighton's death, anxious moments have arisen from time to time as to the future of the house—whether it should be kept up or

[1] Models and dealers who wished to buy the pictures Leighton was prepared to sell, were not admitted by the front door, but made their way to the Great Studio through the servants' quarters, up a staircase and through a door at its eastern end.

[2] Now in the Lady Leverhulme collection at Port Sunlight.

[3] The second casting stands to-day in Kensington Gardens. The original marks Cecil Rhodes's memorial in South Africa.

demolished—and there have been advocates of both courses. At first, it was maintained by the Leighton House Association who set out to refurbish it with as many of the artist's works as possible, an aim which, because of the generosity of many, was largely successful. Then, in 1926, the property was taken over by the Borough Council and the freehold purchased from Lord Ilchester.

So it has remained ever since and though it suffered in the air raids of 1940, repairs were carried out and the house re-opened to the public in 1951. Recently, due to the reforming of the Friends of Leighton House and to the interest taken by the Trustees of the Tate and other galleries, extended loans of a wide selection of paintings and sculptures have been negotiated.

It therefore seems that the future of Leighton House is assured and that it will continue to serve not only as one of the fascinating centres of Victorian Art but also, because of the facilities it can offer, to give service as a place for meetings, recitals, lectures, exhibitions and University Extension Courses.

*

If it had come as something of a shock to find Leighton's exotic Arab Hall in the middle of Kensington, that feeling would have been considerably greater had one entered The Tower House—the home of William Burges[1] F.R.I.B.A. (1827–81) in Melbury Road only a stone's throw from Leighton House—in its heyday for in the décor of the interior that gifted and eccentric architect gave full vent to his ability and imagination with amazing results.

Beginning in 1875 and until his death six years later, he worked assiduously in building and decorating his house, designing and supervising every detail of furniture and décor himself and, it is said, spending £30,000 on his project. A keen follower of thirteenth-century Gothic, he did not hesitate to fuse it harmoniously with rich materials from Turkey, Indian bronzes, Eastern enamels and, like Leighton, musharabiyeh work from Cairo.

An expert designer of jewellery and furniture, some of his productions had a taste of Carl Fabergé, who was creating his precious pieces in St. Petersburg at about the same time. There were bowls inset with silver fishes and butterflies, the taps in the basins were made of bronze figures inlaid with jewels, and crystal balls surmounted the bed and seat

[1] Among his works are Trinity College, Hartford, Conn. U.S.A., St. Finbar's Cathedral, Cork, and St. Anne's Court in Wardour Street, London.

posts. Burges's carved and gilt bedhead carried a painting of 'The Judgement of Paris' and twelve mirrors and many items of furniture had panels painted by his Pre-Raphaelite friends, Rossetti, Burne-Jones and others.

With walls two-foot thick and a roof of green Cumberland slate, the house is solidly built, the main exterior feature being the tower following the form of a fifteenth-century French château. In complete contrast, the front door carried Pompeian panels with 'The Four Ages of Man' in bronze relief and the mosaic floor of the porch incongruously had a design of Burges's pet poodle.

The rooms themselves presented a dazzling blending of gold, stained glass and marble and each door carried a clue as to what was behind it —for instance, a bowl and flask for the dining-room or a rose for the garden door.

In the hall, the subject of the mosaic floor was Theseus slaying the Minotaur within a surround of the Labyrinth, and emblems of the Constellations featured on the ceiling. Most of the cupboards and cabinets throughout the house were built in, and decorated with long painted panels, the design of that in the hall being 'The troubles of the Philosophers', in which one of the incidents appropriately depicted Socrates's wife pouring a pitcher of water over him. A fourteenth-century suit of armour from Burges's large collection stood nearby.

The theme of the décor of the Dining Room was Chaucer's 'House of Fame', the goddess herself being represented above the chimney piece by a carved figure with an ivory head, sapphire eyes, and holding a rock crystal ball in her hand. Devon marble lined the walls, the frieze was a galaxy of fairy-tale personalities—Cinderella, Ali Baba and Jack the Giant Killer—after cartoons by H. W. Lonsdale, and the ceiling, cast in enamelled iron, had an astrological flavour like the Hall, with Sol in the centre, encircled by planets and signs of the Zodiac, with the Four Winds and Four Seasons beyond.

For the library, probably the most sumptuous room of all, the basic subject was Literature and Liberal Arts, the stained glass windows representing Poetry, Music and Architecture, and the pitch pine coffered ceiling portraying philosophers, religious personalities and lawgivers such as Aristotle, Moses, St. Paul, Mohammed and Justinian.

Any wall space there was between the innumerable bookcases was decorated with canvas painted to simulate gold tiles and the deep, painted and gilded frieze above had a floral design, embossed on metal. On each panel of the bookcases was a painting to represent a letter of the alphabet connected with architecture, the first 'A' for the architect, that of Burges himself, 'G' stood for the glazier, 'H' for the hod-bearer, 'Q' for the quarryman, and so on; since Burges was a keen bird lover, the insides of the panels were painted with a variety of exotic species.

The chimney piece, castellated in the Gothic style and sculptored by Thomas Nicholls, was a most elaborate work, depicting the distribution of languages after the destruction of the Towel of Babel. Above, in an archway between the two towers, sat Nimrod in his lion chair and below a crenellated wall joining two more towers, a panel showed the central figure, Mistress Grammar, in medieval costume, despatching the parts of speech. On her left, two trumpeters (The Pronouns) preceded a Queen (the Verb), her train supported by two pages (the Articles), followed by a man carrying a sackful of Nouns; on her immediate right were two men (the Adjective and the Adverb) exchanging money and next to them two lovers (the Preposition and the Conjunction) watched with obvious disapproval by an onlooker (the Interjection). Finally, to add a touch of humour, characteristic of Burges, a small dog, its tail curled to represent a mark of Interrogation, was walking off the stage.

The Drawing or Music Room, which would no doubt have outshone the Library had not Burges died before its completion, came next and had as its underlying theme 'The Fortunes and Misfortunes of Love'.

Here the panelling was green, ornamented with flowers, and the frieze, again the work of Lonsdale, contained some of the well-known lovers of the past—Dido and Aeneas, Pyramus and Thisbe, Lancelot and Guinevere —all in thirteenth-century dress, while three versions of Cupid as a king, pilgrim and conqueror decorated the ceiling. In the arched windows, separated by columns of green serpentine marble, there were pictures of Helen of Troy, Cleopatra and Beatrice.

As in the Library, the chimney piece was remarkable. Built of Caen stone, it carried a hood on which a medieval Cupid, crowned and writing on a scroll, was sculptured and, on a panel below it, scenes from Chaucer's *Romaunt of the Rose* were depicted in relief. The cabinets on either side of the chimney piece were painted inside and out with symbols representing the Winds, Oceans and Flowers.

The décor of Burges's bedroom or Mermaid Room, so called because of the mermaid on the hood of the chimney piece, represented the ocean and the living things within it. Lying in bed, he could look up at a ceiling illustrating the night sky at sea: the twinkling stars were made of plate-glass mirrors and, in the frieze on the wall, all manners of sea creatures swam in the wave motifs.

Chimney pieces seem to have been Burges's special delight, for the one in his bedroom was hardly less ornamental than those in the ground-floor rooms. The mermaid on the hood held up a real mirror, the sprigs about her symbolized seaweed and coral, and in a lower panel, three large fish emerged from the waves, whose crests were tipped with silver.

Burges remained a bachelor all his days, yet he may have prepared for marriage and children at some time, for a spiral staircase led to nurseries in the tower where the chimney pieces were decorated with figures from famous fairy tales and with animals.

Following his death in 1881 as a result of contracting a chill when driving in an open carriage, the house was lived in until 1962 and then, disastrously, for four years it was left unoccupied to become the target of vandals and a refuge for destitutes. A great deal of damage was done. Windows were broken, the splendid carvings defaced and pigeons infested the top rooms; to make matters worse, dry rot had set in and the exterior brickwork had begun to decay. However, in 1965, the Historic Building Department of the Greater London Council obtained a preservation order on the house and its restoration and further modernization was started the following year, with some of the firms who had originally worked under Burges's direction ninety odd years before. Since the utmost care was taken with the wiring and plumbing, no structural alterations were necessary, the elaborate ceilings and chimneys were left intact and the Tower House has been re-presented in much the same order as it was in Burges's time. To-day it is once more in private ownership.

*

Among other personalities to be found in Melbury Road, some of them in Queen Anne-style houses built for them by the architect Norman Shaw— sombre as compared with those of Leighton and Burges—were G. F. Watts O.M. (1817–1904), John Leech (1817–64), William Holman Hunt O.M. (1827–1910), Sir Luke Fildes R.A. (1843–1927), the sculptor Sir Hamo Thornycroft R.A. (1850–1925), Marcus Stone R.A. (1840–1921) and Colin Hunter A.R.A. (1841–1904).

At No. 11 (now No. 31), next door to the Tower House, on the corner of Melbury Road and Ilchester Place, lived Luke Fildes, the painter of State Portraits of two monarchs, Edward VII and George V. In his early years, he contributed a number of illustrations to *The Graphic* and *Cornhill* magazines and also for Charles Dickens's last novel *Edwin Drood*. Profoundly interested in the social problems of the day, his best-known pictures were 'The Doctor' which hangs in the Tate Gallery, 'The Widower', the painting which gained him his recommendation to the appointment of A.R.A., and 'The Casuals', for which he spent many nights scouring the Casual Wards to find his models.

Whereas these are all rather gloomy subjects but representative of the conditions of the times, his 'Village Wedding' is full of gaiety and movement and it was in connection with this painting that Fildes described an incident to Harry How when the latter interviewed him in 1893.

His model for the bridegroom was a young recently married shepherd whom the artist had discovered in a small Berkshire village and, after painting for some minutes, Fildes noticed the man's face had gone deadly white. 'Are you ill?' he enquired, to which the shepherd replied: 'No Sir, I think it be the smell of that stuff you're using.' Fildes suggested a rest but when he resumed painting, he noticed after a short period that his subject looked even worse. 'You don't seem at all well!' he exclaimed anxiously and, to his great surprise, the answer he received was: 'I be a'right Sir, only for holding my breath for so long!'

Little Holland House or No. 6 Melbury Road has long disappeared, but for twenty-five years G. F. Watts, close friend of the Hollands of Holland House and one time married to Ellen Terry, lived there. A man of deep integrity and upright character, who felt he had a message to give to his fellow men, he was both painter and sculptor. To him his art meant much more than money as is proved by the five years he devoted to decorating the Hall of Lincolns Inn with his fresco 'Justice—Hemicycle of Lawgivers', for no more than the cost of the materials. His paintings are mainly historical or portraits and besides those in the Tate, 'Love and Death' for instance, and in provincial galleries, some are on view in the Compton Gallery near his old home at Compton, near Guildford, to which he moved after marrying a second time. Twice he was offered a baronetcy and on each occasion he refused, though he did accept the award of the Order of Merit; he eventually resigned from the Royal Academy.

This was also the time of the Pre-Raphaelite movement and one of the three leaders of the Pre-Raphaelite Brotherhood,[1] who led the revolt

[1] There does not seem to have been any exact definition or meaning of the title 'Pre-Raphaelite', though it did indicate a revolt against the influence of Raphael described as 'the divine painter' and model of all Academies. But besides the revolutionary aspect, the Pre-Raphaelites aimed to introduce a moral intensity to painting, to execute their works from their close study of nature, and to employ such technical methods as painting on a wet white ground to produce a special brilliance, the use of wide areas of vivid colour and a strict attention to detail.

The movement began in secret in 1848, but when its meetings came to light two years later, it aroused the most virulent criticism from many quarters, though some gave their approval to the new style. In about 1853, the Brotherhood broke up though Holman Hunt remained true to its original principles.

against the Academy and its teaching, was William Holman Hunt of 18 Melbury Road,[1] his partners being his great friends John Everett Millais and Dante Gabriel Rossetti. His deep religious feelings are represented in such paintings as his famous 'Light of the World', hanging in St. Paul's Cathedral where Hunt is buried, 'May Morning' depicting the college choir singing on Magdalen Tower and the 'Shadow of Death', the picture of Jesus with his parents, painted after visiting Palestine in 1872.

A close neighbour was the illustrator and caricaturist John Leech, celebrated for his illustrations in *Punch*,[2] for R. S. Surtees's novels such as *Handley Cross*, and for Charles Dickens's *Christmas Carol*. 'Tall, thin and unusually handsome, he was, in dress, manner and bearing, typical of the well-bred English gentleman and man of the world. Neither from his expression, which was always sad even when he smiled, nor from anything he said, would anybody have guessed that, for a quarter of a century', as George du Maurier put it, 'he made the whole nation laugh as it has never laughed before or since.'

No. 2A Melbury Road, almost on the corner of Melbury and Addison Roads and from which the roof of Leighton House used to be just visible, was once the home and studio of Sir Hamo Thornycroft, the sculptor, and brother of John Thornycroft, the torpedo-boat builder of Chiswick and eminent pioneer of naval architecture.

Several of Thornycroft's works are to be seen in London, in the country and overseas. 'Artemis', the sculpture which won him his appointment as Associate R.A., was bought by the Duke of Westminster and stood at Eaton Hall, Cheshire before its demolition in 1961. 'A Warrior carrying a wounded youth', for which he was awarded the Gold Medal, will be found in the hall of Leighton House. 'Teucer', bought under the Chantrey Bequest and now in the Tate Gallery, required three models— an Italian for the general outline, the head from a gypsy he encountered and the arms from those of one of his workmen. 'General Gordon' once in Trafalgar Square and now in Horse Guards Avenue (his first public statue, of which there is a replica in Melbourne), took him two and a half years to complete and his figure of Samuel Coleridge, the poet, stands in Westminster Abbey. The frieze on the exterior of the Institute of Chartered Accountants in the City is always said to be one of his best works.

[1] The Zulu King, Cetewayo, stayed briefly here during his visit to England in 1882.
[2] A lucrative source of income for, it is reported, he received £40,000 for 8,000 drawings.

To enable him to move the gigantic marble blocks weighing several tons to obtain the angles he needed, he created a turn-table in the garden and the carriage on which the virgin blocks were placed ran in and out of the studio[1] as required.

Like a host of his artist and stage friends, Thornycroft was an enthusiastic member of the Artist Rifles and a group drawing in the hall showed him in uniform with Leighton, Forbes Robertson, Val Prinsep[2] and others. Because he and Leighton had the largest heads in the Corps, the Quartermaster was always at his wits' end to find helmets to fit them.

Lastly, in that comparatively small area of Kensington, the Melbury Road–Campden Hill enclave, we find two more Presidents of the Royal Academy in the persons of Sir Francis Dicksee (1853–1928) of 80 Peel Street, the fashionable portrait painter who was particularly popular with women, and who also painted in the historical, romantic and sentimental vein; and Sir William Llewellyn (1858–1941) of Little Blundell House, painter of the State Portrait of Queen Mary and successor to Dicksee as President.

*

Of the many more artists who lived in other parts of Kensington, probably the most familiar to the public of that era was John Everett Millais (1829–96). His career, like Leighton's, was one long success, although he cannot be said to have begun very auspiciously when he was expelled from school for biting a master's hand after he had been beaten by him, nor when, at the age of nine, he was taken to see Sir Martin Archer Shee, and the then President of the Royal Academy acidly remarked, 'Better make him a chimney sweep rather than an artist.' However, on being shown some of Millais's drawings, Shee quickly changed his mind and, when the ten-year-old boy was awarded the Society of Arts silver medal, he was admitted as a student of the Royal Academy.

Extremely handsome in his youth, he grew up to retain his good looks and to keep himself in fine physical condition by tramping the Scottish hills after grouse, deer-stalking and salmon-fishing. His intimate friend, John Leech, also introduced him to hunting, a sport he entered into with verve and, in return, he initiated Leech into the art of casting for salmon.

[1] When a recumbent figure of the deceased Bishop of Carlisle had been commissioned, the model, clothed in the late Bishop's episcopal robes, was reclining in the studio as dusk was falling. A new assistant happened to pass through the room. Terrified, he took to his heels when 'the corpse' raised its head and enquired the time.

[2] Val Prinsep R.A. (1838–1904), Leighton's neighbour in Holland Park Road, studied under Watts and was influenced by Leighton. Versatile, a social success and very wealthy.

Athletically built, Millais was even known to demonstrate his fitness by making a standing jump of five feet in his own studio.

In private life, although a strict disciplinarian as regards his children, he was generous and good-natured and always the life and soul of any party, whether in the Garrick Club, at the theatre, when dining out, or during his holidays in Scotland where he met and married in 1855 Euphemia Gray, previously the wife of John Ruskin.

During the period when he was one of the Pre-Raphaelite Brotherhood, his works were the subject of much insulting criticism from the Press, nor was the Academy favourable to him. Yet, his exhibits in Burlington House were invariably surrounded by admiring crowds and when he painted 'The Vale of Rest', he turned from the Pre-Raphaelite movement with its excessive detail, to become the favourite painter of society.

Criticism did not come only from official sources but during social occasions as well. When attending a dinner party at which Millais sat on his hostess's right, he found himself next to Mrs. X, a charming society lady, whom he had not met before and who had not caught his name when introduced. Since it was the month of May, the conversation naturally veered towards the exhibition at the Academy and Mrs. X, turning to Millais, remarked in not too soft a voice, 'Isn't Millais dreadful this year?' Then, seeing the expression of despair on the face of her hostess, she quickly added, 'Oh dear! do tell me what I have done. Look at Mrs. Y's face. I must have said or done something dreadful!'

'As a matter of fact you have,' replied Millais laughingly, at which Mrs. X, now thoroughly confused, exclaimed, 'Oh, please tell me.'

'You'd better fortify yourself, so drink your glass of sherry first,' said Millais and Mrs. X, after hastily gulping it down, cried, 'Now what is it?'

Millais said nothing but, looking at her fixedly, quietly pointed to himself. The unfortunate lady was dumbfounded, but as Millais treated the incident as a huge joke, her equanimity was quickly restored.

The most popular artist of the day, his works were remarkable for their versatility and realistic presentations of the objects portrayed—landscapes, portraits, historical subjects and animals—and, by 1859, he was receiving £1,000 for a painting.

For his celebrated 'Ophelia', Millais found what he needed for its superb background on the river Ewell, near Kingston. In July when the flowers on the banks and the water weeds were in full bloom, he took lodgings nearby in company with Holman Hunt, who was then at work on his 'Light of the World'. Convenient though the rooms were, the culinary efforts of the landlady, which never went beyond mutton chops for dinner, led Millais to observe that they gave him a strong aversion to sheep in general and 'to revolt at the proximity of woollen socks!'.

Eight o'clock in the morning found him on the river bank and there he remained until 7 p.m., tormented by the midges, menaced from time to time by an angry bull and exasperated by the swans that ate the weeds he was attempting to paint. 'Painting under such conditions,' wrote Millais in a letter, 'would be greater punishment to a murderer than hanging.'

The tall, slender, copper-haired Miss Siddall, the future Mrs. Rossetti, was his model for Ophelia and in order that the artist could obtain the right set of the garments in water, she had to recline in a large bath full of water, kept at a suitable temperature by lamps placed underneath. This do-it-yourself warm water system worked satisfactorily until one day, when the painting was almost completed, the lamps went out. So intent was Millais on his work that he failed to notice that Miss Siddall was gradually becoming stiff with cold, and the consequence was she caught a terrible chill. Her father was furious and wrote threatening an action for damages of £50 for carelessness on Millais's part, but was satisfied when the latter agreed to pay the doctor's bill, and happily the lady was none the worse for her experience.

During his travels, Millais often discovered the necessary background for a painting and when working on 'The Random Shot', for example, he needed a church interior, and found it when on a visit to Winchelsea. What followed was quite unexpected, for on contacting the sexton and enquiring if he might paint the church, that worthy fellow replied rather abruptly: 'You needn't hang about here any longer, young man. The church was all done up last year.'

In 1878, the family moved to the grand new house which Millais built— No. 2 Palace Gate off Kensington Road—and in which he lived until his death. White marble was used for the hall and staircase and on the first floor was a fountain containing a marble sea-lion carved by Sir Edgar Boehm. Because he always required space in which to paint so that he could view his picture from a distance, the studio was vast, forty feet by twenty-five and twenty feet high, with a parquet floor and a dais in the centre for his models. Here he painted Gladstone, Disraeli, Tennyson and Cardinal Newman, and completed his celebrated 'Bubbles', for which he came in for much adverse criticism because it was bought by the soap manufacturers, Pears, and used for advertisement. He did not, in fact, paint it for that purpose but for his own pleasure, using his four-year-old grandson as the model.

Over the years Millais had become a wealthy man and in 1885 he was offered a baronetcy at the same time as G. F. Watts. Watts refused, but Millais, feeling that the honour was one recognising artists as a whole, accepted. Eleven years later, in 1896, Lord Leighton died and Millais was elected President of the Royal Academy, an office he held for less than six months for he died the same year of cancer of the throat and, like his predecessor, is buried in St. Paul's Cathedral.

Some critics have described him as 'commonplace, conceited and sentimental', but the fact remains that his wide circle of close friends, Leighton, Tennyson, Thackeray, Trollope and Holman Hunt, did not think that way, and his exhibits in the Academy were a source of pleasure to a host of admirers.

*

Millais's successor to the high office of President of the Academy was yet another resident of Kensington, for Sir Edward Poynter (1836–1919), whose home was No. 70 Addison Road from 1905 until his death, held the appointment for twenty-four years until ill-health forced him to resign.

Of distinguished appearance and a gifted linguist, as was Leighton, Poynter had a wide and thorough knowledge of art education, having been Director of Art of the South Kensington (Victoria and Albert) Museum and Director of the National Gallery, for which he obtained its first pictures by Dürer and Goya.

In his early years he collaborated with William Burges in the painted ceiling of Waltham Abbey and first exhibited in the Royal Academy in 1861, after which he exhibited annually until the year of his death more than fifty years later. His 'Israel in Egypt' can be seen in the Guildhall Gallery and the mosaic of St. George, for the design of which he was responsible, in the Houses of Parliament.

Described by a critic as 'sound but not brilliant', he was a popular figure in Academy circles and his portrait by Sir Philip Burne-Jones hangs in the National Portrait Gallery. He too is buried in St. Paul's Cathedral.

*

The former No. 1 Linden Grove, now No. 42 Linden Gardens, lying north of Notting Hill Gate and only a short step from the boundary between Kensington and Paddington, can boast of an eminent painter of the same period in William Mulready (1786–1863), whose career was as meteoric in domestic life as it was as a painter. The son of an Irish leather-breeches maker of County Clare, he was brought to London when he was

six years old and, by the time he was fifteen, he had made himself independent of his parents through the income he received for his drawings. Two
years later he married the sister of his tutor, John Varley, and became a
father at the age of nineteen. Shortly after his marriage he was involved in
an incident which made him probably the first to supply an 'Identikit'
drawing to the police to assist them to identify a criminal.

One night, on returning from his studio in the City, he was walking
along Bayswater Road and had just reached the junction with the then
little country lane of Westbourne Terrace, when a man jumped from
behind a tree and, levelling a pistol at young Mulready, demanded his
money and his watch. The 'mugger' was unlucky in his choice of victim
for Mulready had no watch nor could the silver in his pocket have amounted
to much, but there was no option but to hand it over. Angry at the loss
which he could ill afford, as soon as he reached home, he made a pencil
drawing of the man's face as he remembered it in the moonlight, and
taking it to Bow Street handed it over to the police with a report of the
'mugging'. Only fourteen days elapsed before he was summoned to Bow
Street where a sailor was being held for the murder of a toll keeper on
Southwark Bridge and, lo and behold, the thief of Westbourne Terrace
was easily recognizable from Mulready's drawing.

A follower of the Dutch School, he was only eighteen when three of his
pictures were accepted by the Academy. From then on, he exhibited
regularly, being elected an Associate at the age of thirty-one and, remarkably, promoted to Royal Academician within twelve months, such
rapid promotion never known before or since in the history of the Academy.
Besides the many pictures he painted,[1] he was a most conscientious
member of the Academy, putting his duties towards it before his personal
and financial interests and giving much time to advising the young
artists of the day. But his life was a sad one, for his marriage broke up
irrevocably in its early years and his later life was spent in seclusion.

*

Some six years Mulready's junior and a fellow pupil of John Varley, was
John Linnell (1792–1882), who lodged for some time with Mulready
after his marriage and of whom it is said that he learnt more from his
friend and landlord than from his tutor. As the son of a picture dealer and
wood carver he began with some artistic background and quickly showed
his talent in this direction by having two of his paintings accepted by the
Academy when he was only fifteen. Once he had settled down, besides

[1] In 1840, he also designed the penny postage envelope for Sir Rowland Hill.

specialising in portraits and landscapes of scenes near London, he was equally gifted as an engraver, a miniaturist on ivory and in reproduction in mezzotint. For his later life he retired to Redhill and, outliving Mulready by twenty years, he died at the age of ninety.

*

'He painted everything tolerably, nothing excellently,' was Ruskin's comment on the work of Sir Augustus Callcott R.A. (1779-1844), Keeper of the Royal Collection, a resident of The Mall on the south side of Notting Hill Gate, opposite Linden Gardens and adjacent to the narrow street with the delightful name of 'Rabbit Row'. But despite Ruskin's caustic remark, Callcott was not only in his day a popular and expensive artist of English landscape and marine subjects, but also an enthusiastic, well-liked and courteous friend of the rising generation.

Another resident of The Mall[1] was Thomas Webster R.A. (1800-86), popular for his paintings of the schoolboy in all his varieties of class and character. Among his paintings are 'The Truant', 'The Dame's School' and 'The Village Choir', all to be found in the National Gallery.

Of a slightly earlier vintage and living far from those in the fashionable part of Kensington, but none the less a celebrated artist, was George Morland (1763-1804), talented, popular but dissipated, who lived for some time in the secluded countryside of Kensal Green, on the north-west outskirts of Kensington.

Brought up with the strictest discipline by his father, Henry, himself a painter and from whom George Morland inherited his gifts, the stern, hard life the boy was forced to lead no doubt accounted for the fact that when he escaped from parental surveillance, he turned to the high living and intemperance which were to prove his downfall.

So obvious was his ability and promise as a boy, that George Romney offered him an apprenticeship, but the young man had had more than enough of supervision and refused it. Instead, at the age of eighteen, he began to travel around England and on the continent, eventually settling in Kensal Green[2] in his early twenties.

Here he met and married Nancy, the sister of William Ward, the engraver and brother of James Ward, the celebrated animal painter, and

[1] John Dent, the famous clockmaker (1790-1853) also lived in The Mall. He made the clock for the Royal Exchange and though he received the order for 'Big Ben', the work was completed by his stepson, Frederick.

[2] One of Morland's favourite haunts was the sixteenth-century Plough Inn at the junction of the present Ladbroke Grove and Harrow Road. It was in excellent preservation in 1820, but has since been demolished and replaced with a brick Plough Inn.

when the former married George Morland's sister, Maria, the two families set up house together until their respective wives came to loggerheads and the Morlands moved to Great Portland Street.

It may well be that the accounts of his dissipation are grossly exaggerated for it is difficult to understand how a man could work so hard[1] and turn out pictures of such calibre under such circumstances, though the results of heavy drinking did overtake him eventually. It is more likely that his troubles came about through living well above his means to the extent that he and his poor wife were continually changing their address to avoid their creditors.

Many of his best paintings were done in the various sponging houses in which he was put for his debts, and where he usually received four guineas a day for his work with drink supplied by those who exploited him. One of the keepers went so far as to set up an attic for Morland to use as a studio and, consequently, became the owner of one of the finest collections of Morlands in the country. It was in a sponging house in Clerkenwell that he died aged forty-two, his harassed wife following him in three days.

A specialist in the painting of animals in country or stable scenes, the countryside and its people, his 'Inside of a Stable' in the Tate Gallery is usually considered to be his masterpiece.

*

South Kensington too has provided its quota of celebrated artists, for the two Irish-born artists, Sir John Lavery R.A. (1856–1941) and Sir William Orpen R.A. (1878–1931) painted respectively from No. 5 Cromwell Place, opposite the Natural History Museum, and from No. 8 South Bolton Gardens.

Lavery, who was President of the Royal Society of Portrait Painters for nine years and honoured with the membership of most of the Academies in Europe, is, of course, best known for his portraits, especially of women, of whom he painted an enormous number.

The ebullient William Orpen, with his never-ending fund of stories and songs, was appointed the official War Artist in 1917. His pictures ranged from paintings of generals to private soldiers, wartime scenes such as 'Changing Billets', 'Picardy' and 'Bomb by Night' and assemblies during the Peace Conference at the Quai d'Orsay in Paris, and the Hall of Mirrors at Versailles. On the conclusion of the war, Messrs. Agnew staged

[1] In eight years he painted 792 pictures.

an exhibition of Orpen's works and to-day a large collection of his paintings are on view in the Imperial War Museum.

Appointed Royal Academician in 1919, Orpen became a fashionable portrait painter of the day, completing nearly six hundred portraits in his last twelve years, during which he was appointed President, both of the International Society of Sculptors, Painters and Engravers and of the National Society of Portrait Painters.

So finally, to the present day. Gold medallist at home and in the United States, Kensington's sixth President of the Royal Academy (1956–66), Sir Charles Wheeler, P.P.R.A.,[1] had his studio at 22 Cathcart Road in the south-west corner of the Borough. Several of his sculptures are to be seen in London in Trafalgar Square, at the Bank of England, the Royal Empire Society and on Tower Hill—while others will be found in Malta, France and New Zealand.

Just as Kensington was once the centre of English horticulture, for over a century and a half, it has had, within its boundaries, the homes or studios of a very large proportion of the celebrated artists and sculptors, men who have made so great a contribution to the history of Art in this country and abroad.

[1] The first sculptor to be elected President of the Royal Academy. He died in 1974.

CHAPTER SIX

A MULTIPLICITY OF MUSEUMS

I T IS difficult to conceive of a collective word for a complex of museums, but perhaps a 'multiplicity' would be the most suitable, and this term could justifiably be applied to the museums of South Kensington. It is certainly no overstatement to say that, in the area of the Exhibition and Cromwell Roads, there are more museums within shouting distance of one another than anywhere else. They are the Victoria and Albert, the Science, the Natural History and the Geological Museums.

Moreover, all are veritable national treasure chests in their own special way and, within their doors, the general public, students, authors and parents wishing to educate and entertain their young as well as themselves, gain extraordinary satisfaction and enjoyment. Some are also a fitting memorial to a man with boundless enthusiasm for the arts, manufactures and promotion of learning—Prince Albert, the Prince Consort.

Of the four, the first to appear was the Victoria and Albert Museum (then called 'The South Kensington Museum'), yet each had its beginnings elsewhere and it was not until the second half of the 1800s that they began to come to rest on their present sites.

The origin of the Victoria and Albert Museum goes back to 1835, when Parliament set up a Select Committee to enquire into the best means of extending knowledge of the Arts and the principles of design among the people of the country, particularly 'the manufacturing population'; one of its recommendations, highly significant for the future, read: 'The opening of public galleries should be encouraged.'

But some years were to pass before any positive action was taken, and museums remained depositories for a miscellany of precious objects and quantities of relics, generally of interest to connoisseurs only; no effort was made to enlighten those who were not.

The next move was the formation in 1837 of a Government School of Design (later the Royal College of Art), under the aegis of the Board of

Trade, the main centre being Somerset House in which a collection of objects of art and crafts was gradually assembled.

Then, on the closure of the Great Exhibition of 1851, the Government established a Department of Practical Art (soon to become the Department of Science and Art), again under the Board of Trade, and the Treasury authorised the expenditure of £5,000 to buy those items of applied art on display at the Exhibition, which were appropriate either for their excellence or workmanship. These were put on view at Marlborough House in Pall Mall, firstly as 'The Museum of Manufactures' and later as 'The Museum of Ornamental Art'; Sir Henry Cole, who had been the Prince Consort's right-hand man in the Great Exhibition project, was appointed Director.

But, because Marlborough House was required as a residence for the Prince of Wales, later King Edward VII, other accommodation for the Museum had to be found and, in 1856, work started on the building of the South Kensington Museum on land purchased by the Commissioners of the Great Exhibition out of the vast profits which had accrued. Sir Henry Cole, now Secretary of the Science and Art Department, was made responsible for its development, a duty he performed with great dexterity for twenty years.[1]

Constructed of iron and glass, as Joseph Paxton had designed the Great Exhibition, it took a year to build and because of its shape and appearance was irreverently dubbed 'The Brompton Boilers'.[2] It was opened on 24 June 1857 by the Queen, accompanied by the Prince Consort, and the *Daily Telegraph* announced: 'In the midst of an aristocratic neighbourhood—all too far from our most densely populated districts—the South Kensington Museum of Science and Art will be opened to the public to-day.'

In addition to opening from 10 a.m. to 4 p.m. daily, it was open also from 7 to 10 p.m. on Mondays and Thursdays to enable the 'working population' to visit it (an echo of Cole's policy for the Great Exhibition); three days per week were known as 'student days' for which an admission charge of sixpence was made, and a restaurant was a popular amenity. As the rooms were heated, they could be used all the year round and the gas lighting was agreed to be the best yet for showing exhibits by artificial

[1] A memorial to Sir Henry Cole, comprising his portrait in mosaics with an inscription, can be seen on the landing of the Cole staircase.

[2] These were removed in 1867 to form the Bethnal Green Museum and reopened in 1872 to become a satellite of the Victoria and Albert Museum. Syon House and Osterley Park are similarly under the general protection of the Victoria and Albert.

light. The Press, too, gave its approval, one newspaper remarking pompously: 'The poor need no longer mourn that the ample page of knowledge, rich with the spoils of time, is a sealed book to the lowly', and the public responded for, within a month of the opening, 14,000 visitors had passed through the portals of the new museum.

Almost at once, it became abundantly clear that the building would be inadequate to house the collection (the enormous Raphael Cartoons presented by Queen Victoria demanded a gallery to themselves), and so, in the 1860s, perhaps in a somewhat haphazard manner, extensions were begun northwards and westwards to form part of the building as it is to-day.

In the planning and carrying out of the new works, the Army played a prominent part since a Royal Engineer, Captain Francis Fowke, was the official architect, engineer and, later, superintendent of construction; on his death in 1865, he was succeeded by another Royal Engineer, Major General H. Y. D. Scott. Sappers of the Corps of Engineers were also employed to do the actual work[1] and to man the fire appliances.

The Quadrangle,[2] designed by Fowke and enclosing a peaceful garden, profuse with white prunus in the spring, was completed early in 1868; for the decoration of other parts of the Museum, eminent artists, among them Frederic Leighton, were commissioned to paint allegorical scenes in the lunettes at the ends of the vaulted galleries, while mosaics in the Grill Room were constructed from designs by Edward Poynter and artists from the studio of William Morris.

When, in 1891, a design was required for that part of the Museum facing the Cromwell and Exhibition Roads, a competition was held (and duly won by Sir Aston Webb), but nine years went by before the foundation stone was laid, the last official ceremony of this nature undertaken by Queen Victoria, who, at the same time, decreed that the museum would henceforth be known as the 'Victoria and Albert Museum'.

Webb's work occupied eight years and, in June 1909, the Museum as we know it to-day, built at a cost of one million pounds, was opened with great pomp and ceremony by King Edward VII, accompanied by the

---

[1] The bricks used for the north, east and west sides of the Quadrangle are some of the finest in the country.

[2] Not long ago, consternation was aroused when a wild duck, which had nested in a lead cistern in the Quadrangle, solemnly led her seven ducklings through the halls and past crowds of astonished visitors, in search of water. Staff were hurriedly summoned to round up the small family, a suitable box was produced to house them and telephones buzzed calling on the Parks Department of the Ministry of Works for help. At dead of night a van carried the now surfeited mother and ducklings to St. James's Park.

Queen, the Prince and Princess of Wales and other members of the Royal Family. During the proceedings and in the presence of this distinguished company, His Majesty knighted the Director, Cecil Harcourt Smith, and Aston Webb was created a Companion of the Order of the Bath.

The monumental, highly decorated and imposing building, with its central tower surmounted by a lantern in the shape of a crown on which stands the figure of Fame, houses in its galleries one of the world's greatest collections of the fine and applied arts of the post-classical period, covering departments such as Architecture and Sculpture, Paintings, Engravings, Illustration and Design, Metal Work, Ceramics, Textiles, an Indian section, and the National Art Library containing a million books.

Many of the Museum's treasures, superbly displayed and documented, have been bequeathed from fabulous private collections. Among the most outstanding gifts made just before and after the turn of the century are the Sheepshanks Collection of 240 paintings by Victorian artists such as Mulready, Frith, and Landseer, and including Constable's famous 'Salisbury Cathedral'; the Dyce and Forster collections of 32,000 volumes, including Charles Dickens's original manuscripts; the miscellaneous Jones collection of the eighteenth century; the splendid Ionides collection of paintings, dominated by the only publicly owned example of Louis le Nain in the world; the Salting collection of Oriental ceramics, Italian bronzes and ivories, requiring a whole room; three oil paintings and ninety-five sketches, watercolours and drawings by Constable, presented by his daughter, Isobel; and the Schreiber porcelain collection.

The public, of course, only see what is on display in the galleries and few have any idea that a very large proportion of the staff work goes on behind closed doors.[1] Besides the officers of the Museum and their staffs, an army of expert craftsmen and craftswomen—gilders, embroideresses, furniture restorers—are constantly at work, since often a great deal of restoration has to be done before a new exhibit can be put on show. In addition there is the Department of Circulation whose responsibilities include the assembly and despatch of items for exhibition in other museums at home and abroad, and the reception of precious objects sent from overseas for the superb special exhibitions held from time to time in the Museum.

*

[1] To quote the Directory of early days: 'General attendants are required to be able to write fairly and to know the first four rules of arithmetic. Preference is given to those candidates who are under 25 years of age and of active character.' Times have changed and much more is demanded to-day.

The Science Museum has probably had to face more frustration and set-backs than any of its neighbours, and although there is still a long way to go before a satisfactory position is reached, the long queues waiting patiently on Sundays and Bank Holidays are evidence of the painstaking efforts of successive Directors and their staff to overcome them. To-day it ranks with the Deutsches Museum in Munich and the Smithsonian Institute in Washington as the finest of Science Museums.

1837, that important date in museum history, marks its beginning, when the Government School of Design was opened in Somerset House, after which its progress marched with the Museum of Ornamental Art, through Marlborough House and on to the South Kensington Museum in 1857. But because its collection grew at such a pace that accommodation in the 'Brompton Boilers' was insufficient to display all of it, part was transferred into those buildings erected for the 1862 Exhibition in the old Horticultural Society gardens on the east side of Exhibition Road and between it and Queen's Gate. Eventually, in 1884, the Pure Science Department moved into them *en bloc*, to become virtually a separate institution.

Here the Museum languished in the semi-permanent buildings until the situation became so desperate that, in 1909, the Government set up a Committee, under Sir Hugh Bell, to enquire into the measures to be taken to develop the Museum more actively and to house it in accommodation befitting its importance and value.[1] As a result, building began in 1913 with the hope that the first block, the Eastern Block, would be completed by 1918. But with the coming of the First World War, the programme was disrupted and it was only in 1928 that the Eastern Block was ready for its opening by King George V, to give the Museum at least some solid housing. As for the architecture, the façade is solemn compared with the lavishly decorated Victoria and Albert and Natural History Museums, and gives no clue to the remarkable exhibits and wealth of British history within.

Meanwhile, due to the confusion caused by simultaneous demolition and rebuilding and the depleted space that resulted, a severe strain was placed on the staff to keep the Museum going at all and some collections had to be withdrawn or dispersed. Even so, with the increasing effects of science on environment, the annual number of visitors grew at an astonishing rate; from around 400,000 in 1912, it reached a figure of 1,300,000 in 1935 and, to-day, over two million visit the Museum annually.

The period between the wars was one of stagnation, largely due to lack

[1] The plan envisaged three blocks—eastern, centre and western—to be built in that order.

of money, and the Museum was forced to carry on in rapidly disintegrating temporary buildings erected seventy years before.[1] The Second World War not only put a stop to further progress and necessitated the evacuation of two-thirds of the collection, but enemy air raids did considerable damage to the existing accommodation. With the exception of the Library of half a million books which made a useful contribution to the war effort, the buildings were handed over to the Royal Air Force as a Signal School for the rest of the war, after which the situation remained unchanged until, in 1949, the Government gave approval to proceed with the erection of the Centre Block.

To take the decision was one thing, but to implement it was another matter and only the basement and ground floor were constructed for the 1951 Festival of Britain, while ten more years elapsed before work began on the main structure, by which time the number, and often the size, of exhibits had risen enormously. Thus, even with the Centre Block, the available space was still inadequate, but at least it was a move in the right direction.

In 1963, the first of the new galleries was opened making it possible to put on show to the public, in suitable conditions, some of those exhibits which hitherto could not be displayed, as, for instance, the large and comprehensive Aeronautical Collection covering the history of aviation from its earliest days. But bringing complete aeroplanes to the hangar-shaped top floor demanded much ingenuity and was only accomplished by removing the long windows on the north side, lifting the aircraft by crane and easing them carefully through the opening.[2]

Of the Museum's seven departments, calling for a staff of slightly over four hundred men and women, six devote themselves to the collection and its exposition and one—a quarter of the whole—provides the Museum services. In due course, a further responsibility will be added when the Railway Museum at York, now under construction, comes under its wing. Bequests, purchases, permanent loans and gifts from Trade and Industry are the sources from which the vast collection has been made up, subsequently to be placed in the appropriate sections—Motive Power, Road and Transport, Water Transport by Sail and Steam, Agricultural Engineering, etc.

A very popular section is the Road and Rail Transport, in the Centre

[1] Dry rot was now a serious menace. A departmental director arrived one morning to find a vehicle had gone through the wooden floor up to its axles and workmen were scooping out the dry rot in handfuls.
[2] It was a close thing for one aircraft which was manoeuvred through the windows with half an inch to spare.

Block, for here will be seen the evolution of all the means of land pro-pulsion—the horse, steam, electricity and internal combustion engine from the early horse-drawn carriages to the engine used on London's Underground. Among the locomotives are Stephenson's 'Rocket', Hed-ley's 'Puffing Billy' and the magnificent 'Caerphilly Castle'[1] of the old Great Western Railways. Weighing eighty tons and with its tender seventy-two feet long, this example of superb British engineering pulled trains carrying thousands upon thousands of passengers at great speed from London to the West Country between 1923–60, and covered almost two million miles before its retirement. When one looks at its beautiful lines and realizes the power it represents, it is easy to understand why the aspirations of young boys of those days was to become an engine driver.

Horse-drawn carriages of various shapes, sizes and periods, tram cars which gave useful service in our big cities for so many years, the motor car from its inception to the present day, are on view to offer a full and fascinating history of land transport in Britain.

Those whose bent lies in the atomic field will find in the Atomic Physics Section a working demonstration of a cloud chamber showing the tracks made by atoms; gardeners will be interested in the first ever pro-duced lawn mower in the Agricultural Section. There is all one wants to know about Town and Natural Gas and, shortly, housewives will be able to inspect the development of domestic appliances—heating, cooking, washing and cleaning equipment, together with replicas of the Victorian kitchen and an Edwardian bathroom.

But, besides the mere display of exhibits, much more goes on to maintain the Prince Consort's objective of promoting learning among the public. Hardly a day, including Saturdays, passes without a lecture or film in the large or small theatres, on subjects covering a wide field to meet the needs of specialists, students, school-children and the ordinary man in the street. Many of the lectures are given by highly qualified members of the Museum staff, some by guest lecturers with exceptional knowledge of their subject and others by representatives from Industry.

It is by no means an exaggeration to say that it would be difficult to find a subject affecting man's daily life which is not touched upon some-where in the Museum.

*

[1] Brought to the Museum on special vehicles, it was lowered on to railway lines and, surprisingly, required only two men to winch it through the west doors and into its present position.

A search in the telephone directory for the number of the Natural History Museum,[1] as it is popularly known, under that heading, will prove fruitless, for its full title is the 'British Museum (Natural History)' since it was, at one time, an integral part of that world-famed institution.

1753 marks the year from which the British Museum may be said to date, when Parliament rather grudgingly voted funds to buy Sir Hans Sloane's magnificent collection, containing among its innumerable treasures representations of all branches of natural history and the Harleian Manuscripts. A year later the old Montagu House in Bloomsbury was purchased 'for the better reception and more convenient use of the said collections and of the Cottonian Library and of Additions thereto'.

Sloane, in his Will, stipulated that his collection be used 'for continuing and preserving my said collection, in such a manner as . . . most likely to answer the public benefit' and saw it as not only 'tending many ways to the manifestation of the glory of God, the confutation of Atheism and its consequences'[2] but also for the 'use and improvement of the arts, sciences, and benefit of mankind'. And it is from his collection that the Natural History Museum has stemmed.

For over a century it remained in Bloomsbury and, in its early days, admission was by ticket only, with not more than ten persons allowed in every three hours, and then only under the close shepherding of a member of the staff.[3] Gradually these stringent rules were relaxed and by 1879 free access was granted to the public daily. However, because of over-crowding, it had already been decided, in 1860, that other accommodation had to be found for the Natural History Section.

The site chosen was on the land of the Commissioners of the 1851 Exhibition on the west side of Exhibition Road facing the Cromwell Road. Captain Fowke was called upon to design the new building, but died before he could carry out the work. In his place, Alfred Waterhouse R.A. (1830–1905), whose works include the Manchester Town Hall, the

[1] An issue of *Punch* in 1929 contained an illustration of two children sitting on the floor reading books. The caption read:— HE 'Where do animals go when they die?' SHE 'All good animals go to Heaven, but the bad ones go to the Natural History Museum.'

[2] In this connection, Sloane might well have raised his eyebrows on seeing Thomas Huxley's statue in the North Hall!

[3] One foreign visitor complained that he only had leisure just to cast one poor longing look of astonishment on all these stupendous treasures of natural curiosities before being hustled on to the next room.

Prudential Assurance Office in Holborn and the recently demolished St. Paul's School in Hammersmith, was commissioned but, as time in those days seems to have been of little consequence, building did not start until 1873 and the finished article was not handed over to the Trustees until 1880. Other than that Natural History was now physically separated from the British Museum, there were relatively few changes made administratively until, in 1963, the Natural History Museum became entirely independent.

670 feet long, its gigantic proportions counter-balance the Victoria and Albert Museum on the opposite corner of Exhibition Road, but, architecturally, it differs both in style and colour. Constructed in the Romanesque or round-arched Gothic of the seventeenth century, it is largely built of terra-cotta, with designs after William Morris featured in the high-vaulted ceiling[1] of the Main Hall. If it were not for the animal exhibits and the noise of excited chattering children, one might be entering a cathedral complete with side chapels.

Certainly it is an ideal place to take children in the holidays and at week-ends, but the provision of such entertainment, even of an educational value, is not the main function of the Museum. Of a total staff of around six hundred—taxidermists, exposition staff, designers, etc.—more than half are high-grade scientists engaged in research, so as to make the Museum the leading institution for the identification, classification and description of flora, fauna, fossils,[2] rocks and minerals, work which often entails lengthy expeditions to the most out-of-the-way parts of the world.

Comprising five departments—Zoology, Entomology, Palaeontology, Mineralogy and Botany—as well as a library, the collections in each are sensationally wide in range. Between fifteen and twenty million insects, about half the world's known species, are gathered in the Entomology Department, the collection of flowering plants in the Botany section exceed five million and it is because of these, the contributions from other departments and the half-million volumes in the library, that the Museum has emerged as a mecca for consultation and research by scientists,

---

[1] High ceilings and ample room are essential for the larger mammals, pre-historic and present, and the denizens of the sea, to be seen in proper perspective. A good example is the huge, benevolent-looking African elephant which greets the visitor on entering the Museum. The tip of this monster's right tusk, nearest to visitors as they pass by, has been polished by their stroking fingers as the toe of St. Peter's statue in the Basilica at Rome has been by the kisses of millions.

[2] One of the most famous is the late Jurassic Archaeoptery, the earliest bird and a perfect link between birds and reptiles.

9a. Lord Macaulay.
Engraving by C. Cook

9b. William M. Thackeray.
Engraving from a drawing
by Samuel Laurence

10a. Brompton Square, c. 1850. Water-colour by Thomas Hosmer Shepherd

10b. Alexander Square

11a. The Bell and Horns Inn, 1850. Water-colour by Thomas Hosmer Shepherd

11b. The Hoop and Toy Inn, 1850. Water-colour by Thomas Hosmer Shepherd

12a. Hale House. The house, demolished in 1853, stood on the site of the present Queensberry Place. Water-colour by an unknown artist

12b. Kensington House. Built for Mr Albert Grant in 1877 and demolished in 1882, it occupied the site of Prince of Wales Terrace. The previous house was the residence of the Duchess of Portsmouth, mistress of Charles II

13a. William Curtis.
Engraving by F. Sansom

13b. Mr Rubergall's Nursery. It covered five acres and stood near the corner of
Selwood Terrace and the Fulham Road. Artist unknown

14a. 'The Brompton Boilers'. Once the South Kensington Museum and now the Victoria and Albert Museum

14b. The Great International Exhibition, 1862, staged in the Royal Horticultural Society Gardens when they occupied the area on the west of Exhibition Road

15. Lord Leighton. A caricature from *Vanity Fair*, 1872

16. The Arab Hall, Leighton House

naturalists and explorers of all nationalities as well as enthusiastic amateurs.[1]

What is seldom realized is the great contribution made by the Museum's taxonomic service towards combating some of the diseases of man, animals and agriculture through its identification and study of the habits of those insects, mammals and pests which carry the infection. By under-standing the characteristics of these enemies, precautions can be taken to minimize the damage they inflict, as the Commonwealth troops found in Korea after the Museum had supplied detailed information on the field mouse that carries the often fatal scrub-typhus.

Since its arrival in Kensington, the problem of finding sufficient space to display the Museum's ever-increasing possessions[2] has constantly faced the Trustees, and it was indeed fortunate that, in 1937, the second Baron Rothschild bequeathed not only his magnificent collection of mounted birds, mammals, reptiles, fish, butterflies and his comprehensive library of 30,000 volumes, but also the building in which it was housed at Tring in Hertfordshire, plus sufficient land to allow for expansion. Accordingly, the greater part of the Ornithological Section has been concentrated at Tring to establish it as the centre of Ornithological Research.

During the Second World War, the Museum was several times hit by bombs, and though much of the Collection had been dispersed and no casualties resulted, some of the damage was serious, particularly in the Mollusca Gallery; in one of the towers, the ill-effects were not so much due to the actual bombing as to the efforts of the fire-fighters. A part of Sloane's huge collection of dried plants contained in 310 volumes was housed in this tower and when water was hosed on the flames, some seeped into the books and soaked the paper in which the plants had been encased for three hundred years, causing the seeds to sprout, just as those of a much older vintage did when removed from Egyptian tombs.

But apart from loss and damage suffered during the war, the Museum received a serious blow when, despite stringent precautions, the Colenso Diamond was stolen on the night of 29 April 1965, never to be recovered. A gift to the Museum from John Ruskin in 1887, the stone was an uncut

---

[1] Among the many letters received from this group, one reads as follows: 'Dear Sir, I am extremely interested in anatomy and you must have plenty will you please send me one horse's clavicle and a pair of sparrows' kneecaps.' Another, addressed to The Manager, Stuffed Curiosity Department, British Museum, W.C., was safely delivered.

[2] One of the latest additions is Chi-Chi, the panda, which figured so frequently in the Press and gave children such pleasure at the Zoological Gardens.

pale yellow octohedron from Kimberley; weighing 133·1 carats, it was one of the largest crystals ever found and valued in the trade at £7,500.

The thief (a window-cleaner was charged and sentenced) had gained entrance to the Mineral Gallery on the first floor, where the stone was exhibited, by climbing a rain-water pipe; after crossing the roof and sawing through two one-inch iron bars, he cut the glass from the window and extracted the diamond from its case. Even though the police acted immediately in response to the automatic alarm, the intruder made his escape down another pipe, although he left a number of finger-prints behind.

The three hundred lectures given annually to general audiences, the temporary exhibitions staged at frequent intervals and the great attention paid to the young in the Children's Centre, are an indication of the influence exerted by the Museum. Those making use of its facilities during 1969–71 included some 80,000 in the Research Departments, while 48,000 students attended classes in 1971 and one and a half million visitors came for pure entertainment. Since these figures were published, the numbers in each category have greatly increased.

*

A million years or so ago giant mammoths may have plodded along what is now the High Street, Kensington, hippopotami may have wallowed in an earlier Thames, and moose perhaps browsed in the bygone forests of North Kensington. Incredible though this may seem, evidence that these animals, together with rhinoceros and musk ox, existed in the Thames Valley, has been provided by their remains discovered in that area and displayed on the right of the entrance to the Main Hall[1] of the Geological Museum, the last of the Museums to be set up in South Kensington.

The last arrival it may be, yet it came into existence at the same time as the progenitors of the Victoria and Albert Museum, when, in 1835, Henry Thomas de la Bèche (1796–1855), the first Director of Geological Survey, represented to the Chancellor of the Exchequer of the day, that a museum be 'attached to the Geological Survey, in which rocks and

---

[1] Also in the Main Hall is a colossal Portland stone copy of the Farnese Hercules in the Museo Nazionale, Naples. It is not as complete as it may appear for because, in Victorian times, certain ladies took exception to its display of masculine virility, to meet their objections, the offending parts of the statue were removed one night and a fig leaf substituted. Since they were not thrown away many requests have been made for their restoration and, perhaps at some future date, Hercules may regain his original form.

minerals which had a bearing on the application of geology to industry should be exhibited'.[1]

Beginning in a small way with de la Bèche's private collection—building stones assembled by the Royal Commission of 1838 appointed to ascertain the most suitable materials for the new Houses of Parliament, ores of the metals, especially from Devon and Cornwall, and metallurgical products— the museum quickly became so valuable as to merit its opening to the public in 1841. Then, in May 1851, a new museum of Practical Geology was opened by the Prince Consort at 28 Jermyn Street, where Simpson of Piccadilly now stands. And again it was Prince Albert, who, through his influence and encouragement, laid the foundations of what was to become, in modern times The National Museum of Earth Sciences, the premier museum of its kind in the world.

In his speech in reply to an address by de la Bèche, the Prince Consort stated emphatically: 'It is impossible to estimate too highly the advantages to be derived from an institution like this, intended to direct the researches of science and to apply their results to the development of the immense mineral riches granted by the bounty of Providence to our isles and their numerous colonial dependencies.' Colonial dependencies may have vanished, otherwise this statement remains as true to-day as it was then.

For fifty years the Museum remained in Jermyn Street and, though structurally damaged during the First World War and by 1923 falling into a calamitous condition, it did not move to South Kensington until 1935. Built at a cost of a quarter of a million pounds it was officially opened by the Duke of York, later King George VI, on 5 July 1935, the date coinciding with the centenary of the Geological Survey.

Situated in Exhibition Road, adjacent to the Natural History Museum (in fact the two will shortly be physically connected by a passage-way), it lies next door to the Science Museum and opposite the western walls of the Victoria and Albert Museum. A good deal smaller than its neighbours but less severe in appearance than the Science Museum, its façade is decorated with Corinthian pillars supporting a pediment, the tympanum carrying a design of an oculuo or small window surrounded by laurel leaves, scroll foliage and palm fronds and surmounted by an enriched blank escutcheon. Furthermore, it differs from them in that it is not a museum on its own but has become since 1965 an integral part of the Institute of Geological Sciences which combines the Geological Surveys

[1] At that time the Geological Survey was accommodated in 6, Craig's Court, on the east side of Whitehall, a few yards short of Trafalgar Square.

of Great Britain and Overseas. Consequently, it performs a dual function, for, besides providing a National Museum, it also gives service to other sections of the Institute—the geologists, geophysicists, petrologists, palaeontologists and others—who work in close co-operation with Industry generally in the field of research.

Many may feel that the Museum has little to offer to the young, but although this contained an element of truth in the past, steps have now been taken to bring the exhibits and lay-out up to date. Daily, the halls are thronged with adults, school parties and even children on their own, to the extent that the number of visitors has risen dramatically towards the half-million mark.

The exhibits, splendidly displayed, annotated and collected over 140 years, have come either from bequests or from discoveries made by the staff, since the Institute has its field representatives all over Great Britain and throughout the world. The collection of rock, minerals and fossils alone numbers over a million specimens.[1] The Kidston Collection is made up of fossil plants of 310 million years ago, the Ludlow Collection contains over 20,000 minerals, while the gem-stone display is one of the finest anywhere. This last display, occupying the central part of the Main Hall, is of exceptional interest since it shows the evolution of precious and semi-precious stones from their original parent rock association, in the natural form when extracted and, finally, in their cut state ready for the craftsman to prepare his jewellery designs; while some of the smaller diamonds are real, the glass models of the larger ones are exact.

A recent addition which has attracted large numbers of visitors and caused a stir in the museum world, is the 'Story of the Earth' Exhibition, on the ground floor, the largest exhibition of basic earth science in the Western hemisphere. Because it is the first major permanent exhibition to be built in a national museum by a famous designer working in co-operation with the curatorial staff, it is unique. Previously, other permanent exhibitions have been constructed by museum staff alone or have been built and presented by Industry.

This absorbing new conception, designed by the eminent industrial designer and consultant James Gardner (he also designed the interior of the New Commonwealth Institute and the 'Britain To-day' section of the British Pavilion at Expo '67), cost £125,000 and took three years to build. A gigantic precision casting of Precambrian rock in a road cutting on

[1] It may appear that the Natural History, Science and Geological Museums overlap in certain ways, for instance in mineralogy. This is not so, because though they may deal with similar subjects, they do so from different aspects.

the Fort William–Mallaig road in Scotland, marks the entrance to the Exhibition at the western end of the Main Hall.

Altogether there are five sections, each dealing with a part of the Earth's evolution and the living things on it, beginning with 'Earth in Space' in which will be found a sample of the Moon Rock presented by the United States Government and a moving panorama, with sound track, of the first thousand million years of the Earth's history; in later sections there are an animated diorama of a volcano, a film of a volcanic eruption and an earthquake simulator capable of vibrating a room; in the final section, a large piece of the World's oldest rock—3,800 million years old—discovered in Greenland in 1971, is the outstanding exhibit.

As is the case in all South Kensington Museums, the Library is among the finest in existence, its hundred thousand volumes, thousands of pamphlets, maps of the greatest importance, photographs and journals, giving invaluable service not only to the Institute itself but to outside bodies such as town planners, the world of Industry, and to students and lecturers; somewhat unexpectedly it is extensively used by children.

Because geology plays an increasing part in modern life (in no small measure due to television coverage of the moon shots), the public generally take a deeper interest in this subject than ever before and the Museum staff are inundated with queries from all strata of society and the most unpredictable quarters.

A lone example concerns a proposed visit to Venice by someone whose fear of earthquakes was very real and who needed assurance before setting out. The concluding paragraph of the letter read: 'Then there is the dread of fissures opening up and swallowing people alive and buildings! Is Venice and the rest of Italy likely to stay intact now?' Whether the assurance given, that all would be well, led to the journey being undertaken is not recorded.

CHAPTER SEVEN

A MOUSETRAP TO A STEAM-ROLLER

IMAGINE SLOANE Street without a single shop, for such was the case in 1849. In the Brompton Road there were only a few insignificant shops to serve the daily needs of the few local residents, who, if they decided on a proper shopping spree, took a carriage to Marshall and Snelgrove in Oxford Street and other large shops in the West End. No one could have foreseen that in less than fifty years the site occupied by Middle Queen Buildings, 150 yards along the Brompton Road from the corner of Sloane Street, would become one of the best known stores in the world.

In 1849, Middle Queen Buildings comprised a few dwelling houses with front and back gardens, inhabited by those professionals so important in a small community—the surgeon, the solicitor, the apothecary and the parson; beside a small draper's shop and two shoemakers' shops, a little grocery, owned by Mr. Philip Burden, stood at No. 8.

Burden lived a quiet, humdrum life, as did his fifty-year-old friend Henry Charles Harrod when he took over from Burden in 1849. Ruddy-complexioned and generally well-covered, Harrod had started life as a miller in Clacton. He had married Elizabeth Digby, a pork butcher's daughter, and moved to London where he was quite content to do a little trade without aspirations to anything higher.

His son, Charles Digby, however, was of an entirely different calibre. Endowed with foresight, enthusiasm and a determination to work hard, he followed his father in ownership when he was twenty, and in 1861 the sign 'C. D. Harrod. Grocer' was blazoned across the shop front. Young Harrod paid his father for the business over a period of three years; he also got married and moved into the house behind his premises, now 105 Brompton Road.

The success that came to him was in no small measure due to his personal qualities. Handsome, obliging and so honest that he suffered from his refusal to bribe the servants of the big houses, customers were always pleased to be served by him, particularly the ladies who registered much disappointment when they could not be attended to by him in person because 'Mr. Harrod had gone to the City for the day'. Arrayed in shirt sleeves with a billycock hat on his head—he never wore his top hat while working—he had a welcome for everybody.

Competition was growing but, through his charm of manner, industry and judicious advertising, he more than held his own and within three years was employing five assistants. He also installed a new shop front with plate-glass windows—not that any goods were displayed there since in those days such blatancy was considered not at all *comme il faut*.

By 1869, when his turnover was £1,000 per week and his assistants numbered sixteen,[1] he moved his family to Esher to enable him to convert his house into extra storage and sales space. Furthermore, he widened his selection of wares by stocking perfumes, stationery and medicines, as well as groceries.

The next ten years showed further advances. First, a two-storey building was erected in the garden of No. 105 and, in 1874, the leases of two adjacent shops, Nos. 101 and 103, were acquired. Wire blinds carrying the notice 'Harrods Stores' were erected and a delivery van taken into use. Thus Harrods began to establish its present-day shape, for customers could now buy from the display of delicatessen, game, fruit, flowers, confectionery and china.

None of this could have been achieved, however, without the long hours put in by Harrod and his assistants, whose number had risen to one hundred by 1880. Arriving sharp at seven o'clock in the morning, he himself set the example and, to curb unpunctuality, an assistant was fined one penny for every quarter of an hour he or she was late.

In one aspect Harrod did not move with the times, for he had a rooted objection to electricity and gas jets burned all night, both for security reasons and to provide the staff with light on dark mornings. Whether it was a gas fault or whether some naked flame had been left unattended is not known, but just after midnight in December 1883, when the store was stocked up with Christmas fare, the building was enveloped by flames and completely gutted in three or four hours. While it was still dark, Charles Harrod arrived on the scene to face what appeared to be total disaster.

But he was not the kind of man to dissolve in despair. Instead, he quickly established a temporary office in a nearby public house and,

[1] His wage bill was just over £15 per week plus 10/- each to two boys in caps and white aprons who delivered goods to customers' houses either in baskets or in a cart pulled by hand.

loyally assisted by his staff, began to resuscitate his seemingly ruined Christmas business. Messengers went in all directions, twelve hansom cabs were engaged to fetch fresh orders from the wholesalers and an office organization was set up in Humphrey's Hall opposite the ruins of more than twenty years' effort. So efficient were the arrangements that Harrods was functioning again in Humphrey's Hall, albeit on a reduced scale, within three days and on paper with the heading 'Harrods, 101 and 5, Knightsbridge', Harrod wrote to his clients in the following terms:

'I greatly regret to inform you that in consequence of the above premises being burnt down, your order will be delayed in execution a day or two. I hope, in course of Tuesday or Wednesday next, to be able to forward it. In the meantime, may I ask for your indulgence.'

Impressed by Harrod's initiative and courage, the public were quick to grant him the indulgence he sought. Old and new customers rallied round with such alacrity that the Christmas turnover that year exceeded all previous years and new premises with more departments were opened the following year, when turnover doubled.

It was about this time, too, that Harrod introduced two reforms. The first was the provision of cash desks to stop customers experiencing interminable waits for their receipts and change (previously these had been returned in small screwtop cases from a central cash office on a small overhead railway or had depended on small boys, employed as runners, wriggling their way through hordes of customers). Adults may have been glad to see the last of these old-fashioned methods, but it was a bitter disappointment to the children that they could no longer watch the fascinating railway. The other reform was to grant limited credit to certain approved customers.[1]

By 1889, when the turnover had passed the half-million mark and Charles Harrod had celebrated his fiftieth birthday, the strain of the preceding thirty years was beginning to tell on him. He was tired and felt the time had come to retire, so turning the business into a Limited Liability Company and taking his golden handshake, he looked forward to a rest. But it was not to materialize for, when a sudden and alarming drop in trade came about he was hurriedly recalled to restore the situation until Richard Burbidge was found to succeed him as General Manager.

Harrod died aged sixty-five. He had been a stern master but, none the less, his staff liked him and gave him astonishingly loyal service. Demanding he may have been, yet he was also a generous man as is demonstrated

[1] Lily Langtry, Ellen Terry and Oscar Wilde were among the first of the chosen few. To-day the number is in the region of 120,000.

by the story of the obviously badly off customer who, he noticed, was worrying about what she could afford. Calling the assistant to one side, he whispered: 'Let her have anything she wants within reason and charge my account.' From a very modest beginning he had laid the foundation of the world-famed institution that Harrods is to-day.

*

The non-smoking, teetotal, rigid self-disciplinarian, but nevertheless genial Richard Burbidge was forty-four when he came to his new post in 1891. With him he brought the expertise he had acquired as a member of the staff of the Army and Navy Stores and Whiteleys, plus amazing energy and ability. Assisted by a strong board of directors, Harrods continued to prosper under his leadership.

In common with his predecessor, he believed in setting an example for he was always in the store, in his frock coat and striped trousers by 7 a.m. He also attached great importance to the welfare of his staff and, besides abolishing the penny fine for unpunctuality, he reduced working hours by closing the store at 7 p.m. each night and 4 p.m. on Thursdays: in fact, he might be termed the pioneer of early closing days.

With a man such as Richard Burbidge in the chair, development could be expected, his main project being to create the 'island' on which Harrods stands by buying up adjacent property. Sordid tenements were pulled down to be replaced by decent flats and sale-rooms, but progress in this direction was naturally gradual and even in 1898 the Brompton Road façade showed little difference from that of Middle Queen Buildings many years before. However, by 1911 Burbidge had built his 'island' and Doulton's terracotta had made its appearance on the outside of the store.

Lifts were anathema to Burbidge and, in November 1898, the first escalator went into action as far as the first floor.[1] The opening day brought much excitement and a feeling of satisfaction for Burbidge as seven hundred staff ascended in fifteen minutes and four thousand customers per hour.

Although the device bore little resemblance to the modern escalator, the Press were loud in their praise and one report described how one ascended forty feet up a gradual slope on a conveyer belt between two hand-rails, to be met at the top by attendants armed with sal volatile and brandy to restore those whose nerves had been shattered by the thrilling experience. Later, as the escalator was extended, the *Sketch* wrote: 'By a delightful movement, which is both exhilarating and fascinating, you are

[1] There are now thirty-two lifts and escalators giving access to the first five floors.

carried from floor to floor without the least effort and without any of those unpleasant thrills which lifts always succeed in giving to nervous persons.'

Then came the Boer War and Harrods was called upon to provide much of the equipment for the City Imperial Volunteers—including 1,600 helmets, a hundred sets of mule harness and a hundred saddles. On their return from the war in 1900, 1,250 packed lunches were sent to Southampton by special carriage to welcome and sustain them on the final stages of their journey.

The early 1900s showed remarkable growth in the number of employees, in turnover and innovations—the installation of a twenty-four-hour telephone service, free delivery in England and Wales, and the provision of a sports ground for the staff. Every day, the store overflowed with ladies of fashion, wasp-waisted and wearing immense hats and long skirts sweeping to the floor. In 1913, the Royal Warrant was granted to Harrods by Queen Mary.

At the outbreak of the First World War, Richard Burbidge was sixty-seven and his son Woodman was gradually taking over from him. Encouraged by the Chairman's policy of no discharge for those who volunteered and of help to the families of married men who enlisted, a large number of the staff joined the Services. Asked to equip a base hospital within a week, Harrods completed it in three days; one million shirts were supplied to the Army and a quarter of a million pipes for Princess Mary's Fund.

Created a baronet in 1916, Richard Burbidge died the following year, to be replaced by Woodman who, besides taking his father's seat on many public committees, had the responsibility of steering Harrods through the slump that occurred between the wars, a task he performed with resounding success.

Living in an elegant flat above the store, all the Burbidge family, including the children, were wrapped up in Harrods. It was part of their daily life as Mrs. Enid Venables, one of Woodman's three daughters, recalls. 'As young children, every morning exactly at the appointed time, we had to escort father to the private door to the Store, which we were never allowed to use unless accompanied, and hand him his top hat. When the sales were on and the day's figures were phoned up each evening, one of us had to copy them down and take them to father; we had innumerable personal friends among the staff with whom we exchanged Christmas cards and if retirement came to any member of the staff, we always went to say good-bye, a practice that I and my sister continue to-day.'

Such time as Woodman could spare for outside activities was taken up with coursing (he owned a runner-up in the Waterloo Cup), racing and golf, in all of which he had a deep interest and some success. During his régime, the Harrods empire was extended by the acquisition of D. H. Evans, Swan and Edgar and certain small businesses, and at the same time more attention was paid to the staff by establishing a staff council, pension fund, medical facilities within the store and amenity rooms for those off duty.

In 1945, having guided the store through the difficult war years, Woodman died, after thirty years in office, and was succeeded by a third Burbidge, Richard, his son, who maintained Harrod's connection with the Services by becoming the civilian director of the Board of the Navy, Army and Air Force Institute.

For the succeeding fifteen years, during which the centenary was celebrated in 1949 by the erection of a replica of Charles Harrod's original shop in the Central Hall, Richard Burbidge occupied the chair until, in 1959, the House of Fraser won the take-over battle with the Debenham Group. But, although structural alterations have of necessity taken place from time to time, yet much of the original Victorian architecture has been preserved. Some of the plaster ceilings indeed are original, as are the mosaic friezes in the lofty, airy Meat Hall, and certain aspects of architectural interest in the Gentlemen's Hairdressing, and the Ladies' Powder Room on the first floor.

To-day the emporium that was once a very modest grocer's shop covers four and a half acres with three times that area as selling space and a staff of over five thousand. Instead of two storeys it comprises six, with 240 departments catering for all conceivable needs from a zoo to a beauty salon to a lending library. There are few 'services' that Harrods cannot provide—insurance, banking, tourism and the like. The store's motto, *Omnia, Omnibus, Ubique* ('Everyone, everything, everywhere') is indeed appropriate.

*

'Within the boundaries of aristocratic Kensington—the chosen home of a large selection of London's fashionable society—are to be found at the present day some of the most extensive businesses in the Metropolis.'

So wrote the author of an article in *Illustrated London* in 1893, about the High Street and, in particular, Derry and Toms. And, after remarking that streams of carriages almost blocked the way to the shop, the article went on:

'There is no more complete emporium of ladies' goods in London than the immense establishment conducted at the above address (Nos. 99–115) by Messrs. Derry and Toms. In these windows are promptly exhibited, from time to time, all the choicest novelties of the day, and a lady has only to pass Messrs. Derry and Toms two or three times a week to keep fully posted on every point of interest in the great world of fashion.'

But this description was written some thirty years after Mr. Charles Derry and his brother-in-law Mr. Charles W. Toms opened their small shop in Wrights Lane in 1862.

It was very much a family affair for each partner had two sons who, when they reached a suitable age, became partners in the firm, and the responsibility for running the business—finance, development, advertising and transport—was apportioned between the three Derrys and the three Toms, a set-up that remained active until, in 1921, the store was sold to Messrs. John Barker, though the name Derry and Toms continued to figure on the façade.

A combination of enterprise and advertising resulted in the addition of twelve more shops by the turn of the century. Advertising on a large scale was only in its infancy and Alfred Derry, one of the sons, realizing the advantages to be gained from the National Press, was one of the first to take the whole of the front page of the *Daily Mail*. As the Underground Railway came into being, coloured posters were designed and pasted on the station walls; but, since these proved to be of insufficiently high quality, with the collaboration of the railway authorities, reputable artists were commissioned to draw them.

The introduction of the unexpected and the provision of high-class goods at reasonable prices was the keynote. For instance, to meet the demand for furs, Alfred Derry journeyed to Russia on a number of occasions, to negotiate with a Siberian company for skins to be despatched by river and across the Arctic Sea (the heavy cost of rail transport was thus avoided, and the price of furs was cut considerably). Father Toms, too, found a method of producing the fashionable, lavishly trimmed ladies' hats of the day at the modest price of 12s. 9d., and such was their popularity that hundreds were sold each day.

As a further encouragement to customers to visit the store, a Moorish restaurant and a picture gallery were installed. The gallery exhibited works by well-known artists, while the restaurant, sited on the fifth floor and reached by an open lift, was presided over once a week by an Indian chef from Veeraswamy's of Regent Street, who created his exotic curries, attired in full Indian dress.

Charles Toms, another son and an enthusiastic horse lover, was appointed manager of the firm's transport, the horses, carts and vans, and soon became well known as a judge at the Olympia, Richmond and Dublin Horse Shows. He was also the inaugurator of the popular Cart Horse Parade held annually in Regents Park and, during the First World War, joined the Remount Service with responsibility for buying horses and mules for the Army.

*

Not long after Charles Derry and Stanley Toms opened their shop, another young man, sensing that the development of the High Street offered great opportunities, was searching the district with a view to starting a shop of his own. His name was John Barker, still in his twenties, and the son of a small Maidstone brewer.

Either he or his parents came to the conclusion that brewing was not to be his future, and so he had been apprenticed at the age of thirteen to a draper in Maidstone and, like the artist Mulready, rapidly made himself financially independent of his father. After trying out his hand in shops in Dover and Folkestone, he migrated to London, where he felt he was more likely to make his fortune, and soon obtained employment with a firm in Marylebone.

But his stay here was short and, moving on to Whiteleys in Westbourne Grove, a locality often referred to by drapers of those days as 'bankruptcy row', he quickly made his mark by rising to departmental manager in a few years at a salary of £300 per annum.

As trade improved so did his salary, and, feeling that he was due for promotion, he applied to be made a partner. Although Mr. Whiteley offered to raise his income to £1,000 a year, he refused to consider a partnership, and this was not good enough for John Barker.

By now he was married and, deciding that his future was no longer with Whiteleys, in October 1870 he opened a shop on Barker's present site in partnership with James Whitehead, later to be knighted and to become Lord Mayor of London in 1889. So successful was the venture that extensions were soon called for both in the High Street and Ball Street, which ran south and parallel to the High Street but has now disappeared. In a little over twenty years Barkers comprised twenty-eight shops served by a staff of one thousand, and a delivery service requiring eighty horses to pull the vans. It was at this time, 1893, that the Barker–Whitehead partnership came to an end, when the former's son-in-law, Tresham Gilbey, bought out the latter, to form a Limited Company with John Barker as its first Chairman.

The fortune that Barker had set out to make was his. He owned a property in Buckinghamshire where he bred polo ponies and raised a flock of Syrian sheep; he had also been elected Liberal Member of Parliament for Penryn and Falmouth. Nevertheless, he was a very active Chairman, for Barkers acquired Pontings in 1906 for the sum of £84,000. Two years later a baronetcy was conferred on him.

So far, the history of Barkers had been remarkably free from set-backs but, in November 1912, disaster fell as it had on Charles Harrod, when fire destroyed that part of the store adjoining Young Street; although not as devastating, it had worse consequences, for five of the resident staff were burnt to death.

Following Charles Harrod's example, John Barker immediately took steps to keep in being those departments which had suffered, by obtaining a site on the opposite side of the road on which to erect a temporary wooden structure, eventually to become the furniture store.

The effect of the 1914 war on Barkers was in some ways very similar to that on Harrods in that Barkers found itself closely connected with supplying the Services, the first colossal contract being the feeding of fifty thousand of Kitchener's Army before its units embarked for overseas. That year also marked a change in the Chairmanship when John Barker, having reached the age of seventy-four retired and was succeeded by Sidney Skinner, who remained in office until 1940.

A wise and far-seeing man, whose early training had been on the drapery side, many of Skinner's ideas and plans had a lasting effect on the turnover and shape of the store. A year following his appointment, he bought Derry and Toms for £600,000; whereas, in 1914, the capital value of Barkers had been one and three-quarter million pounds, by 1920 it had reached four million, with sales rising at an astonishing pace—three million yards of linen in six months, one million reels of cotton in two, and one hundred thousand dresses in three.[1]

It was Skinner who agitated for the widening of the High Street, giving up several yards of depth of frontage for the purpose. The necessary re-building, however, was inevitably delayed by the advent of the Second World War. During his time as Chairman, Derry and Toms was entirely rebuilt in three and a half years, under the direction of Bernard George, the architect, whose offices were in Thackeray's old house in Young

---

[1] The contrast in prices of goods in 1926 as compared with to-day are amazing. A hand-painted dinner-service of several pieces cost 59s. 6d., and one could buy a grand piano for thirty-five guineas, while a pair of the best shoes could be had for 19s. 6d. and a bottle of whisky and champagne for 20s.

Street. To celebrate the opening in March 1933, a banquet for 250 was held in the Rainbow Restaurant, attended by, among others, the Chairmen of the rival firms of Harrods, Selfridges, Gamages and Austin Reed.

A keen supporter of the Territorial Army, Skinner encouraged the formation of Barkers' own gunner battery—162 Anti-Aircraft Battery (London), recruited entirely from its employees—to whom Skinner paid full salary during their fortnight's annual camp and special allowances to those who were married. During the General Strike of 1926, the unit served as a Civil Constabulary Reserve and, when mobilized in 1939, it saw service both in Britain and abroad.

During these years of Skinner's Chairmanship, Trevor Bowen was steadily moving up the promotion ladder of Barkers. Born in 1878, Bowen had his first introduction to the confectionery trade in his father's pastry shop in Monmouth where he put his training to so good a purpose that, in his twenties, he was winning Gold Medals at Cookery and Confectionery Exhibitions at the Albert and Agricultural Halls. The post of junior manager at Messrs. Lyons, Cadby Hall, followed and then, in January 1914, he joined the staff of Barkers as Manager of the Food Department.

To gain further experience for the benefit of both Barkers and himself, Bowen was sent in 1919 on the first of his many visits to America and Canada to examine the organization and design of transatlantic shops and, impressed by what he saw, he put a number of innovations in train on his return. He did not forget the welfare side, for a sports ground was acquired in Wimbledon and a hostel for the staff in Kensington, with a trained nurse in attendance.

An important assignment was brought to Barkers in 1922, when the store was commissioned to make the wedding cake for the marriage of Princess Mary and the Earl of Harewood, a task for which Bowen himself was responsible. How much was Bowen's own handiwork can only be guessed, but the result was a triumph. Seven and a half feet high, the four tiers were lavishly ornamented with intricate decorations comprising Grecian temples in which stood statuettes, panels carrying the two family crests, crests of regiments with whom the Princess and her husband were connected, flowers, scrolls of music, shields with the initials of the bride and bridegroom and, on the fourth tier, a drum from which hung silver slippers. The finished masterpiece was much acclaimed by the Royal Family when it was delivered to Buckingham Palace.

In 1940, when Skinner had completed thirty-three years with Barkers, of which twenty-six were spent as Chairman, he handed over to Bowen, and within a year the store suffered its first bomb damage when a 250 pounder fell on the Roof Garden of Derry and Toms. Although the garden, the making of which had been Bowen's idea, was hardly affected as the bomb passed clean through the roof, it exploded on reaching the fourth floor where the damage was considerable.

For a variety of reasons beyond the effect of enemy action, the war placed a great strain on the big stores, but Bowen thrived on long hours and exacting work, with the result that, on its termination in 1945, the profits of Barkers had reached the million mark, a record in its long history. He was considering extending the Store's empire and, although he lost the battle for the control of Selfridges, a new branch of Barkers was opened in Eastbourne in 1953. When his reign came to an end in 1957, the store was employing a staff of four thousand, of whom nearly half worked mainly behind the scenes. These included those who work in the offices and telephone exchanges, man the power house which supplies all the heating and lighting, in this case under the garden of the old Ball Street, the cold storage for perishable goods, the despatch and delivery services, in fact all those who generally make the wheels go round in the sales department.

In 1957, Barkers, as such, went out of existence when the House of Fraser took over the store and Bowen handed over to his old friend Sir Hugh Fraser. But, even if the management has changed, the name of the man who founded this famous shopping centre is not forgotten, since 'John Barker' is still prominent on the shop-fronts to-day.

*

The final big store in Kensington High Street was Pontings, a popular rendez-vous for shoppers for more than thirty years. In 1873 three brothers Ponting, from Gloucestershire, began in a small way by opening their shop at 125 Kensington High Street and twenty years later added the old Scarsdale House to their property.

But Pontings was not on the same scale as Harrods, Derry and Toms and Barkers for, even at the beginning of the century, its peak profits were only in the region of £7,000 a year. Strong competition clearly had its effect as the original firm went into liquidation in 1906 and accepted John Barker's offer of £84,000 the next year. Nevertheless, the name of Pontings is still evident on Barkers' façade, and business carries on in the basement.

CHAPTER EIGHT

WALK ABOUT

WHEN CHARLES HARROD was laying the foundations for his store, a public house, the Red Lion, stood on the corner of Lloyds Place (Brompton Place) where back sword play, for a prize of a gold lace hat and a smock, was a popular pastime; from the Red Lion to another inn, the Bunch of Grapes, at the northern end of Yeoman's (or Yeomanry) Row—built in 1767, the southern side of Brompton Road, composed almost entirely of residential property, was known as Brompton Grove. On the site of Ovington Gardens and Ovington Square was a large mansion, Grove House, the home of William Wilberforce in 1823. Yeoman's Row led to the Grange Estate, occupied by Michael Novosielski, the architect of the Royal Italian Opera House and the houses of the old Michael Place, opposite Brompton Square. Egerton Terrace and Egerton Crescent, originally Brompton Crescent, replaced the Grange Estate when it was broken up in 1846, and Egerton Gardens now occupy Michael Place, demolished forty years later.[1]

No doubt the hosts of the Bell and Horns[2] bought their fruit and vegetables from the market garden on the opposite side of the Brompton Road, and, later, their candles from the wax candle factory which followed it (it too was superseded, in 1827, by a school). Behind the school rose the spire of Holy Trinity Church, the foundation stone of which was laid in 1826, but it is now hidden from the Brompton Road by the massive Brompton Oratory, the centre of all great Roman Catholic functions until Westminster Cathedral was opened in 1903.

Although the congregation of the Oratory was founded by Saint Philip Neri during the age of Raphael, Michelangelo and Shakespeare, the movement did not make its first proper appearance in England until the middle of the nineteenth century as a result of the efforts of John Henry Newman, later Cardinal Newman. Starting in a small way in Birmingham

---

[1] The occupants of the elegant houses of Egerton Terrace and Egerton Crescent may be surprised to learn that the whole of that area was known as 'Flounders Fields', because of the usual swampy, muddy state of the ground.

[2] See page 49

in 1849, he sent Father Faber in the same year to open an Oratory in London; this, incongruously, had its beginnings in a converted whisky store, on which site the Charing Cross Hospital was later erected.

Expansion was rapid and soon a move became a matter of such urgency that Newman, in 1854, despite fears that Brompton might be too far in the country, agreed to the building of a temporary church on the present site until the permanent church could be opened in 1884.

Designed by Henry Gribble, the Oratory has one of the widest naves in the country, even wider than that of St. Paul's Cathedral. The summit of the cross above the dome is two hundred feet from ground level. A variety of materials, such as steel, timber and concrete, were used in its construction; sixty tons of lead comprise the dome; the pilasters and columns in the nave are of Devonshire marble; the huge statues of the Apostles made from Carrara marble were carved by a pupil of Bernini and stood in Siena Cathedral for two hundred years.

By far the Oratory's greatest artistic treasure is the Lady Altar in the east transept, constructed by Frances Corbarelli and his two sons in 1693 for the Dominican Church in Brescia. The background to its arrival in this country lies in the revolution of 1797 when the Venetian Republic, the ruler of Brescia, was driven out of the town, and the property of the Dominicans seized by the Government to be sold in the open market with many artistic treasures from other suppressed religious orders. Then, through the stimulating energy of one Father Keogh, who discovered the altar in Brescia, it was bought for £16,000 and fortuitously fitted exactly into the position selected for it. A feature of its decoration, other than the fine marbles of which it is composed, is the inlay of semi-precious stones—lapis lazuli, rock crystal, agate, amethyst and red cornelian—combined with mother-of-pearl.

Music has always played an important part in the life of an Oratory, as Saint Philip Neri, convinced that music and song stirred the highest and noblest emotions, laid great emphasis on them (the Oratory in Rome, in his time, was celebrated for its high standards). This tradition has been carried through the ages and the Brompton Oratory has always had the services of choir-masters and organists of distinction.

*

The Albert Hall and the Gore, often regarded as part of Kensington, are, in fact, not so, because the boundary between the Royal Borough and the City of Westminster, which follows the Broad Walk and the southern side of Kensington Road, turns south at Queen's Gate. In days gone by, the line of demarcation was obvious, for a toll gate, near the junction of Palace Gate and Kensington Road, controlled the traffic entering Kensington Road from the City, in the same manner as its opposite number, near Holland House, looked after the traffic from the west.

Consequently, the first houses to be viewed on the way to the High Street from Knightsbridge are those of Hyde Park Gate, an open expanse known as Butt's Field until development took place between 1820 and 1840.[1]

Two great houses, Noel House and Kensington House, once stood immediately west of Hyde Park Gate. The former, a pleasant square-shaped building with fine views of the Surrey Hills from the drawing-room windows, was built in 1804 on property of the Noel family, heirs of Baptist Hicks, on the west corner of Hogmore Lane (Gloucester Road) where it emerged into Kensington Road, and covered four acres near the site of De Vere Gardens.

Kensington House, adjacent to Sir Thomas Colby's house and built about the same time as Kensington Square, stood in what is now Prince of Wales Terrace and, during the reign of George I, was the residence of the beautiful Louise de Quérouaille, Duchess of Portsmouth and mistress of Charles II, during her visits to London after the King's death.

In Doctor Johnson's time, it housed a school under the headmastership of his friend, James Elphinstone, whom he often visited, and who published a translation of some Latin epigrams which some said were more difficult to understand than the original. Following Elphinstone came a French Jesuit school presided over by the—Prince—Abbé de Broglie, described by one of his pupils as a small, slender man in perfectly fitting clothes, with silk waistcoat, black stockings, small silver-buckled shoes and a smile registering both guile and weakness. Many of his scholars, among them the Duc de Gramont, were French *émigrés*, while others were of French West Indian origin. Here, Mrs. Inchbald, formerly of Earls Terrace, spent the last years of her life, dying, it is said, as the result of tight lacing.

But this fine old house met its end in 1872 when Alfred Grant, a wealthy financier and sometime Member of Parliament for Kidderminster, not only pulled it down together with the next-door Colby House, but, to make room for his garden, demolished the unsightly, sordid tenements behind them, known as Jennings Buildings or Jennings Rents. In so doing he evicted the 1,200 tenants and forced them to move to Notting Hill.

Built in a mixed Renaissance and Italian style, the exterior and interior

[1] It was also the London home of Sir Winston Churchill at the time of his death.

of Grant's house were constructed regardless of expense, the total cost
of the mansion and its appurtenances amounting to more than £300,000.
The seven acres of skilfully laid out garden, with which it was surrounded,
comprised lakes furnished with canoes, plantations, lawns, flower-beds,
an orangery and greenhouses; and among the outbuildings were stabling
for twenty horses and a bowling alley.

The interior was palatial. From the high-ceilinged, mosaic-floored
central hall, marble staircases rose to left and right and side-halls gave
access to a gallery containing a splendid collection of pictures bought at
Christies; a vast music salon, the ceiling painted in the French manner
with cupids playing musical instruments—panpipes, lyres, fiddles and
violin-cellos; an even larger ballroom; two drawing-rooms—the Blue
and the Yellow; a dining-room, library and billiards room. Above were
three floors looking out on Kensington Palace and Kensington Gardens,
and the whole was equipped with central heating under brazen grilles.

Yet, whatever his intention when he bought the property, Alfred Grant
never took up residence when the house was completed, and, instead, it
was used by a committee of gentlemen connected with two of the fashionable recreational clubs. From time to time it was also the scene of various
social activities, charity bazaars organized by the aristocracy and patronized
by the Prince and Princess of Wales and, on one occasion, for a grand
Bachelors' Ball given by certain noblemen and gentlemen for 1,300 guests,
the house and grounds splendidly illuminated with limelights.

In spite of the enormous sums spent on this colossal mansion, its life,
though gay, was a short one, for Grant put it up for sale in 1877. Because
the bids were insufficient it was demolished five years later and the
Italian marble columns, the staircases and other building effects were
sold at auction for ridiculously small prices.[1]

*

In the 1830s, the Victoria Road district was not the much sought after
residential area it is to-day: instead it was open fields extending towards
the villages of Brompton and Earls Court. Victoria Road itself, or Love
Lane as it was called, was a mere footpath leading from Kensington Road,
down Victoria Grove to join the Gloucester Road. But between 1837 and
1855, the area was developed, to emerge as what was known then as
Kensington New Town.

In 1804, when the threat of Napoleon was a very real one, the

[1] The staircase went to Madame Tussauds and the front railings to Sandown
Race Course.

Kensington Volunteers paraded for an inspection by the Duke of
Clarence, William IV to be, in a field behind the present site of the College
of Estate Management in St. Alban's Grove, carrying their Colours
worked by the Duchess of Gloucester and her daughter Princess Sophia
Matilda.

Some fifty years later, Victoria Road was enlivened by exciting and
noisy entertainment when first a circus and then what might be described
as London's first airport opened on land between it and De Vere Gardens.

The 1851 Exhibition was responsible for the circus, or Batty's
Hippodrome, so named after William Batty, the proprietor, and as it was
only a few minutes walk from Hyde Park, it became a popular venue for
visitors. Comprising an elliptical-roofed pavilion accommodating a very
large number of spectators and an open-air arena, it started operations in
May 1851 and came to an end with the closing of the Exhibition.

To the accompaniment of two brass bands, the performances, usually
in the evening, with a minimum charge of sixpence for admission, were
chiefly of the equine variety. There were chariot races, the *pièces de
résistance* being one in which the brothers Debach each drove six horses,
and a race involving twelve riderless horses. Balloon ascents and acrobats
also appeared on the programme, and it may have been the former which
led to the airport project of 1855 which succeeded the Hippodrome.

A contemporary newspaper report gave details of 'The Eagle', describing it as 'the first aerial ship' and 'stupendous as a first-rate man-of-
war'. A hundred and sixty feet long, fifty feet high and forty feet wide it
was manned by seventeen 'experimental sailors' and carried 2,400 yards
of oil silk. Ropes secured the six-foot wide cabin to the inflated balloon
and propulsion was by means of four flappers.

Lying in 'the dockyard' of the Aeronautical Society in Victoria Road
opposite Kensington Gardens, it was scheduled to sail on its first flight in
August 1855, carrying Government despatches to Paris. Further flights
were planned to Vienna and St. Petersburg on which passengers were 'to
be admitted for the pleasure of the voyage', but, alas, the project was
abandoned and the airship never left the ground.

*

A few steps west of the entrance to Kensington Palace, police and green-
uniformed men in top hats stand guard at a barrier closing the entrance to
Palace Green and Kensington Palace Gardens, one of the most elegant
and exclusive of London's private roads.

From the time when William and Mary first acquired Kensington

Palace, and for 150 years, the land on which the vast mansions now stand was the Royal Kitchen Gardens, and the old barracks, built in 1689–90 for the Palace Guard, occupied Palace Green. Then, in 1840, when the decision was taken to turn the area into a residential one, a seventy-foot-wide avenue[1] was laid out connecting the High Street with the Bayswater Road. Stringent conditions were applied to those who wished to build on the thirty-three plots, estimated to bring a revenue of £2,300 per annum.

First, the plans for the houses had to be submitted to the Commissioner for Works for approval; secondly, not less than £3,000 was to be spent by the lessees, and thirdly, the buildings were to be erected at least sixty feet from the front of the plot. These stipulations were accepted, though with some reluctance, and by 1860 all the original houses were occupied, except numbers 4 to 10, erected in the early part of this century in the substantial manner they present to-day.

Initially the occupants mainly belonged to the building, railway, civil engineering and steel manufacturing professions and, whereas they may not have been of aristocratic birth, they were men of considerable wealth, with the result that the avenue earned the sobriquet of 'Millionaires Row'.[2]

By 1890, it appears that the original lessees were largely replaced by bankers and financiers, but in 1930 the invasion by foreign embassies began, despite complaints by the residents that diplomatic immunity might be claimed if the prevailing rules and regulations pertaining to the area were broken, complaints which the Foreign Secretary of the day refused to consider.

The first of the embassies to arrive was the Soviet, which now occupies five houses, and it was followed quickly by others, so that now only three houses in Palace Green and three in Kensington Palace Gardens remain in private hands.

Of recent years, this highly distinguished avenue has lost some of its quiet elegance through the demonstrations staged outside certain Embassies in protest against the actions taken by the Governments they represent.

*

Opposite the Royal Garden Hotel, whose top-floor restaurant offers marvellous views over London, some of the upper storeys of the old

---

[1] The occidental plane trees, the branches of which join to form a canopy over the avenue, were planted by the residents, at their own expense, ten years later.

[2] The average household at that time numbered ten, including the servants, which usually accounted for six. In ten years this number had increased to twelve.

Georgian and Victorian houses of the High Street are still visible and are in great contrast to the modern shop fronts that have replaced the ground floors. In Old Court Place, on the same side of the street as the hotel, the Royal Kent Theatre, with a seating capacity of between three and four hundred, flourished intermittently between 1831 and 1846. Apparently the performances were marred by frequent rowdy scenes, so much so that the proprietor was compelled to state in his advertisements that 'constables are stationed in every part of the house to prevent disturbances'.

One hundred yards further west on the corner of Church Street, famous for its profusion of antique shops, stands the church of St. Mary Abbots, the centre of community life when Kensington was a village.

The present church is at least the third to occupy the site, its two predecessors having been pulled down, the first because it became too small to meet the needs of the growing population, and the second because the building deteriorated to such a degree as to be pronounced unsafe.

Regrettably, no records exist of any church of Saxon times, and it may have been that the De Veres erected the first church, mentioned in a charter of 1100–7, but it is known that, in 1260, Fabritius, the Abbot of the Benedictine Abbey of St. Mary, Abingdon, established the church at Kensington as an independent vicarage. Thirty years later it was valued at £17 6s. 8d.

In the early years of the seventeenth century and until 1772, the tower, only fifty feet high, was crowned with a turret carrying the clock surmounted by a small spire, very different from the present one. Within, additions were constantly made to accommodate the rising number of parishioners, and Walter Cope, for example, added a gallery for the exclusive use of his tenants. However, by 1696 it was obvious that not only would further enlargements be a waste of money, but that the structure was growing increasingly unsound. So, complete rebuilding was agreed upon and, to meet the cost, William III, Princess Anne, the Bishop of London, the Hollands and others of the aristocracy made considerable contributions. But, from the point of view of the Bishop of London at the time, the finished article was 'the ugliest church in London'.[1]

In addition to the church, a small building at the western end of the churchyard (pulled down in 1827) housed the parish watch and, at a

[1] There also seems to have been a good deal of traffic in the buying and selling of pews, to the exclusion of the less affluent, until, after complaints to the Bishop, an end was put to the practice by the wardens.

later date, the guard employed to combat the activities of the body-snatchers of the nineteenth century. Another building provided the lock-up or cage for malefactors and, on the south side, facing the High Street, were the stocks and the village pump.

Whether or not the Bishop's adverse criticism of the appearance of the church was merited, the work and materials were certainly not up to standard because insufficient money was put into them and within eight years the building was again declared unsafe. Although repairs were carried out, by 1752 the tower was declared dangerous and was completely rebuilt after 1770. In 1811, an inspection showed that the structure had seriously deteriorated, but no positive action, other than running repairs, was taken until 1869, when plans were made to build an entirely new church at an estimated cost of £53,000. Sir Gilbert Scott was appointed the architect and, once more, members of the Royal Family contributed generously.

Built of London stock brick faced with Kentish ragstone from the Medway, with mortar made partly from ground-up brick from the old church, stone dressings from near Bath, columns of Irish marble, roof timber from Danzig and Russian oak from Riga for the seats in the chancel, the church,[1] less the spire, was ready for consecration in May 1872.

The spire, claimed to be the ninth tallest in the country and rising to 254 feet, followed seven years later, its final stone being laid in somewhat perilous circumstances. On a blustery winter's day, 'the scaffolding swaying slightly but perceptibly in the wind', as The Times correspondent stated, the vicar, escorted by twelve undaunted parishioners, the two churchwardens, five clergy, the contractor and three of his workmen, and the intrepid Times correspondent, climbed the scaffolding by means of canvas-covered ladders. On reaching the summit, 250 feet above the congregation in the nave below, the vicar, his cassock and surplice billowing in the strong gusts of winds, laid the final stone and held a short service of dedication, after which the party descended without mishap.

Much of the church plate, a large part of which is in the Victoria and Albert Museum, dates from 1599–1690 and the register has been carefully kept since its first entry in 1539; but, with the exception of the pulpit and the marble effigy of the seventh Earl of Warwick, Addison's stepson, in the south transept, and a few smaller memorials, little remains of the Renaissance church. In the north transept one of the stained glass windows, erected by the Royal College of Surgeons, portrays memorials to Sir Isaac Newton, who died in 1727 in his house in the Campden Grove of to-day,

[1] It has a seating capacity of 1,800.

Sir James McGrigor of Elm Lodge and John Hunter[1] of Earls Court. The Processional Cross, presented by Princess Beatrice in 1921, is believed to be of sixteenth-century Spanish origin.

This fine church, so often attended by members of the Royal Family, was indeed fortunate to survive the war, for it was severely damaged by incendiary bombs in 1940, the roof being almost entirely destroyed and crashing on the pews. Happily, restoration has been such as to leave little evidence of the wounds it suffered.

*

Beyond the west end of the church is one of those unexpected oases frequently found in London which take one back several years in time. The small colourful garden, once the churchyard, though separated from the noisy High Street by only the width of the Town Hall, is a haven of peace and quiet, except when the school-children come out to play. On the south side stands the old Vestry Hall built in 1852 (later to house the Central Library but at present part of the offices of the Council administration), adjacent to the Charity School, designed by Nicholas Hawksmoor, one of Wren's pupils. A relic of that period, high up on the wall of the present school, is two blue-uniformed figures of a charity boy and girl, the former holding a pen and scroll on which is written 'I was naked and ye clothed me', and the latter with a prayer book in her hand. The Town Hall now occupies most of that site.

Continuing the old-world atmosphere is the narrow, picturesque Kensington Church Walk with its antique- and book-shops, leading from the north side of the churchyard into Holland Street, where many of the houses are of the Queen Anne period, some still retaining their powder closets and original panelling.

Within a few yards of Kensington Church Walk is Gordon Place, a charming cul-de-sac, on its south side approachable only on foot, in which, some say, the coachmen and grooms of Kensington Palace were once accommodated. On either side of the pathway, the three-storied early Victorian houses have their small front gardens, in the summer ablaze with sweet-scented flowers, and one might well be in some country town far from the noisy, busy environment of London.

*

The increasing needs of the ever-expanding population, together with the amalgamation of Kensington and Chelsea into one Borough, have

[1] See page 123.

outmoded such institutions as the Town Hall and a site on the west side of Hornton Street, which slopes steeply down from Campden Hill to the High Street, will shortly become the Borough's Civic and Cultural Centre. A splendid new library, probably the best equipped and furnished in London, has already been built, while grinding excavators, cranes reaching skywards, bulldozers and a continuous stream of lorries passing in and out of the site adjoining the library, combine towards the construction of the new Civic Centre, in which the whole of the administration will be concentrated instead of being spread over a wide area.

The imposing Central Library, built over five years at a cost of £680,000, and opened by Queen Elizabeth, the Queen Mother, on 13 July 1960, was designed by S. Vincent Harris R.A., the Gold Medallist of 1931. While the core is of steel and concrete, it is finished with red Berkshire brick and Portland stone in the modern English Renaissance style; comprising six stories, with an eventual capacity for 600,000 books, it has already 30,000 biographies, a collection, perhaps, second only to that in the British Museum.

A tall arcaded portico gives access to the public library and, here, there is immediately a sense of space, light and orderliness, and the impression that no effort has been spared to make it easy for the visitor to take out a book or to study in comfort. Particularly is this so in the reference library on the first floor where the mass of material, together with the very knowledgeable and helpful staff, do much to meet the requirements of authors, students and others bent on research.

Whereas, in 1880, £54,000 was sufficient to build the present Town Hall, close on three million pounds will be needed for the new one under construction on the 'Abbey' site.

Designed by Sir Basil Spence R.A., it will be complementary to the Central Library in that it will be built of brick, which will blend equally well with the red-brick residential property opposite. It is comforting to note that many of the trees at the northern end are being preserved and that the area between the Library and the Civic Offices will be an open space and ceremonial court.[1] An unusual feature will be the pool of water over which the Council Chamber is to be built.

Thus, Hornton Street, once entirely residential, will soon become one of the more important thoroughfares in the Borough and a greater scene of activity than ever before.

*

[1] A multi-storied car-park for public use is to be installed underground.

From the upper deck of any slow-moving bus travelling along the High Street, an observant passenger will normally have ample time to take stock of his surroundings. Should one of the many halts occur between Earls Court Road and Edwardes Square, he will notice, on the north side, a cluster of multi-coloured flags of the Commonwealth Nations, thirty-three in all, flying from tall poles standing in front of, or in, ornamental water which surrounds a large well-kept lawn on two sides. In spring and summer, whether in the water or on the grass in the shade of the old original trees of Holland Park, ducks, with their ever-busy broods, take full advantage of the scraps of bread thrown to them by the children eating their sandwich lunches on the near-by seats.

This is the entrance to the Commonwealth Institute, the latest of Kensington's new buildings and successor to the old Imperial Institute in South Kensington.

The necessity to build a Commonwealth Institute arose in 1953, when the Government of the day decided to demolish the Imperial Institute to allow for the expansion of the Imperial College of Science and Technology and, because of the great amount of research, discussion and planning entailed, the project required ten years to come to fruition. The result, the combined efforts of the Chairman and Directors, the architects, Messrs. Matthew, Johnson-Marshall (responsible also for the Festival Hall), James Gardner, the designer,[1] and Harold Midgeley, the research worker and script writer, has been well worth every minute spent in preparation and the million pounds expended on the building, its furniture, exhibitions and equipment.

The underlying purpose of this Commonwealth Institute was two-fold: to strengthen the friendship between the Commonwealth peoples by helping them to know more about one another; and, through visual means —permanent exhibitions, films and displays of contemporary art from all parts of the Commonwealth—to instruct the young generation and to teach their instructors how to put the subjects across.

Since the Institute was to occupy three and a half acres of Holland Park, the architects based their plans on blending the structure as far as possible with its surroundings; hence its tent-like appearance with five hyperbolic paraboloids in the roof and the extension of the park atmosphere right up to the High Street by means of lawns, water and forecourt.

But this exciting building, designed to emphasize the change from the old 'Imperial' to the new 'Commonwealth' era, is not entirely a British effort. It is a co-operative one for, besides financial contributions, many

[1] See page 98.

of the materials for its construction have come from Commonwealth countries world-wide. For instance, the twenty-five tons of copper for the immense roof was a gift from the old Northern Rhodesia Chamber of Mines; the aluminium and cedar wood were presented by Canada and the wide selection of timber was donated by Australia, New Zealand, the East and West African countries and Guyana; in the Board Room and adjoining Jehangir Room, used for social gatherings, the floor is made from Loliondo blocks from Uganda, and the curtain, designed by Gerald Holtom after eighteenth-century Indian paintings, was presented by the Indian Government.

The stone avenue of varying levels, flanked by tall trees, and terminating in a bridge over the water, leads to the main entrance of the Exhibition Block. At first, the impression is not a stimulating one for the two passages communicating with the main hall are unimpressive. Then, suddenly, the vast main hall comes into view and the surprise effect, intended of the architects, is phenomenal.

For the first time in this century, it was possible in London to design an interior for housing permanent exhibitions, and James Gardner made full use of the opportunity.

Crossing a ramp to the large circular central platform, its floor of marble rescued from the front entrance of the old Imperial Institute, one has a general view of the exhibition from this vantage point. High overhead, the remarkable roof structure is illuminated by two clerestory windows in its peak, the only daylight in the Hall, and all around are three tiers of galleries, one below and two above the platform, glittering with lights. Radiating from the platform are staircases up to and down to the galleries and the excellent system of sign-posting enables visitors to find quickly the exhibition of their choice. Ample room has been allowed to see the exhibits in comfort, in this case for up to as many as 4,000 people at any one time.

As for the exhibitions themselves, each country has its allotted space to display its history, geography, economy, scenery and peoples by various excellent visual means, dioramas, photographs, maps, films with sound-tracks and scenes comprising life-size models of men, women and animals in natural surroundings. Whereas about half the stands were laid out by James Gardner himself, some countries, such as Canada, designed their own and sent them to this country.

The emphasis is on children of all colour and creeds, as is evident from the crowds of the small and not so small boys and girls, armed with note-books, and drawing materials, either sitting on the floor writing and sketching or listening intently to talks by their teachers. In spite of children's natural tendency towards untidiness, the whole exhibition is a model of cleanliness which reflects great credit on the staff, who spend long hours after closing time polishing the floors and cleaning the exhibits.

Adjoining the Main Hall is the Art Gallery, an airy spacious room with a large picture window overlooking Holland Park; here exhibitions are staged from time to time of all that is best in Commonwealth Art, and shown to the best advantage by means of the flexible lighting system in the roof. On the floor below, the cinema, with a seating capacity for 450, is normally used for daily programmes of documentary films, but can easily be converted for frequent performances by singers, dancers and actors from overseas.

Although the aesthetic aspect played an important part in the minds of the Governors, they did not forget the comfort and needs of visitors, especially the children. Schools are provided with their own reception centre, cloakrooms and a 'tuck shop', stocked with soft drinks, ice cream and sweets, together with a large refectory table for 160 to eat their packed lunches. Adults have their own cafeteria with tables and chairs outside on the lawn, a much appreciated spot in fine weather.

*

Almost opposite the Commonwealth Institute, the Earls Court Road runs south to join the Brompton Road. A few yards past the Underground Station, on the opposite side of the road, there once lived one of the most remarkable men in the history of medicine. He was John Hunter, the distinguished surgeon and anatomist who, in 1764, built himself a country retreat from which he could commute to the City, on two acres of land at the junction of the modern Barkston Gardens and the Earls Court Road.

Since his absorbing hobby was the study of the habits of various kinds of animals, birds, reptiles and insects, and he wanted to pass on his observations to the Royal Society in book form, he established a small zoo within his grounds. Here he kept buffaloes, domestic cattle, sheep and goats from foreign parts, zebras, jackals, leopards, ostriches, eagles and snakes; and to house the fiercer type of fauna he erected a large mound in the garden (still visible in 1888), in which he built dens and pits. In the conservatory was a hive of bees whose activities he could watch from his drawing-room, and a flock of geese roamed the garden and provided eggs for his experiments during their incubation.

A small man, but full of energy and capable of great exertion both physical and mental, Hunter displayed the former characteristic to a marked degree in his extraordinary practice of wrestling with bulls, particularly with a fine small one given to him by the Queen. It was while one day exercising with this animal that he nearly met his end, for the bull got him down and, had not a passing servant driven it off, no doubt Hunter would have been no more.

As an anatomist, one of his greatest triumphs was to acquire the body of Bryne O'Brien, the eight-foot Irish giant, for which, it was alleged, he was forced to pay £500. In extreme secrecy he boiled down the corpse in sections, in a large cauldron, reassembled the skeleton and placed it with the other exhibits in his Museum.

This unique collection, comprising several hundred items, is now in the keeping of the Royal College of Surgeons of England, and just inside the entrance doors of the Hunterian Museum stands O'Brien's skeleton in its glass case. John Hunter's portrait by Sir Joshua Reynolds, in which the lower part of the skeleton's legs and feet features in the top right-hand corner of the painting, occupies a prominent position in the Council Chamber of the College.

In 1793, while visiting a friend one morning, Hunter complained of a pain in his chest and took a dose of opium to relieve it. Later in the day, when attending a meeting in St. George's Hospital, whether he saw something which annoyed him or had a heated argument—and both theories have been suggested—the pain returned and, after hurriedly leaving the room, he died a few hours later, possibly from a heart attack.

*

At the points where the never-ending streams of traffic leave the western boundary of Kensington near Olympia and the southern end of Brompton Cemetery to enter Hammersmith and Fulham respectively, pedestrians once had to tread warily and horses splashed through the brook which, for four hundred years, formed the boundary between Kensington and its neighbours. Rising near Kensal Green, it flowed parallel to what are now Latimer and Warwick Roads, before emptying itself into the Thames through Chelsea Creek.

Although generally called 'The Creek', its northern portion was known as 'Counters Creek', over which ran the road to Windsor from what is now Kensington High Street by means of Countess Bridge (possibly so named after one of the de Vere ladies), later Counters Bridge. From there to Sandford Bridge (the bridge at sand ford), which in turn carried the Fulham Road over the stream, it became 'Billings Ditch' and thence to the Thames, 'Chelsea Creek'.

On both banks, orchards and market gardens flourished and 'the water-cress was large and good', but as London expanded, so pollution of the streams and wells became so disgusting as to lead Dean Swift to remark in the early eighteenth century: 'Drowned puppies, stinking sprats all drenched in mud, dead cats and turnip tops tumbling down the flood.'

By the turn of the eighteenth century great changes were taking place as canals began gradually to replace the horse as a more profitable method of transportation and, in 1820, Lord Kensington, in company with some friends and backed by a capital of £45,000, prepared a scheme to transform 'The Creek' into a canal joining the Thames with the Grand Junction Canal at Paddington which had been opened in 1801.

One hundred feet broad with sufficient depth for craft up to one hundred tons burden, the Kensington Canal was completed in 1828 and opened, amid much excitement, on 12 August, the birthday of King George IV. When describing the scene, the *Times* correspondent wrote: 'Witnessed by a number of persons, the Rt. Hon. Lord Kensington and a number of his friends of the undertaking, embarked on a stately barge at Battersea Bridge and proceeded up the canal. The whole party entered the basin amidst the cheers of the multitude assembled, the band on board playing "God save the King". We learn that Lord Kensington and his friends partook of a sumptuous dinner after the ceremony and provided for some two hundred of the work people a substantial dinner with a butt of porter.'

But with the arrival of the railway era the project came too late to be profitable. Revenue dwindled and, though in 1839 the canal passed into the hands of the Birmingham, Bristol and Thames Junction Railway, it continued for another twenty years, not as a canal, but as a carrier of sewage, a far better money-making concern.

So this once sweet water stream became a stagnant ditch with a few disheartened marguerites, daisies and thistles growing on its banks, and its dereliction was accelerated when the Secretary decamped with £1,000 or more, nearly a year's takings. Because of its filthy state, and because it was thought to be the probable cause of a case of cholera in Fulham, the Commissioner of Sewage condemned it as dangerous in 1854 and it was filled in. In its place, railway lines were laid over it in 1863, marking the western boundary of the Borough.[1]

[1] One of the original lock-keeper's cottages still stands under the bridge that carries the West Cromwell Road over the railway and is used by the Kensington Rifle Club.

CHAPTER NINE

THE PIGGERIES AND THE POTTERIES

AN AERIAL view of North Kensington, that part of the Borough lying north of Holland Park Avenue, makes it hard to believe that, a little more than one hundred years ago, the congestion of bricks, mortar and concrete that now covers the area, was delightful countryside; that even in the 1850s, Portobello Lane, now Portobello Road, leading to Portobello Farm,[1] was much favoured by Londoners as 'one of the most rural and pleasant walks in the summer in the vicinity', and that cornfields and meadows lay on either side of the path meandering on to Kensal Green; that, in 1837, the year of Queen Victoria's accession, one could back a horse on the Hippodrome Race Course and mix with London's high society in their splendid equipages or with the pedestrians on the hill on which St. John's Church was to be built, to watch one's selection carrying one's money to victory or defeat and, when the race was over, to celebrate or drown one's sorrows in the marquees serving iced champagne; that, at the same time, if the wind was from the south-west, whiffs of piggeries and the smoke of Mr. Adams's pottery kilns from Notting Dale might assail the nostrils.

As Kensington may once have been 'Chenisinton', so Notting Hill may have derived its name from a Saxon tribe, the Cnottingas, sons of Cnotting, who settled in a clearing in the great forest of Middlesex, north of Holland Park Avenue, some time in the seventh century, but who vanished before the arrival of the Normans. Over the years it has been described in old deeds as Knottynghull, Knotting Bernes, Nuttyng Barnes, Notingbarns and Knottyngbarons, and some of the pastures, woods and enclosures went by the picturesque names of Nuttyng Wood (St. John's Hill), Darkingby Jones, Balserfield and Baudclands. Knotting Barns, with its farm, situated approximately half-way between Holland Park Avenue and the Harrow Road, and still evident in 1880, was the Manor House of olden days.

---

[1] So called to commemorate Admiral Vernon's victory over the Spaniards in 1739, when the fine port of Puerto Bello, in the Gulf of Mexico and adjacent to the present Panama Canal, was captured.

Nevertheless, from the end of the eighteenth century and, indeed, until towards the beginning of the nineteenth, there were many among the well-to-do in the rest of Kensington including some administrators, who were reluctant to acknowledge that North Kensington existed, much less to recognize the shocking conditions in which the population lived. This was in large measure due to the unsavoury reputation it had gained through the inhabitants who had settled in parts of it and the occupations they followed.

Until 1820, building had been confined to the houses immediately on either side of the Uxbridge Road (Notting Hill Gate and Holland Park Avenue). Richard Ladbroke owned two farms on the north side and, to the west of the stately Royal Crescent, built in the early years of Queen Victoria's reign, was Norland House, for many years a Military Academy for the education of the sons of the gentry desirous of entering the Army. Within the precincts of this large property of twelve acres, which included a riding school, cricket ground and fives court, the young men were taught languages, mathematics, geography, dancing and such military subjects as fortification, navigation and fencing. An unfortunate fire in 1825 destroyed the house and, in its place, Norland Square and Norland Place were built.

By now, London was expanding so rapidly that the demand for housing further afield became so great as to encourage the development of the district,[1] but, even so, encroachment into the countryside was gradual and spread over some sixty years. In 1848, the area north of Arundel Gardens and Westbourne Grove still remained open country, while fifteen years later there were no buildings beyond the Silchester and Lancaster Roads, other than the two farms of Notting Barns and Portobello; west of St. Mark's Road and north of Walmer Road was unspoilt one hundred years ago.

Of the big estates comprising the greater part of North Kensington, on which new houses began to appear, the most important were the Norland Estate on the east, the Ladbroke Estate in the centre, the Portobello Estate on the west and the St. Quintin Estate to the west of St. Mark's Road and north of Lancaster Road. Some of these names appear occasionally in the naming of roads and squares, but that of Ladbroke features again and again in Ladbroke Square, Road, Terrace, etc., although no member of the family seems ever to have lived in Kensington.

Since 1780 a brickfield has been in existence in Notting Dale, the

[1] Between 1820 and the end of the century, the population of Kensington rose by 164,000.

northern portion of the Norland Estate, but it was a Mr. Adams who, in the 1820s, founded the Norland Pottery Works,[1] for the manufacture of tiles, drain pipes and flower pots, in addition to bricks, on the low-lying ground west of St. John's Church hill and to-day covered by Henry Dickens Court, Avondale Park, Walmer Road and Pottery Lane. Here, unlike the gravel of Kensington, the soil was of stiff yellow clay, ideal for Adams's purpose, but when the clay was dug out, large holes remained in which water collected to stagnate through the absence of drainage.

In itself this was not too obnoxious a problem at the outset but when Samuel Lane, a chimney-sweep and night-soil collector, moved into the area, it quickly became one of the most appalling, pestilential districts in the country, let alone in the City and its environs.

Lane, who lived and carried out his unpleasant business in Tottenham Court Road, was no doubt compelled by the complaints of his neighbours to move to a spot where his occupation would cause less offence and, on arrival in Notting Dale, he also took to keeping pigs. In a year or two he was joined by one Stephens, a bowstring maker who, having bought some of Lane's land, also changed his profession to that of pig-keeper.

Whereas the piggeries began in a small way, the number of humans and pigs increased astronomically when Stephens made contact with a group who went under the exalted name of 'the pigkeepers of the West End Establishment'. This group, a collection of families, resided with their animals in Connaught Square near Marble Arch, a position well placed to collect the waste food of the grand houses and hotels of Mayfair to feed their pigs; but, as London expanded and the developers turned their eyes to Connaught Square, when Stephens offered them some of his land with the promise they could do as they wished on it, they gladly accepted and moved in with their pigs, ducks, geese and turkeys.

Because at that period the local authority, in other words the Kensington Vestry, had no control over the standards and quality of buildings, nor the nuisances that could consequently arise, the results of this influx were deplorable. Shanties, hovels, sheds, low brick buildings, followed by discarded carriages and vans, sprang up indiscriminately without thought to sanitation or drainage. Families with hordes of young children lived cheek by jowl with the animals and the stench of boiling fat and offal, combined with that of human excreta and rotting refuse, hung over the whole sordid locality. Many of the families had their own pony or donkey

[1] The last vestige of this once flourishing industry is an original kiln standing in Walmer Road, opposite to the entrance to Avondale Park.

carts and early each morning they set off to the West End to collect the swill as before; on their return the results were sorted out, the best being kept for their own consumption while the fat was boiled down and what was left was given to the pigs.

From the start, living conditions were atrocious but, as time passed, and the populations of humans and pigs increased, so they became immeasurably worse. An investigation by the Poor Law Commission in 1838 revealed that, in some cases, the hovels had been built over stagnant water and when the floor collapsed one end of the room lay to rot in the fouled water, while the family slept as best they could on mattresses at the comparatively dry end. The cavities left after digging the clay had now become receptacles for liquid pig manure and all kinds of rotting matter and there they remained for lack of any form of drainage.

Of course there were complaints from the newly arrived nearby residents of Lansdowne Road and Crescent[1] and from the property developers, but to little avail, one of the complainants being told that he and he alone was responsible for the drainage.

And so it went on until, within ten years, the locality had become a complex of open evil-smelling ditches surrounding the dwellings, or running down the unpaved, deeply rutted lanes, which were so choked with garbage that they were impassable at times. To make matters worse, the wells became contaminated and the inhabitants were forced to fetch their drinking water from a distant pump and pay the landlord for the privilege. As the new big houses were erected in the vicinity, so their sewage seeped into the piggeries and Avondale Park was an acre of stagnant water, locally known as 'The Ocean'.

It seems incredible that such conditions were permitted to continue when, a short distance away, the residents of Campden Hill and Lansdowne Crescent lived in affluence in their elegant houses. No wonder disease and high mortality were prevalent among this rough but, at the same time, hardworking and honest section of the community.

By 1846, the population was estimated at 130 persons per acre with three thousand pigs, and the average age of death was eleven and a half years compared with thirty-seven years for the whole of London. Three years later the mortality rate was sixty per thousand of the population and twenty-one deaths occurred during a serious cholera epidemic.

But 1856 marks the date from which the first Medical Officer of Health to be appointed to the Vestry, Dr. Francis Goodrich, and his successor Dr. Thomas Orme Dudfield made bold efforts to urge the Vestry to take

[1] Built between 1840 and 1850.

some action. At first, they had little success. Although the occasional prosecution of pig owners was instituted, magistrates were loathe to deprive the defendants of their living and this leniency encouraged the pig-keepers to engage their own lawyer to protest, largely on the grounds that they were the first arrivals and, if the pigs were a nuisance to the new better-class residents, they, in turn, were equally offensive to the pigs and their masters.

Very gradually an improvement was noticeable and the pig populations began to decline, not always without physical resistance from their owners. The mortality rate, however, remained high, seventy-nine per cent of the deaths of children in 1856 being among those under the age of five. At last, in 1883, the final 'official' pig disappeared by order of the Vestry, though a few remained in private ownership. But, further and drastic improvements to the whole locality had to wait until the new Borough Council replaced the Vestry[1] in 1899 and the first Mayor of the Royal Borough, Sir Henry Seymour King, made a personal, interest-free loan, towards these projects.

*

Throughout this period, the pig-keepers had led an uneasy co-existence with the brick-makers, whom the former despized, so much so, that a woman of the pig-keeping colony was heard to remark: 'Now pig-keepers is respectable, but them brick people bean't some of them no wiser than the clay they works on!' However true or false that may be, the brick-making families worked hard to make a living and, for five months in the year, father, mother and those children old enough to help toiled for fifteen to sixteen hours a day, digging out and carrying away heavy loads of wet clay, quenching their thirst with vast quantities of beer.

For the rest of the year, work was difficult to come by and families were hard put to it to keep themselves alive. 1856 was a particularly bad year for unemployment and resulted in the springing up of an entirely new industry that was to outrival the pigs and the bricks, namely laundries. This was brought about by the enterprise and initiative of the women of the district, who became the families' chief wage-earners. The consequence was that great competition existed among the men to marry a laundry woman for, it was said, to marry one of them was as good as making a

[1] In 1896, a special committee, on reporting to the Vestry, put the blame on the local population when they said: 'The bad conditions . . . are due to the evil habits of the inhabitants themselves, largely made up of loafers, cab-runners, beggars, tramps, thieves and prostitutes.'

fortune, and this attracted a number of layabouts and rogues from other parts of London.

In such a situation, family life suffered, because the mother went out to work, locking the door behind her and leaving the children to fend for themselves—regrettably a custom not unknown in modern times. Furthermore, whereas, in the past, alcohol had been generally confined to the menfolk, the mothers, having spent long hours washing and ironing, needed a stimulant on reaching home and took to the gin bottle, absurdly cheap in those days. The family, particularly the children, suffered accordingly.

Another shifting community to frequent the district in the 1850s was that of the gypsies, who began arriving in their caravans in the autumn of each year to settle and make their encampment[1] in and around Avondale Park, only to leave again in the following summer (but, by 1870, many had settled permanently with a roof over their heads). In addition, a large labour force was required for the construction of the Hammersmith and City Railway through the centre of North Kensington and hundreds of labourers moved into the area to increase the congestion, the demands for accommodation and the need for improved roads. Latimer and Walmer Roads were then merely rough tracks in which, in wet weather, carts sank up to their axles in mud and it was not unknown for pedestrians to stumble in the dark and drown in the deep pot-holes.

But, by degrees, the plight of the pig-keepers, the brick-makers, the gypsies, the labourers and those working at other trades, was to some extent relieved through the agencies of a number of charitable, religious and welfare organizations, individuals appalled at the frightening conditions, and the Vestry. Schools and public baths were built, churches were erected, mission halls introduced for social gatherings, but, as late as 1893, the correspondent of the *Daily News* described the area adjacent to Avondale Park and Henry Dickens Court as the 'West End Avernus', adding that he had never seen anywhere in London 'more hopelessly degraded and abandoned than life in these wretched places'. An illustration of the existing congestion was the discovery that no less than 723 persons were accommodated in eleven lodging houses, while the report of the Medical Officer of Health showed that out of every thousand children, 432

[1] In her *Nottinghill in Bygone Days* Mrs. Gladstone tells the story of a young gypsy woman who came to Mr. Moore, a local farmer, in a state of great agitation, because she could hear a strange man snoring loudly in her tent and was afraid to enter. In gallant fashion, Moore returned with her to find that one of his elderly sows had escaped and, finding a comfortable resting place on the woman's bed, was fast asleep!

had died before attaining the age of one. Obviously a great deal more remained to be done, and a walk around the district is not only fascinating but shows what has been achieved over the years. Whereas, Kenley Street, with its row of dustbins, does not present the most pleasing of sights, both Pottery Lane and Portland Road have some charming small houses, mixed with somewhat dilapidated and crumbling buildings. Bright new homes and Council Estates have taken the place of many out-of-date premises and the judicious blocking of roads has eased the traffic problems.

Avondale has changed beyond recognition since those dark days. Magnificent trees have grown up including a particularly fine willow in the playground. Flower beds and well kept grass greet the visitor, the young from the nearby Council Estates have a place to give vent to their high spirits, and seats are provided for the elderly. Sitting on a seat in the sunshine, the spry seventy-one-year-old Mr. Frank Spendlowe, a resident all his life within one hundred yards of the park, recalled that his grandfather owned the old cottages that stood in St. Mary's Place and, that as late as 1914, he used to watch squealing pigs driven along the Walmer Road to Tom Van's slaughter houses further up the road. He also told of the excellence of the sandwiches made from their offal which could be bought for next to nothing, and of Mr. Arnsby who kept a cow in one of the nearby houses.

*

Other than as a money-making concern, the provision of a race course to rival Epsom and Ascot, particularly through its proximity to the rich and poor of the racing fraternity of London, was the primary object that prompted the enterprising Mr. John Whyte of Brace Cottage, Notting Hill, to lease two hundred acres of the Ladbroke estate in 1836.

According to maps of 1841, the course was vegetable-marrow-shaped and bounded approximately by the Portobello Road and Lancaster Road as far as Counters Creek and on the south side by Ladbroke Square. A seven-foot-high fence enclosed the area and the main entrance was through an arch at the junction of the Kensington Park and Portobello Roads. But what Mr. Whyte did not take into account when erecting the fence, was that by so doing it closed a public right of way which allowed the residents in the district to avoid the slums of Pottery Lane when travelling on foot between Notting Hill and Kensal Green. This was a bitter bone of contention, for besides having to endure the offensive smells emanating from the piggeries, pedestrians were often attacked and robbed in 'Cut

Throat Lane', as it was termed, and at times forced to hide in the disgusting ditches in their best clothes to avoid the attention of roving gangs of toughs. This was to be a contributory cause for the failure of the undertaking which only lasted from 1837 to 1841.

In laying out the course everything was done on a grandiose scale, to make it 'a racing emporium more extensive and attractive than Ascot and Epsom', as an article in the *Sporting Magazine* described it; and, to provide it with a greater air of respectability, Whyte gave its address as 'The Hippodrome, Bayswater'.

Steeplechase and flat courses, an area for training or exercise, and stabling for seventy-five horses were constructed, and the hill now occupied by St. John's Church made an admirable natural grandstand. The pallisade round the area protected the racegoers from the intrusion of 'improper persons', a band was to play at appropriate intervals, and refreshments were to be available in the marquees, though no drinking or gambling booths were permitted.

On non-racing days, horses could be hired for hacking, a pastime specially recommended by the Press for ladies, as 'for females, it is without danger or exposure of the parks'. Ponies and donkeys were available for the children and space was let to those wishing to amuse themselves at archery or cricket.

Despite strong opposition from residents of all categories, the project was carried through for the opening meeting held on 3 June 1837 with Count d'Orsay and the Earl of Chesterfield as stewards; but, although on that day the company was brilliant, the standard of the racing came in for severe criticism from the Press, one correspondent describing the horses as 'animated dog's meat'. Another wrote: 'Stakes low and horses poor. Save "Hokey Pokey", there was nothing that could climb or hobble, much more leap over a hedge, and as to a hurdle, it was absurd to attempt one!'

Furthermore, the occasion was marred by crowds of locals who, having broken down the fence where the footpath entered the course, forced their way in without paying for admission, an act which caused the Press again to comment: 'A more filthy or disgusting crew than that which entered, we have seldom had the misfortune to encounter ... relying upon their numbers, they spread themselves over the whole ground, defiling the atmosphere as they go and carrying into the neighbourhood of the stands and carriages, where the ladies are most assembled, a coarseness and obscenity of language as repulsive to every feeling of manhood as to every sense of common decency.' So, by and large, the first meeting could hardly be deemed a success and, because King William died shortly afterwards, further meetings were temporarily abandoned.

For two years, Whyte, supported by his friends of the sporting community, continued his efforts to keep the footpath closed, and a series of summonses, counter-summonses, petitions to Parliament, wordy warfare in the Press and rowdy scenes, were the sequel.

Local feeling ran high. Objections were raised on the grounds that Sunday racing was a desecration of the Sabbath and that the course attracted the scum of London, with the consequent rise in the number of gin palaces and gambling dens of which there were already enough in the area. Finally, in 1839, Whyte agreed to give up the area under dispute and to remodel the course by extending it northward to St. Quintin's Avenue; he also agreed to abolish the name 'The Hippodrome Race Course' and to substitute that of 'Victoria Park' in honour of the young Queen.

The expenses of the alterations were high, and to meet them, a management committee of noblemen and gentlemen was set up with £50,000 raised from the sale of £10 shares, the holder of two shares being allowed a transferable ticket of admission. The prices of admission were doubled by charging pedestrians 2s. 6d. and four-wheeled carriages 10s., while further encouragement was given when a number of foreign notabilities gave their patronage and the Grand Duke of Russia presented a cup.

Now that the footpath problem had been overcome and with more money to hand, the future looked rosy, but another and more serious blow fell when it came to light that the heavy clay soil made the course so dangerous at times, that jockeys refused to ride. This was too much as the committee were unable to meet the expense of a drainage system. So, the last of the thirteen meetings held between 1837 and 1841, a steeplechase, took place on 2 and 4 June 1841, and Whyte who, by then, had lost a great deal of money, was compelled to call it a day. Epsom and Ascot could once again breathe comfortably.

All that remains as a reminder of this project are Hippodrome Mews and Place, off Portland Road, the site of the old racing stables. It was a sad end to a bold venture, but it was enjoyable while it lasted.

*

Cemeteries may not be a cheerful subject on which to ponder, yet no story of Kensington would be complete without mention of the Cemetery of All Souls, Kensal Green, the first and largest cemetery to serve London and whose chapels and mausolea are very representative of the architecture of the Victorian era.

The idea of building a cemetery so far from the City arose in the 1820s, when the authorities began to realize that to bury the dead within its precincts was both insanitary and unhealthy, and that the time had come to site burial grounds away from the dwellings of the living.

In consequence, a committee of interested persons was formed in 1830 to give thought to what should be done and, in due course, by means of an Act of Parliament, they were incorporated into the General Cemetery Company as it is to-day.

Naturally, the primary consideration was the selection of a suitable location and though Primrose Hill was the first choice, it was discarded for various reasons and, instead, fifty-four acres of good sheep-grazing land in Kensal Green on the highest point in North Kensington—150 feet above sea level—were purchased in 1831.

The scheme was now launched and the Committee agreed that the lay-out should follow the lines of Père Lachaise in Paris, but much argument ensued as to the style of architecture to be employed for the entrance and chapels—whether it should be Gothic or Grecian—until eventually Grecian won the day.

Since some time would elapse before permanent buildings could be ready and because the consecration of the ground was an urgent matter, on the insistence of the Bishop of London, who refused to carry out the ceremony without at least a temporary chapel, one was built specially for the occasion. The cemetery was consecrated on a cold winter's day in January 1833 and the first interment took place in the same month.

Its desirability as a burial ground was immediate and Edward Walford remarked in his *Old and New London*: 'No sooner was the cemetery opened than the boon was eagerly embraced by the public and marble obelisks and urns began to rise among the cypresses in all the variety which heathen and classical allusions could suggest.'[1]

For many years, dissenters were not permitted to be buried in the same area as members of the Church of England, so a portion of the eastern end, cut off from the remainder of the cemetery by a high hedge stretching the full width, was allocated to them, and a special chapel, its façade of Doric columns supporting a plain pediment, was built for non-conformist burial services. The hedge has gone but the chapel, listed as of historic interest and to-day presenting a sorry aspect, is used as a store for coffins required in an emergency.[2]

[1] Two watergates were made in the southern wall of the cemetery for the reception of coffins arriving by the Paddington Canal.

[2] It is said that sufficient are held to meet a fatal accident of a fully loaded Jumbo Jet.

The main feature of the cemetery is the chapel standing high above the obelisks and mausolea, in the centre of the grounds; built in the Grecian style, it comprises the chapel itself, a series of piazzas containing memorials, with vast catacombs below. Facing the entrance, but on a lower level, are the mausolea of Princess Sophia, daughter of George III, and the Duke of Sussex, her brother, who, because in his opinion the delays, confusion, protocol and etiquette at the funeral of William IV were disgraceful, stipulated that he should not be buried at Windsor. Strangely, the mausoleum of another Royal Duke, the Duke of Cambridge, cousin of Queen Victoria and Commander-in-Chief of the British Army for no less than thirty-nine years, 1856–95, finds a place on the west side of the chapel, at some distance from his relatives.

Among the many celebrities, other than Royalty, whose graves will be found at Kensal Green, are artists, men of letters, members of Parliament and representatives of the theatrical profession and the world of entertainment. In the first category came William Mulready and John Leech; in the second, William Thackeray, Anthony Trollope, Leigh Hunt and Shirley Brooks, the one time editor of *Punch*; in the third, the tempestuous Feargus O'Connor, M.P., who led the Chartists to Kennington Green on 10 April 1848, compelling the Duke of Wellington to call out the soldiers to disperse them; and, in the last, Charles Kemble, Madame Vestris[1] and Charles Blondin.[2]

At a certain period of its existence, when the magnificent trees and the shrubs were in full leaf, when the roads, the paths and the grass were kept in good condition and until over-crowding set in, the cemetery must have displayed the dignity that the environment originally intended. But, now, lack of money, the rising cost of labour and, not least, vandalism have made it impossible to maintain many of the monuments, the grave-stones and the surroundings in proper state. Decay and corrosion have taken their toll, grass and brambles have gained the upper hand, so that, at times, it is difficult to find the grave one is seeking. It is a sad thought that the last resting places of those who have given so much to the country, should be allowed to go to ruin, but cemeteries are clearly a dying asset.

*

[1] Lucia Mathews, the actress possessed of 'one of the most luscious of low voices, a beautiful face and an almost faultless figure'.

[2] The tight-rope walker, who crossed the Niagara Falls four times between 1859–1860, once blindfolded, once trundling a wheelbarrow and once with a man on his back.

As Paris has its Flea Market, Cairo its Mouski, Marrakesh its Souks, and
Delhi its Chandi Chowk, so London has its Portobello Market and, though
they may differ in character, they have something in common with one
another, for the merchandise for sale in the shops and on the stalls is as
varied as the crowds that throng the streets and alleyways.

It is difficult to give an exact date when the Portobello Market emerged,
but it was some time in the late 1860s or early 1870s, by which date
houses had already been erected in the Portobello Road. From its opening
it has always been a popular shopping centre for those who live locally
and for several years a Saturday morning attraction for many Londoners
and foreign visitors.

Originally, it functioned only on a Saturday, though the street traders
carried out a lengthy feud with the Vestry, later the Borough Council,
and the shopkeepers, to allow business every day of the week, and many
wordy battles were fought over the width of the costermongers' stalls.
Then, Boroughs were powerless to designate any street a market or to
issue licences for trading, but no doubt the pressure brought by the
street traders' small union, the members of which sported an ivy leaf
in their buttonholes, helped towards the passing of a London County
Council Act of 1927, to enable Councils to do precisely that. So, the market received official recognition and licence holders were permitted to trade
from 8 a.m. to 8 p.m., Monday to Friday, and until 9 p.m. on Saturdays;
an Inspector was nominated to ensure that the regulations were obeyed.

In the old days a Saturday night in winter used to be the big occasion,
when the atmosphere was not unlike that of a fair ground. Hoarse-voiced
vendors behind their stalls and barrows laden with food of excellent quality
and lit by means of brilliant naptha flares, advertised their wares; the
crowds spilling into the road made wheeled traffic impossible and in the
side streets leading off 'The Lane', side shows, singers, conjurors and
quacks did a handsome trade. Disorderly incidents were few and far
between and the police were seldom called, for the world and his wife
were not there only to buy but to enjoy an evening out.

To-day, on any Saturday morning, especially if the weather is fine,
crowds of men, women and excited children stream north along the
Portobello Road from the direction of Notting Hill. At the start of his
walk, a stranger, bent on straightforward shopping or on searching for a
bargain or merely to look on, will see nothing to indicate what lies ahead
as there are no shops or stalls for the first few hundred yards. On the right is
a row of pleasant original residential properties with small front gardens
and, opposite, high modern blocks of flats look down on them.

Suddenly the scene changes on reaching Chepstow Villas and the market begins.

At first, antique shops line the street, while on both sides of the road a continuous row of stalls display silver, porcelain, bronze and brass articles, jewellery, clocks, paintings and general bric-à-brac, to attract those looking for a bargain.[1] The bargain hunters may have succeeded in their quest some years ago, but now traders are extremely knowledgeable and the chances of picking up something really good for a song are rare.

The crowd is a mixed one and the languages to be overheard match those of the Tower of Babel. At one stall, an elegantly dressed lady, with a blue rinse and transatlantic accent, examines a trinket or a piece of silver; at another, a trendily dressed young man tries on a nautical hat and, after enquiring the price in broken English, discusses the problem with his girl friend in French. On the pavement, an organ grinder, his instrument hanging from a strap around his neck, strolls up and down entertaining the shoppers and occasionally talking to the red and blue macaw perched on his shoulder; further on, a couple of men show off tiny marmosets, dressed in little multi-coloured woollen coats to keep out the cold, and at a musical instrument stall a young man tests out the tones of an antique trumpet. On the outskirts of the milling crowd, a tall young man in skin-tight trousers, equally tight-fitting long red boots and a wide Stetson, takes photographs with an expensive-looking camera and, behind the stalls, a broad-shouldered, jovial, bearded man, sporting a naval officer's cocked hat, chats and jokes with his friends and customers.

About a third of the way along the market, the antique shops and stalls are replaced by the normal shops to be found in any London street, while the stalls, loaded to the gunnels with fruit and vegetables, do a roaring trade with families buying their weekly shopping. Again, a multitude of colour, race and creed is represented. Among a group of Indian women arrayed in saris, one tests the quality of a sweet pepper with her fingers; at another stall, a collection of Mongolian-featured women, accompanied by a quiverful of sloe-eyed children, laughingly show each other their purchases; West Indians are busy buying for the week-end.

Of the licenced stalls, some have been handed down from father to son and, though temporary licences are issued, there is a long waiting list to take the place of any of the permanent licence holders who may give up. As in the old days, there is a general atmosphere of good humour and the few police encountered appear to be on excellent terms with the street

[1] A brigadier, actors and actresses, and students selling the results of world travel, are numbered among the stall-holders.

traders. Beyond the hum of conversation and the occasional musical instrument, noise is at a minimum, since traders no longer shout to draw attention to their wares.

The Portobello Market has come a long way since it was first opened, especially in the realm of antiques, which received a considerable boost when the Caledonian Market was temporarily closed in 1948. An expedition to it on Saturday morning is certainly a fascinating, and possibly also lucrative, experience.

CHAPTER TEN

THE SEAMY SIDE

THE YEARS of the eighteenth and early nineteenth centuries were hazardous ones for travelling on the roads leading into London, especially after nightfall, for robbery with violence was a common occurrence and highwaymen did a thriving business with the coaches and private carriages. It must also be remembered that in those days there was no street lighting, no efficient police force, and some of the tavern keepers on those main roads were not above co-operating with the highwaymen by giving them shelter and disposing of their spoils.

Kensington was no exception and, while Brompton and Knightsbridge had their share, the favourite haunt of the robbers seems to have been the Uxbridge Road between Bayswater and Shepherd's Bush, particularly in the vicinity of Lancaster Gate, where the shadows of the trees and wall of Kensington Gardens gave good cover from which the highwayman could emerge to pounce on his victims. Such a reputation did it earn that it was given special mention in the Turnpike Act of 1769, which described it as 'frequently infested in the night time with Robbers and other wicked and ill-disposed Persons, and Robberies, Outrages and violence are committed thereon, which in great measure be prevented if the said Highway was properly lighted and watched'.

Some of the highwaymen who made history have been portrayed as of gallant behaviour, sweeping off their hats and bowing low to the ladies in the coaches before riding off with their valuables and money; others were of a very different character.

Between two and three o'clock on a Saturday morning in 1760, the postboy who set out with the Portsmouth Mail from the General Post Office, was stopped near Kensington by a single highwayman, who ordered him to dismount and, having tied the lad's hands and legs, threw him into the ditch. Removing the mail and fastening the bags to his saddle, he returned to the boy and, levelling a pistol at his head, asked him if he was prepared to die, on which the wretched youth begged for mercy. 'All right,' replied the highwayman, 'I will not take your life now but, if I should be taken for this affair and you give evidence against me, you may be sure of being shot soon after, as there are eight or nine in the gang'; and, with that, he mounted his horse and rode off in the direction of London. Luckily for the boy, a horseman riding past, on hearing his groans, released him and that same morning a number of letters were found torn up in Moorfields.

It is surprising that some of these 'Knights of the Road' did not mind how conspicuous they or their mounts appeared, as witness the highwayman who, a year later, held up two gentlemen in a postchaise near Knightsbridge at about 10 p.m. on a Friday night. He sported a blue surtout coat with a white one underneath, while his light chestnut horse carried a white mane and white tail—almost a Palomino—and the gentlemen had no difficulty in giving the police at Bow Street a description of the ruffian. A mounted posse went off in hot pursuit in the direction of the Kensington Gravel Pits in the Uxbridge Road and here they caught up with their quarry, who, levelling a pistol at the leading constable, galloped off in the darkness to give his pursuers the slip. Although warning was given to all the turnpikes, he escaped, it is thought, by taking refuge with his friends in one of the alehouses or in an inn near London.

Poor William Wilberforce had a tiresome experience when his carriage, carrying his luggage from Bath, was halted in the Kensington Road, just short of his house in the Gore and his trunk bundled out by footpads. They were, however, spotted by Peter Antrobus, a patrol man on duty in that section of the road, and on his enquiring from the two men what the trunk contained, they replied by knocking him down and ran off leaving the loot behind them. But the patrol man was tough and, setting out in pursuit, apprehended one of the robbers; meanwhile their accomplices made off with the trunk, which was found next morning in a field three hundred yards from the scene of the robbery. Whether Mr. Wilberforce ever regained his possessions is not revealed.

Nevertheless, success did not always go to the highwayman. In 1836, a gentleman of the Custom House, accompanied by some female passengers, was on his way from Kensington to the City, when the coach was held up by a single highwayman near the lane that turns off to Brompton. After relieving the terrified ladies of their jewellery and money, the ruffian, turning to the gentleman, shouted, 'Damn ye, Sir, your watch', and when the latter replied that he had none, he swore he would shoot him for leaving it at home, at the same time thrusting his pistol into the coach. With great courage and presence of mind, the gentleman wrested the pistol from his assailant and, opening the door, prepared to deal with him; upon which, the robber mounted his horse and fled, leaving his pistol and hat, with the valuables in it, behind him. The money and jewels having been returned to their respective owners, the journey was completed without further incident and the pistol and hat given wide publicity in the hopes of bringing the criminal to justice.

In the sphere of housebreaking, the intrepid and elderly Mrs. Wilson, in 1765, gave her unwelcome guests more than they bargained for, and the incident is best told by quoting the report that appeared in the papers. 'On Saturday morning last, between the houis of Two and Three, some rogues attempted to break into the House of Mrs. Wilson of Kensington Gore, in the Manner following: They set up a ladder against her Bed-Chamber Window, in order to gain admittance that Way, but providentially Mrs. Wilson heard them and immediately got out of Bed, and took up a Gun which she always kept ready charged in the Room she lay in, and presented it to them, and at the same time swore if they did not go away directly she would shoot them dead: this intimidated them so much that they took their leave of her, but not till they had made the following speech, "You old Bitch, though we have been disappointed To-night, we will visit you another Time". It is a constant method of this old Gentlewoman to walk round her Garden every Night, which is very extensive, with a Mastiff Dog by her Side, and a Gun across her shoulder, to see that everything is safe before she goes to Bed.' One cannot but feel that the threat to visit this formidable old lady again was pure bombast.

In lighter vein is the notice that appeared in the *Kensington Press* the previous year: 'Stolen or strayed, on Tuesday Night or Wednesday Morning last, from Bayes-water Brewhouse, a blue Hen with eight Chickens about three weeks old, seven of the Chickens are inclinable to be Piles, and the other one Blue. Whoever will bring them to Mrs. Sharpless, at the Swan at Bayes-water, or gives Information so that they may be had again, shall receive Ten Shillings Reward.'

*

Two shots rang out at eight o'clock in the morning of 14 March 1804, to disturb the silence of the meadows on the west side of Holland House, not far from 'The Moats', and one of the two men engaged in a duel fell to the ground. It was Lord Camelford, a man of fiery temper and eccentric habits and grandson of Governor Pitt. Born in 1775, he had proved intractable as a child and as he grew up he became involved from time to time in a number of ugly incidents which earned him a reputation for extreme pugnacity and wild behaviour.

17a. The Tower House,
9 Melbury Road

17b. William Burges' bedroom (or Mermaid Room) in the Tower House. The mermaid on the hood of the chimney piece holds up a real mirror. On the lower panel, three large fish emerge from waves whose crests are tipped with silver

18. Mr and Mrs G. F. Watts in the studio of New Little Holland House, later
6 Melbury Road

19a. Charles Digby Harrod, who laid the foundations of the world-famous store

19b. Sir Richard Burbidge, 1st Baronet. General Manager and later Managing Director of Messrs. Harrods 1891–1917

19c. John Barker. Founder of John Barker and Company

20a. Harrods' frontage, 1897

20b. Kensington High Street, 1906

21a. Flamingoes in the roof garden of Derry and Toms, now Biba

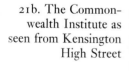

21b. The Commonwealth Institute as seen from Kensington High Street

PARTICULARS AND CONDITIONS OF SALE

OF

THE ADMIRED

SUBURBAN VILLA

OF

THE MARQUIS OF BUTE,

WITH ITS

Extensive Grounds and Gardens

AND

LITTLE PARK PADDOCK,

SITUATE ON

CAMPDEN HILL,

APPROXIMATING UPON

KENSINGTON,

WITHIN A SHORT DRIVE OF

The Houses of Lords and Commons.

THE VILLA

HAS BEEN DENOMINATED ONE OF THE

MOST RECHERCHE IN LONDON'S ENVIRONS,

AND IS ADORNED BY

A CONSERVATORY & HOT-HOUSE.

IT WILL BE SOLD BY AUCTION, BY

MR. GEO. ROBINS,

At the Auction Mart, London,

On WEDNESDAY, 1st of JUNE, 1842, at Twelve,

BY DIRECTION OF THE NOBLE MARQUIS.

It can only be viewed by Particulars, to be ready twenty-one days prior to the Sale, to be had of Messrs.
ROY, BLUNT, JOHNSON, and WALTON, Solicitors, Lothbury; the Auction Mart; and at Mr. GEO. ROBINS'
Offices, in Covent Garden.

SMITH and ROBINS, Printers, King Street, Long Acre.

22a. Particulars advertising the sale
of Bute House, Campden Hill, in
1842

22b. William Batty's advertisement
for his Hippodrome at the north
end of Victoria Road

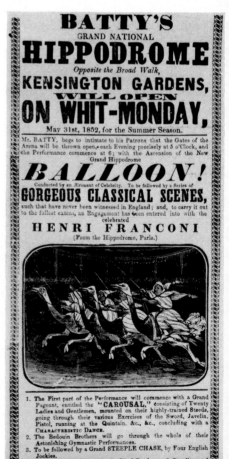

23a. The Piggeries and the Potteries. Tucker's Cottage. From Mary Bayly's 'Ragged Homes and how to mend them', 1859

23b. Royal Crescent, part of the Norland Estate, c. 1840. Engraving by B. Corcoran

24a. John George Haigh, the
'Acid Bath' murderer

24b. Ronald True

As a young man he was sent into the Royal Navy to sail with Captain Vancouver in the *Discovery* but, because of his strong aversion to discipline, he was subjected to severe punishment and this he bitterly resented. On his return to London, a scene which could have had serious consequences was narrowly averted when, as he was walking down Bond Street with his brother one morning, they met Camelford's Captain and a scuffle ensued. It was only the intervention of his brother that prevented him striking his erstwhile commanding officer.

Two unseemly incidents followed in quick succession in 1799, when he was fined £500 by the Court of the King's Bench for savagely assaulting a gentleman in Drury Lane, and shortly afterwards he finished up in the Watch Tower, to which he was escorted by no less than twenty Watchmen after leading an attack on four of their colleagues in Cavendish Square, a fight which lasted for a whole hour.

One of his favourite haunts was the Prince of Wales Coffee House in Conduit Street and here, on 6 March 1804, he encountered his friend Captain Best, reputed to be the finest pistol shot in the country. It was this chance meeting that gave rise to the fatal duel.

His Lordship had for some time been acquainted with a Mrs. Simmonds who, it is said, 'lived under the protection of Best', and it had come to his knowledge, possibly through Mrs. Simmonds herself, that Best had made certain derogatory remarks about him to her. So, on entering the Coffee House and seeing Best in the crowded room, he advanced upon him and, in a very loud voice that all could hear, said: 'I find, Sir, that you have spoken of me in the most unwarrantable terms.'

Best, who was greatly taken aback, denied the charge, saying he had no knowledge of what Camelford was talking about, but the latter would have none of it, proclaiming Best to be 'a scoundrel and a rogue'.

The fat was now really in the fire for, after such insults in the presence of so many people, Best had no option but to challenge Camelford and, later that evening, after he had dined boisterously with his friends, the necessary note was sent to Camelford's apartments in Bond Street.

For a day or two Best tried his utmost to bring the matter to a satisfactory conclusion without resort to duelling, saying that he would be satisfied if his adversary would withdraw his remarks, but Camelford refused because he considered that in view of Best's reputation as a pistol shot, to retract would reflect badly on his own courage.

Although the quarrel and challenge had been brought to the notice of the Marlborough Street police, no action was taken until the night of 13 March, when constables went to Camelford's apartments only to find he had left for an unknown address. He did, in fact, spend that night in a tavern with the specific object of avoiding the law.

Early next morning the opponents, accompanied by their seconds, met in a Coffee House in Oxford Street, and here Best tried again to prevail on Camelford to apologise, but without avail. To all his persuasions Camelford replied: 'This is child's play—the thing must go on.'

So, there was no alternative but to get on their horses, Best riding a mount he had recently won from Camelford at a target contest with pistols; following behind in a postchaise went the seconds who, on arrival at the appointed place in Kensington, measured out the ground, and the adversaries took up their posts thirty paces apart.

The signal being given, Camelford fired first, but the ball went wide and for a moment Best appeared to be asking his opponent if he was satisfied, to which Camelford must have replied that he was not. Best then fired and His Lordship collapsed on the ground, the ball having entered his right side, penetrated his lungs and lodged in one of his vertebrae.

Calling upon Best to come near and clasping him by the hand, he exclaimed: 'Best, I am a dead man; you have killed me but I freely forgive you,' and to those who came to his assistance he several times asserted that he was the aggressor. After lingering in great pain for three days, Camelford died. At the Coroner's inquest, a verdict was returned of death at the hands of 'some person or persons unknown', and Best was acquitted.

*

Between the Wars and since the Second World War, Kensington has either been the scene of some of the more sensational murders, which aroused considerable public interest at the time, or the domicile of the murderers themselves. Ronald True, Neville Heath, John Haigh, Christie and Evans are some of the names that hit the headlines in the Press.

Born in Manchester in 1891 of an unmarried and very young mother— she was only sixteen—Ronald True was brought up in comparative affluence, his mother contracting a favourable marriage when her son was eleven years old. But very early on he evinced a disagreeable tendency towards lying, truancy and cruelty to animals, habits which some children develop but grow out of; but not so True, whose propensity towards these failings increased as the years went by.

Other than showing an inability to concentrate, his life at school, where he remained until he was eighteen, was uneventful. When he left it was decided to ship him off to the Colonies as was often customary in those days when sons displayed no outward signs of suitability for any particular profession and there was money available to pay the fare.

Farming in New Zealand was his first venture, but he was back in a year; after a short and unsuccessful period at trying his hand on a farm in Yorkshire, he set off for the Argentine, but again was home in twelve months. Shipped off to Canada, he joined the North West Mounted Police for a few months before drifting on to Mexico and eventually to Shanghai, where he arrived just prior to the 1914–18 War. And, at some period during this six years of travel, he became a morphia addict.

Returning to England shortly after the outbreak of war, True, in due course, joined the Royal Flying Corps and, managing to conceal his morphine habits from the doctors, he became a cadet at the Gosport Flying School, where, after several failures, he finally passed his exams. But two crashes quickly brought his stay to a halt and he was invalided out of the Service, ostensibly on the grounds of injury, though there were indications that he had had a syphilitic condition.

It is amazing that a man who had already been invalided out and had shown eccentricities amounting to an imbalance of mind, should have been able to find employment in the aeronautical world. True succeeded by obtaining a post, first as a pilot in a Government concern at Yeovil, where his shortcomings rapidly came to light, and later as a flying instructor in the United States, where he met an actress, married her and returned to England, before taking a job in West Africa, the last he ever had.

Supported financially by his mother, his life was now spent in and out of nursing homes as a very unpopular patient (his drug addiction had become considerably worse, as had his mental condition), or as a man about town; but as the money he received from his mother was insufficient for such an existence, True resorted to petty theft and confidence tricks to keep himself in funds.

Tall, dark, quite good-looking, endowed with a plausible manner, an ability to create a good impression plus the fact that he was good company, he had little difficulty in persuading his acquaintances to part with their money or give their services, confident they would be remunerated. By robbing Peter to pay Paul, True succeeded in keeping his creditors quiet.

It was sometime in the middle of 1922, that he first met Gertrude Yates, alias Olive Young, ex-shop girl turned prostitute, who lived by herself in a basement flat, No. 13A, in Finborough Road, a turning off the Brompton Road, east of Brompton Cemetery. Where they actually met is not certain but it is thought to have been somewhere in the West End, and

True, having obtained Miss Yates's address, paid his first visit to the flat on Saturday, 18 February: this visit coincided with a social call by a woman friend of Miss Yates to whom True was introduced as 'Major True', but she shortly left the flat.

The occasion was not a success because True took more than a polite interest in his hostess's jewellery and made known that he carried a loaded revolver on his person. For these reasons and since a five pound note was missing from her bag when her guest departed, the girl was determined not to see him again.

However, True was persistent, telephoning unsuccessfully each day to arrange another meeting; but he did discover that Gertrude Yates was in the habit of leaving a light on in the hall when she went out and of switching it off on her return.

At this time, True's finances were at a low ebb and again and again he visited the flat to find the light burning; but at midnight on 5 March, all was darkness when he arrived. He knocked at the door and, when Miss Yates opened it, she reluctantly let him in because a woman of her profession could not afford to create a disturbance at that time of night.

She could not have entertained any suspicion of True's intentions for at seven o'clock on the Sunday morning, while she lay half asleep, she could have heard the noise of rattling tea cups in the kitchen where True was preparing early morning tea. But making tea was not his only occupation—he was searching for a weapon, which he found in the shape of a heavy rolling pin.

Returning with a cup of tea, he handed it to the unsuspecting woman and then struck her violently on the head. This was sufficient to stun her and, although four more vicious blows virtually killed her, True was taking no chances and, forcing a towel down her throat and tying the cord of her dressing-gown tightly around her neck, he suffocated her.

What followed was evidence of his distorted mind. There was plenty of time to dispose of the corpse and take what money and valuables he could find before the daily woman, Emily Steele, came in about nine o'clock: yet, True, having dragged the body into the bathroom, chose to remain until her arrival. Seeing a man's overcoat lying on a chair did not surprise the daily woman, nor was she taken aback when True appeared from the direction of the bedroom, because she had seen him before. 'Don't disturb Miss Young, we had rather a late night. I will send the car for her at midday,' was his parting remark as she helped him on with his coat. He also pressed half-a-crown into her hand for getting him a cab on a previous visit, apologising for not having tipped her before. Watching from the window, Emily Steele saw him hail a cab; some minutes later she came upon Gertrude Yates's body in the bathroom and immediately telephoned the police.

Convinced he could easily throw the police off the scent, True spent the early part of the next day disposing of his bloodstained clothing, buying a new suit, visiting a barber for a shave and pawning his victim's jewellery for the paltry sum of £25. Later he joined up with friends, and was in Croydon for tea, where he bought a paper on the front page of which was the headline news of the murder. When one of his companions asked if there was any news, True replied, 'Nothing of interest.' On returning to London, he and a friend dined in sufficient time for the opening of the second house of the Hammersmith Palace of Varieties.

But the police, who had acted with outstanding rapidity, found little difficulty in tracking down the wanted man to the theatre and were fortunate to find him and his friend in a private box, for to arrest an armed man in the crowded stalls would have been a hazardous undertaking. In these circumstances the arrest passed off unnoticed by the audience.

Brought before Mr. Justice M'Cardie on 1 May, True was tried, found guilty and sentenced to death, but on 8 June the sentence was rescinded on the grounds of insanity. Confined in Broadmoor Criminal Lunatic Asylum for the remainder of his life, he died there in 1951.

*

On the evening of 20 June 1946, a tall, well-built, handsome and well-dressed young man of twenty-nine, with wavy hair and blue eyes, entered the Panama Club in Cromwell Place, South Kensington, in company with a Mrs. Margery Gardner.

Looking back over the years, Neville Heath's career, since leaving school, had been a chequered one and, in the course of his service in the armed forces, he had been cashiered or dismissed from the service no less than three times.

1936 found him with a short service commission in the Royal Air Force but, within eighteen months, he was sentenced to be cashiered, later reduced to 'dismissal', on a number of charges. A series of crimes varying in seriousness followed, leading to a three-year Borstal sentence, but, on the outbreak of war in 1939, he was released, joined the Royal Army Service Corps, was commissioned and posted to the Middle East.

Again, in less than a year, he was court-martialled and sentenced to be cashiered for absence without leave and for certain fraudulent offences but, on the way to England, he left the ship at Durban and, although his past record was discovered, he was granted a commission in the South African Air Force. When seconded to the Royal Air Force, his only operational commitment ended in his having to bale out when his aircraft was hit.

In December 1945, by which time the marriage he had contracted in South Africa had come to an end, he faced his third Court Martial, which sentenced him to be dismissed from the Service, and he returned to England.

So much for Neville Heath's past. At about midnight on 20 June 1946, Heath and Mrs. Gardner left the Panama Club, hailed a taxi and drove to the Pembridge Court Hotel, Notting Hill, where Heath had taken a room; as he had a key to the front door, nobody saw them enter, nor was Heath seen to leave at any time.

The next morning, the chambermaid was not unduly worried that no sounds were coming from the room, but early in the afternoon she knocked at the door and, on getting no answer, she entered, to find Mrs. Gardner lying on one of the beds covered by the bedclothes. She had been murdered in the most revolting manner. Of Heath there were no signs as he had left London by train for Worthing, to meet a woman to whom he was un-officially engaged and with whom he had once spent the night at the Pembridge Court Hotel.

By evening the story of the brutal murder was in all the papers and Lieutenant Colonel Heath, as he now called himself, discussed the case with his fiancée as they sat at dinner, saying that not only had the killing taken place in the room that he and she had occupied, but that he had seen the body with the police. He also expressed the view that the murder was the work of a sexual maniac.

Fortunately for her, Heath announced his intention of returning to London the next day and she never had anything further to do with him. Instead, he took a train to Bournemouth, where he put up at a hotel under the name of Group Captain Brooke, and from there he wrote to Scotland Yard explaining that he had met Mrs. Gardner during the week of her death and on the fatal night had lent her his room at the Pembridge Court Hotel to sleep with a man to whom she was under some sort of obligation. He went on to say that when he returned to his hotel at about 3 a.m., he found Mrs. Gardner dead and also the instrument with which she had been beaten (a riding whip with a metal tip); this, he said, he was forwarding that day, but never did.

Within a short space of time after his arrival in Bournemouth, Heath made the acquaintance of a Miss Doreen Marshall of the Women's Royal

Naval Service, who was convalescing after a bout of influenza, and they dined together at Heath's hotel on the evening of 3 July, after which she left the hotel in his company. This was the last time the poor girl was seen alive for, five days later, her savagely mutilated body was found under some bushes in Branksome Chine.

On 5 July, the manager of Miss Marshall's hotel became anxious and notified the police that she was missing; he also got in touch with his opposite number at Heath's hotel since he thought Miss Marshall might have dined there on the 3rd and, as this proved correct, Heath was advised to contact the police.

Scotland Yard, meanwhile, had issued a description and photograph of Heath. Consequently, when he went to the Police Station, he was recognized, detained and a search was made of his belongings.

In the pocket of his jacket, the police found a cloak-room ticket issued at Bournemouth West Railway Station on the day of his arrival in the town and in the suitcase, retrieved from the cloak-room, there was plenty of evidence, including the riding whip, to connect him with the murder of Mrs. Gardner. In addition, they discovered a first class ticket to London, later proved to have been Miss Marshall's, together with a single pearl from her necklace; on searching his room at the hotel, a blood-stained handkerchief, with a few of Miss Marshall's hairs attached to it, came to light.

Taken back to London, Heath was identified on 19 July by the receptionist at the Panama Club and by the taxi driver who had driven him and Mrs. Gardner to the Pembridge Court Hotel on 20 June. On 8 August, he was charged with both murders.

Tried before Mr. Justice Morris at the Old Bailey on 24 September, he was found guilty and executed on 26 October 1946.

*

'The Acid Bath Murder', as it later came to be known, probably caused a greater sensation than any crime in the '40s and, though at first it involved only the Onslow Court Hotel in South Kensington, in the course of the investigations, it transpired that the word 'Murder' should have been in the plural since at least five other similar types of murder of which three took place in the basement of 79 Gloucester Road, were committed by the same man in a space of five years.

Sometime in 1945, a presentable man in his late thirties, with black hair, a small moustache and good manners became a resident of the Onslow Court Hotel. His name was John George Haigh.

Among other residents were two elderly ladies, a Mrs. Durand-Deacon, a comfortably off widow in her sixties, and a Mrs. Lane, who, though they sat at different tables in the dining-room, had formed a close friendship over the years. Since Haigh sat at the next table to Mrs. Durand-Deacon, they talked about this and that, as is frequently the case among residents, and were on generally friendly terms.

One day in February 1949, the 14th to be exact, Mrs. Durand-Deacon, in the course of conversation, expressed an interest in the manufacture of plastic fingernails used by women to affix to their natural ones and so improve their appearance, and Haigh, scenting an opportunity to make some money, said he would enquire into the possibilities. Unknown to Mrs. Durand-Deacon, her friend was in serious financial difficulties with an overdraft at the bank and an outstanding hotel bill for just under £50, for which he was being pressed for payment.

At that time, Haigh, who described himself as an engineer, had some business connection with a light engineering company in Crawley, trading under the name of the Hurstlea Products, among whose property was a building in Leopold Road, Crawley, used occasionally as a kind of work-shop or store-room. It was usually kept locked but, from time to time, Haigh was permitted to use it for, as he claimed, experimental purposes and to do so he had to obtain the keys from a Mr. Jones, the Managing Director.

On the day following his conversation with Mrs. Durand-Deacon, Haigh called on Jones to tell him about the plastic fingernail project and, though the latter displayed no great interest, Haigh said he would bring the client to see him later in the week. He must have been on very good terms with Jones for he was able to borrow £50 from him on condition that it was repaid by the 20th, in other words in five days' time. The hotel bill was now accounted for, but to repay the loan Haigh had to act quickly to find the money.

Returning to London, he told Mrs. Durand-Deacon that he had followed up her suggestion of the fingernails and proposed that she came down to the factory at Crawley to discuss it. During the next three and a half days he occupied himself in making methodical preparations for her visit to the store-room by purchasing a forty-five gallon drum, a quantity of sulphuric acid, a pump to transfer the acid from its container to the drum, an apron and gloves and some red paper for the mythical artificial fingernails.

At about 2 p.m. on the afternoon of 18 February, Mrs. Durand-Deacon left the hotel wearing a Persian lamb coat and personal jewellery.

Presumably she drove with Haigh to Crawley, where they were seen together in a hotel sometime between 4 p.m. and 5 p.m., and to leave it in a car driven by Haigh.

The events which occurred between then and Haigh's return to London can be quickly described. Taking Mrs. Durand-Deacon into the store-room he shot her in the back of the head as she was examining the red paper, emptied the contents of her handbag, removed the jewellery and Persian lamb coat and, according to Haigh himself, made an incision in her neck, drew off some of her blood in a glass and drank it, before going to a café for tea. After tea, he went back to the scene, filled the drum with acid and dumped his victim's body into it. Since this took a good deal of time, he arrived at the George Hotel only just in time for a late dinner before driving to London.

The next morning, with the utmost *sang-froid*, he approached Mrs. Lane, the friend of Mrs. Durand-Deacon, to enquire if the latter was ill, as she had arranged to meet him at the Army and Navy Stores in Victoria Street the previous afternoon, but had failed to turn up. When enquiries were made, it was discovered that Mrs. Durand-Deacon had not slept in the hotel that night, nor was there any clue as to where she had gone. And with that Haigh departed to dispose of Mrs. Durand-Deacon's belongings in various places in Sussex and Surrey.

The following day, a Sunday, Haigh again enquired from Mrs. Lane if there was any news of Mrs. Durand-Deacon and, on learning that she, Mrs. Lane, was going to report the disappearance to the police, he offered to drive her to Chelsea Police Station himself, where they made the report.

It was consequent upon information received from the hotel, which elicited the fact that Haigh was not a popular guest, that the police became suspicious and the more so when, checking with the Criminal Record Office, it was discovered that he had previously been in prison for fraud on more than one occasion. After that they were persistent in their enquiries and in questioning Haigh, who stuck to his story of the Army and Navy Stores and Mrs. Durand-Deacon's failure to appear.

Then, as a result of further investigations, the police not only found incriminating articles in the store-room, including a recently fired revolver and a receipt from a firm of cleaners for a Persian lamb coat, but also discovered that, on the day after Mrs. Durand-Deacon's disappearance, Haigh had sold her jewellery to a jeweller in Horsham. With such important evidence to hand, Haigh was picked up while in his Alvis car outside his hotel on the afternoon of 28 February and taken to Chelsea Police Station for further interrogation.

At first Haigh resorted to falsehood and contradiction, but suddenly without warning, though he had received the caution that he need say nothing, he came out with an entirely unexpected statement. 'I will tell you all about it. Mrs. Durand-Deacon no longer exists. She has disappeared completely and no trace of her can ever be found again. I have destroyed her with acid. You will find the sludge which remains at Leopold Road. Every trace has gone. How can you prove murder if there is no body?'

After a further caution, Haigh declared he wished to make a statement and, in doing so, revealed an amazing account of a further eight murders he had committed either at the Gloucester Road address or in the store-room at Crawley.

The first concerned the McSwan family, the father, who owned an amusement arcade, his wife and their son, by whom Haigh had been employed for a period in 1936 in Wimbledon as chauffeur cum secretary. Eight years after he left their employment he met William, the son, by chance in a public house in Kensington and learned from him that his father had sold the amusement arcade and with the proceeds had acquired other property. He also discovered that the family lived in Claverton Street, S.W.1., where he became a welcome visitor and went out on many occasions for the evening with the son.

Then, on 9 September, William McSwan disappeared and Haigh explained to his parents that the young man had made himself scarce to avoid being called up for military service, whereas he had in fact murdered him in much the same way as he was later to dispose of Mrs. Durand-Deacon. They had met in the Goat public house in Kensington High Street that evening and later went on to 79 Gloucester Road, where Haigh hit William McSwan on the head, drew blood from his throat to drink, put him in a tank of acid and got rid of the sludge down a manhole.

Some ten months elapsed before he killed William's father and mother —in the same manner but on different occasions—and having thus eliminated the whole family, he realized their assets by means of forged documents, to become the richer by approximately £4,000. Peculiarly, these three unfortunates were never reported 'missing', and the method of their disappearance did not emerge until Haigh, himself, told the story.

Besides claiming to have murdered a young man and two young women between 1945 and 1949 (he gave the police insufficient details for their identification), there can be no doubt that he killed a Dr. Archibald Henderson and his wife Rose, in 1948.

By September 1947, Haigh had run through the money he had obtained by the murder of the McSwan family and was once more in financial trouble. Through an advertisement offering their house in Ladbroke Square, W.11., for sale, Haigh made the acquaintance of the Hendersons and, despite the fact that he could not find the money to purchase the house and the sale fell through, they became great friends as a result of his ingratiating manner and solicitous attentions.

In the ensuing five months Haigh's finances were such that he owed a substantial sum to various creditors, including the Onslow Court Hotel, and the money had to come from somewhere. On this occasion his target was the Hendersons who by then had sold the Ladbroke Square house and moved to Fulham.

On 7 February 1948, for some unknown reason, presumably for a holiday, the Hendersons set off for Broadstairs for a few days and then on to the Hotel Metropole, Brighton, where Haigh also stayed with them for two nights until the morning of 12 February. On that day he drove Dr. Henderson to the store-room at Crawley, shot him in the head with his victim's own revolver, trussed him up and placed him in a drum of acid. Returning to Brighton, he told Mrs. Henderson that her husband had suddenly been taken ill and offered to drive her to him as he was asking for her. That was the last time she was seen alive as he disposed of her in the same way, asserting that he drank blood from each as he had done on the other occasions. Needless to say he appropriated the valuables they had on their persons.

By dint of forging Mrs. Henderson's handwriting and signature, sending a letter to say that, because of unspecified difficulties, they had emigrated to South Africa, he kept her relatives in the belief that the doctor and his wife were still alive, while he set about realising their assets.

Having obtained all their belongings from the Metropole Hotel, by means of forged authority, he not only sold Mrs. Henderson's jewellery and her husband's car, but having acquired their house in Fulham he sold that also, making himself the richer by almost £8,000 on all the transactions.

An examination of the first twenty-four years of Haigh's life gives no inkling of what the future was to hold. Born of Yorkshire parents, fervent members of the Plymouth Brethren, he was brought up in the strictest fashion and any form of sport or entertainment was looked upon with disfavour. A lonely type, who did not mix with other children, music was his passion, to the extent that he became an able pianist, the organist for the smaller services in Wakefield Cathedral, and was selected from his school choir to be a member of the Cathedral choir.

As he grew up he displayed no signs of outright dishonesty or of sexual perversion. At the age of twenty-four he married, not least with the object of escaping from parental discipline, and it was then that he took to a life of crime as a means of obtaining easy money. Between 1934 and 1941, he was convicted three times for dishonest crimes, serving a total of six years in prison and, after his first conviction, he never met his wife again.

When charged and awaiting trial in Lewes Prison in March 1948, Haigh remarked that it was not the victims' money he was after but their blood and went on to say that, after drinking it, he felt much better.

At his trial, which opened on 18 July, the jury only took a quarter of an hour to reach their verdict and, when asked whether they found the prisoner guilty or not guilty of murdering Mrs. Durand-Deacon, or guilty but insane, the foreman answered, 'Guilty.' Condemned to death, John Haigh was executed at Wandsworth Prison on 6 August 1949.

*

On the western side of St. Mark's Road, Notting Hill, and just before its junction with Lancaster Road, is Ruston Close, a small cul-de-sac comprising ten small, rather dingy three-storeyed houses on each side. But Ruston Close was not its original name, for it was once Rillington Place, and here, at No. 10, the last house on the left, eight notoriously brutal murders were committed between 1943 and 1953, and the bodies disposed of almost under the eyes of the neighbours and occasional workmen employed in the house.

In 1938, when forty-year-old John Reginald Christie and his wife came to live there, it consisted of three flats, of which the Christies occupied the ground floor. Christie, one of a family of seven, in which daughters predominated, was the son of highly respectable parents, his father, an austere and strict man, being a pillar of many of the local organizations in the Halifax area, such as the Conservative Party, the Scouts and the St. John Ambulance Brigade.

During his adolescence, John Christie was frail, inclined to keep himself to himself, and with so many sisters, was very much under female influence; nevertheless he took part in games, sang in the church choir and rose to be assistant scoutmaster of the local troop. As he grew older he discovered himself suffering from sexual frustration and inadequacy with the girls with whom he came into contact and, developing an antagonism to women generally, he could find satisfaction only with the prostitutes with whom he began to consort.

At the conclusion of the First World War in which he served for two years, 1916–18, and during which he suffered various repercussions to his system when a mustard gas shell burst close-by, he returned to Yorkshire where he married and obtained a job as a postman. But this employment was short-lived when, in the same year, he was sentenced to three months' imprisonment for stealing postal orders. A probation order for false pretences and violence was followed by a sentence of six months for violence to a prostitute with whom he was living in London, to which he had moved five years before, leaving his wife in Yorkshire. And this was not the end as, in 1933, he was given three months' hard labour for stealing a car belonging to a Roman Catholic priest from whom he had received a helping hand.

In the intervals, he gave satisfaction at his work by day, while at night he spent the time with prostitutes and their accomplices, until his wife joined him in Rillington Place in 1938.

With the outbreak of war in 1939, he sent his wife back to Yorkshire and, in the surprising absence of any investigation into his past record, he was accepted into the Emergency Reserve of the London Police and based on Paddington Police Station in the Harrow Road. Here he gave efficient service, receiving two recommendations, before applying for his discharge in 1943. It was then, or just prior to his discharge, that the murders in No. 10 Rillington Place began.

Ruth Fuerst, an Austrian girl, who was a student nurse and part-time prostitute, lived close by in Oxford Gardens. Possibly she met Christie on his beat and, perhaps to avoid a charge of soliciting, was persuaded to visit him at his home where he strangled her during sexual intercourse. The disposal of her body became a matter of unexpected and extreme urgency when a telegram was delivered to say that Ethel, his wife, and her brother were arriving that evening. The back garden was an obvious choice but since time was pressing, as a temporary measure, Christie hid the body under the floor boards in the front room. The next day, when his wife and brother-in-law had left the house, he dug his victim's grave while the neighbours looked on and passed the time of day with the man who had created a very favourable impression on them by his manners and superior education. The grizzly work was completed in darkness before Ethel's return and no enquiries seem to have been made.

In August 1944, when his wife was once more back in Yorkshire, Christie was employed by a radio works in Acton, where he met the thoroughly respectable, thirty-one-year-old Muriel Eady, to whom he became physically attracted; but, as she had a regular boy friend, his problem was how to lure her to Rillington Place alone. Discovering that she suffered acutely from catarrh and posing as a man with medical knowledge, he suggested in October that she came to his house for treatment. The treatment comprised the inhalation of coal gas and under its effects the unfortunate woman submitted to sexual intercourse, after which, as with his previous victim, Christie strangled her. Once again the back garden became the depository for the body and, though enquiries after the missing woman were instituted, no evidence was forthcoming and she was presumed to have been killed in a bombing raid.

In 1945, Ethel Christie returned to permanent residence with her husband, who had by then been re-employed by the Post Office, a job he retained for four years until his previous record was brought to light and he was discharged. For the next three years, nothing untoward occurred at Rillington Place and the garden kept its grim secret.

Then, at Easter 1948, new occupants took possession of the top flat above Mr. Kitchener, an elderly and almost blind man, who lived on the second floor. They were Timothy Evans, an insignificant little man of poor physique and inferior intellect and his pretty pregnant wife, Beryl, whom he had married when she worked at the Grosvenor House Hotel.

Evans, who had been rejected for service with the Forces on medical grounds and had spent a good deal of time in and out of hospital, was a van driver and spent much of his out of working hours consorting with prostitutes and drinking in public houses.

In October, Beryl gave birth to a daughter, Geraldine, but, in the following summer, finding she was pregnant again, was determined to end her pregnancy by abortion, against her husband's wishes. Christie, again claiming to have medical knowledge, offered his help to bring the abortion about. This he tried to do on 8 November, while Evans was out at work but, when the patient struggled, he not only brutally knocked her about, but strangled her and attempted sexual intercourse.

That evening, when Evans returned to find his wife dead, Christie invented a story which Evans believed and suggested they hid the body, a proposition to which Evans agreed with reluctance. Christie also suggested that the baby be sent to some mythical foster parents with whom he said he was acquainted; but she, in turn, was murdered two days later.

Because Mr. Kitchener's flat was unoccupied at that moment, the body of Beryl (and later her daughter) were put into the flat for three days before Christie moved them into a recently decorated wash-house and hid them behind some piles of wood.

On 30 November, Evans, who had returned to his native Wales, made a confession of both killings to the police as a result of which the bodies of his wife and daughter were found at 10 Rillington Place. Charged with the murder of his daughter, he withdrew the confession at his trial at the Old Bailey in January 1950, at which Christie was the chief prosecution witness, but was found guilty and hanged at Pentonville on 9 March. Later there was considerable disquiet over the strong possibility that an innocent man had been sent to his death, but the enquiry that took place upheld the verdict.

Two more years passed before Christie returned to his evil practices: the next victim was his wife, Ethel, whom he strangled in December 1952, burying the body under the floorboards in the front room. Although he then sold his furniture with the exception of a deck-chair which he kept for his perverted activities with women, he continued to live in the house and, between January and March 1953, three prostitutes, Rita Nelson, Kathleen Malony and Hectorina McLennon, went to their death there. All three were strangled after the administration of coal gas, and on each occasion Christie had intercourse at or after death. For the disposal of the corpses, Christie used an alcove, once a cupboard, in the kitchen and, having propped up his victims inside it, he papered it over.

He was now in financial difficulties and, on 21 March, he moved out of the flat and obtained a bed in a house in King's Cross. On Christie's departure, the West Indian owner of the house gave a fellow countryman, who now had the flat upstairs, permission to use the ground floor kitchen; it was then that the foul deeds of the previous owner were disclosed.

While tapping the walls to find a satisfactory position to install his radio, the new occupant came upon a hollow place and, when he tore the paper away, the bodies of three naked women were revealed. During the police search that ensued, the skeletons of two women were unearthed in the garden and Ethel's body found under the floorboards.

A description of Christie was immediately circulated, and he was apprehended on 31 March, on Putney Bridge, by an astute constable who recognized the down and out figure peering over the balustrade. Throughout the four-day trial, which began on 25 June, Christie, while admitting the killings of the women, denied murdering the baby, Geraldine. He was hanged in Pentonville Prison on 15 July.

CHAPTER ELEVEN

THE OLD COURT SUBURB TODAY

DESPITE the fact that since the conclusion of the Second World War and especially during the last ten to fifteen years, the character of Kensington has changed considerably in some respects, the Royal Borough remains essentially a residential area for all strata of society. But it has been and will continue to be a struggle to keep it so with all the pressures to which it is subjected. The drift westwards from the City and West End, so prominent in the last century, still goes on and the demand for accommodation, both public and private, has by no means diminished.

In fact, the conflict has been intensified as residential property beyond the Borough's eastern boundaries disappears to make room for hotels, offices, restaurants and places of entertainment, a situation which has, to a great extent, been aggravated by the vast influx of tourists into London annually. From this angle alone, Kensington, because of its museums, historical assets, parks and shopping centres, is particularly vulnerable.

Until recently, there was nothing to prevent an antique-, book-, or food-shop, for example, changing hands overnight to become a restaurant and, following the popularity of the Borough with the tourist avalanche, many took advantage of the opportunity for financial gain. The results of this absence of control were soon obvious and by 1969 the situation was rapidly getting out of control to the detriment of the residential population whose amenities were seriously affected.

In consequence, the Borough Council promoted a Bill, the Kensington and Chelsea Corporation Act, which successfully passed through Parliament three years later, giving it powers to regulate the number of hotels and guest houses within the Borough; further legislation in the same year enabled it to control the number of restaurants and 'take-away' food shops and thus put a stop to a practice so damaging to the environment.

But before this action was taken, the spirit of Oxford Street had moved to the west, to the High Street, the southern part of Church Street, the

Earls Court Road and Notting Hill High Street, so that all these now have much in common with the King's Road, Chelsea.

Myriads of small boutiques and restaurants jostle one another for space, the pavements are thronged with tourists and visitors from other parts of London and the country generally, while the costumes of some who parade along these busy thoroughfares recall the days of the 'Macaronies' of the nineteenth century. Yet it is not always the clothes and adornments that spring surprises, as those who witnessed the extraordinary incident that occurred in Hornton and the High Streets while this book was in preparation, will testify.

Astonishment and confusion undoubtedly prevailed in Hornton Street at about 4 p.m. one afternoon in May, when both pedestrians (including the author) and drivers alike were startled by the sight of a completely naked woman walking south along the pavement towards the High Street, quite oblivious of the chilly wind and the consternation she caused to those on foot and in cars.[1]

The reaction of both sexes, when coming face to face on the pavement with this totally unexpected phenomenon, varied greatly. Some took no notice whatsoever; some registered utter incredulity but continued on their way; others walked past as if they had noticed nothing untoward and then, suddenly realizing what they had seen, halted and turned round to stare. A woman with a small girl, perhaps her daughter, having convinced herself that it was really a naked woman approaching, hurriedly snatched her charge away.

On the road, accidents were narrowly avoided as drivers ignored the rule to keep their eyes on the road. Meanwhile the cause of all the excitement continued on her way to the High Street, nobody making any attempt to stop her, until she was eventually halted in a supermarket and the police were summoned. There was no need for any to invoke the claim of the man arrested in 1913 for a conveyance as a privilege of the Royal Borough: it was clearly a necessity.

*

Of course, the old-established and world-famed Harrods and Barkers continue to draw the crowds as they have always done, even before the tourist boom, and although Derry and Toms is no more, a new store, of a very different character, has taken its place in the shape of Biba's, with its modern décor and 1930s atmosphere. The story of how it rose from very

[1] Since 'Streaking' has recently become a popular pastime, incidents of this nature are not so uncommon.

small beginnings to become a multi-million pound store, in the space of nine years, is remarkable.

It all began in 1964 when the Polish Barbara Hulanicki, a fashion designer, and her husband Stephen Fitz-Simon, an advertising executive, opened a small dress shop in an old chemist's shop in Abingdon Road, off the High Street and close to Earls Court Road; they christened it Biba's after the nickname of one of Barbara Hulanicki's sisters.

Their object was to cater for the younger generation by offering them 'fun' clothes at moderate prices and, so successful was the venture that, in two years, larger premises had to be found, this time in an erstwhile grocer's shop in Church Street. By 1969 the business had expanded to such a degree that a third move was a necessity so, transferring it to the High Street, they opened a small departmental store, selling jewellery and household goods as well as clothes and accessories for both sexes.

Again their enterprise met with success and in 1971, in conjunction with British Land, Derry and Toms was bought from the House of Fraser at a cost of just under four million pounds for the site alone. It took two years to make the massive interior alterations they needed and on 10 September 1973, accompanied by a fanfare of publicity, the new Biba's opened its doors to the public.

Covering a selling space of about 100,000 square feet, ten times that of the old premises, three of the floors were marbled, seven miles of carpet were laid and although the appearance of each floor was drastically changed, the splendid old lifts and staircases of Derry and Toms, the well-known Rainbow Restaurant, and the even more famous Roof Garden have been retained. This last opened again in the spring of 1974 and the flamingoes, who have spent the interim period staying with friends, have one more returned to their old haunts; it is also rumoured that they will shortly have penguins as neighbours.

An expedition to Biba's is an entirely new experience for shoppers and a popular one for the younger generation. Plenty of space, especially on the ground floor, has been allowed to enable the goods on display to be seen in comfort; the lighting is subdued, glass and chromium abound and, for those who appreciate music in these circumstances, there is an abundance of it all day through the amplifiers installed on each floor.

*

The redevelopment of the High Street to alleviate the ever increasing congestion both on the road and on the pavements, to keep a balance of shopping facilities between the requirements of the local population and the tourists but at the same time to reconcile that with the demand for additional office space, yet retain the best of Victoriana, is an urgent necessity. But in other parts of the Borough there is another problem of equal importance, namely the accommodation of those who, by virtue of their employment in the essential services and industries, such as transport, gas and electricity, require to live within easy reach of their place of work.

The solution is beset with obstacles, of which the first is the number of conservation areas in the Borough on which new building is quite properly subject to severe control, and as a general rule only minor redevelopment is allowed. The second is the vicious circle that arises when old property, not worth the expense of conversion, needs to be rebuilt and the lower income group residents who occupy them are compelled to move out while this is done. When they wish to return they find that rents have been raised for the better accommodation to a scale they cannot afford and the middle income group move in instead. And so it goes on. Furthermore, the living standards in some of the old houses, especially for the old, infirm and those with large families, are so unsatisfactory, that rehabilitation is of high priority.

Earls Court and North Kensington are the worst affected. In the former, many of the houses that were originally in private family ownership have been split up for multiple occupation, while in the latter overcrowding and bad housing are just as, or perhaps more, serious.

Since the early 1870s, North Kensington has always attracted Orientals —students and others—so much so that the area enclosed by Westbourne Park Road in the north and Colville Terrace in the south at one period earned the sobriquet of 'Little India', through the number of Indians who occupied rooms in the many boarding houses that sprang up during the development of the Portobello district. Yet, twenty years earlier, the Portobello Pleasure Garden, which lay astride Talbot Road running through the centre of the area, was the scene of balloon ascents, fairs and a variety of displays accompanied by the strains of martial music. Now, the large numbers of immigrants from the Caribbean who have settled in the area have accentuated the problem.

To help combat this extremely complex situation, the Borough has the invaluable assistance of, and works in close co-operation with, two voluntary bodies, the Kensington Housing Trust, operating north of the Motor Way running through North Kensington, and the Notting Hill Housing Trust, whose responsibility lies south of it, though overlapping sometimes occurs with the agreement of all parties. Both are non-profit-making concerns.

Although it was in operation in 1922 as part of the Kensington Council of Social Service and obtained its funds through donations, the Kensington Housing Trust was properly registered as a Public Utility Society in 1926 (this came about as the result of pressure brought by Lord Balfour of Burleigh that same year). The aims of the Society as set out were to provide new dwellings at low rent, to ease overcrowding by skilled management and to select as tenants for their properties those with young children, those that lived in exceptionally sub-standard conditions and those who could not afford to pay higher rents. The result has been that the Trust now owns 950 units.

The Notting Hill Housing Trust, on the other hand, is of a later date and did not emerge until 1963, when the Rev. Bruce Kendrick, also the founder of 'Shelter', founded the Trust, with aims very similar to those of the Kensington Trust. It largely came into existence following the bringing to public notice of the Rachman scandals and the exposure of the plight of those who had accommodation in those properties.

Initially, like the Kensington Housing Trust, the Notting Hill Housing Trust was entirely dependent on charitable sources for its income and, although donations continue to flow in, each now obtains loans, repayable within a stipulated time, from the Greater London Council and the Borough of Kensington and Chelsea, to enable them to buy property either for demolition and rebuilding or conversion to proper living standards. In the case of the latter Trust, over 3,500 persons have been rehoused since its foundation ten years ago.

Both Trusts have distinguished Boards of Management, comprised of volunteers, men and women, who, besides their deep interest in these pressing problems, are experts in many fields of benefit to the Trust. Naturally, each organization has its salaried staff to deal with the day to day problems and future planning, but the permanent staff would be quite unable to do what has to be done without the enthusiastic assistance of a very large number of volunteers who give their services free.

It can be argued that the work undertaken by these organizations is the responsibility of the Borough Council, and so it is, but the task is such a vast one and time of such importance that it would be impossible for the Council to give the necessary service with the staff at its disposal. Moreover, the Trusts have a more personal contact and deal with individual questions of which, in many cases, the Council may be unaware. The research sections carry out most valuable studies, while the welfare sections do much to alleviate the hardships of those who occupy their dwellings by providing essentials in the way of cookers, blankets, etc., and arranging social occasions for the elderly, the children and the very poor. There can be no doubt that without these voluntary organizations, conditions would be considerably worse and improvement much slower.

Fortunately for the Borough as a whole and for the residential population in particular, planning philosophy has recently undergone a welcome change. Whereas in the past it was the policy to demolish and rebuild, the emphasis is now on conservation and preservation. Where changes in purpose are desirable and acceptable, fine old buildings will be maintained as far as possible for future generations, by retaining the façades and remodelling the interiors under strict planning permission. It is also the intention to preserve the small village areas, such as Kensington Square, Holland Street and Gordon Place, Edwardes Square and the environs of Kensington Palace.

So, by a combination of these methods, it is to be hoped that what remains of the charm, appearance and style of the Old Court Suburb will continue in perpetuity and its fascinating history be kept alive for those who live in the Borough and for those who visit it.

Grant of the Title of Royal to the Metropolitan Borough of Kensington

EDWARD THE SEVENTH BY THE GRACE OF GOD of the United Kingdom of Great Britain and Ireland and of the British Dominions beyond the Seas King Defender of the Faith TO ALL TO WHOM these Presents shall come Greeting WHEREAS by an Office in Council of Her late Majesty Queen Victoria dated the fifteen day of May One thousand nine hundred made by the authority of the London Government Act, 1899, it was ordered that the area of the Metropolitan Borough of Kensington therein constituted should be formed into a Metropolitan Borough under the name of the Metropolitan Borough of Kensington and that there should be established a Council for the Borough which Council should be a body corporate by the name of the Mayor Aldermen and Councillors of the Metropolitan Borough of Kensington and that the said Order in Council should come into operation on the day on which the first election of Borough Councillors should be held under the said Act AND WHEREAS the first election of Borough Councillors as aforesaid was held on the first day of November One thousand nine hundred and the said Order in Council came into operation on the same day accordingly AND WHEREAS for divers good causes and considerations Us thereunto moving Our will and pleasure is that a Royal Charter shall issue granting to the said Borough so constituted the title of Royal NOW KNOW YE that We of our especial grace DO by this Our Royal Charter grant to the Metropolitan Borough of Kensington the title of Royal and do declare and appoint that the said Metropolitan Borough of Kensington shall henceforth be called and styled the Royal Borough of Kensington and do further declare and appoint that the said Council established by the Order in Council aforesaid as a body corporate shall henceforth be called and styled 'The Mayor Aldermen and Councillors of the Royal Borough of Kensington' instead of the 'Mayor Aldermen and Councillors of the Metropolitan Borough of Kensington'

IN WITNESS whereof We have caused these Our Letters to be made patent WITNESS Ourself at Westminster the twentieth day of November in the first year of Our reign.

BY WARRANT UNDER THE KING'S SIGN MANUAL.

L.S.   (Signed) MUIR MACKENZIE.

APPENDIX II

The Borough Arms

(Photograph or drawing of the Arms)
The Motto:- "Quid nobis Ardui"
(Nothing is too difficult for us).

The Armorial bearings, granted to the Borough on 23 May 1901, were, in the main, made up from those who were Lords of the Manor or in some way connected with the history of Kensington from the beginning of the reign of William the Conqueror to the time Holland House was bought by Henry Fox in 1786.

The silver star on a red ground, in the first quarter, is taken from the armorial bearings of the de Vere family, while the golden celestial crown and fleur-de-lys are symbolic of the Virgin Mary, to whom the Church of St. Mary Abbots is dedicated.

In the second quarter, the black cross and four martlets are represented in the arms of the Abbey of Abingdon, to whose Abbot, it will be recalled, Aubrey de Vere granted a portion of the Manor of Chenesinton in the second half of the eleventh century.

The four red roses and the red cross displayed in the third quarter, are derived respectively from the arms of Sir Walter Cope and his son-in-law,

Henry Rich, both of whom became Lords of the Manor: the golden mitre on a red ground in the fourth quarter is emblematic of the mitred abbot of the Abbey of Abingdon.

A golden fleur-de-lys was part of the armorial bearings of Henry Fox, first Baron Holland, and that below the celestial crown can be regarded as representative of the Fox family's connection with Kensington.

Some past celebrities who have lived in Kensington since the seventeenth century

1. The following are commemorated by blue plaques affixed by the Greater London Council* to the houses in which they were at one time resident.

Field Marshal Viscount Allenby. Famous Commander of the First World War.

24 Wetherby Gardens. 1928–36.

Sir Edwin Arnold. Poet and journalist.

31 Bolton Gardens. 1832–1904.

Sir Max Beerbohm. Artist and writer. 1872–1956.

Andrew Bonar Law. Prime Minister 1922–3.

24 Onslow Gardens. 1858–1923.

Charles Booth. Pioneer in social work.

6 Granville Place. 1840–1916.

George Borrow. Author.

22 Hereford Square. 1803–81.

G. K. Chesterton. Poet, novelist and critic.

11 Warwick Gardens. 1874–1936.

Albert Chevalier. Music-Hall comedian.

17 St. Ann's Villas. 1861–1923.

Muzzio Clementi. Composer.

128 Kensington Church Street. 1752–1832.

Walter Crane. Artist.

13 Holland Street. 1845–1915.

Sir William Crookes. Scientist.

7 Kensington Park Gardens. 1840–1921.

Goldsworthy Dickinson. Author and humanist.

11 Edwardes Square. 1862–1932.

Henry Dobson. Poet and essayist.

10 Redcliffe Street. 1840–1921.

Sir Luke Fildes. Painter.
  11 Melbury Road. 1878–1927.
James Froude. Historian and man of letters.
  5 Onslow Gardens. 1818–94.
Sir William Gilbert. Dramatist.
  39 Harrington Gardens. 1836–1911.
George Godwin. Architect, journalist and reformer.
  24 Alexander Square. 1815–88.
Kenneth Grahame. Author (*Wind in the Willows*).
  16 Phillimore Place. 1901–8.
William Holman Hunt. Painter.
  18 Melbury Road. 1827–1910.
William Hudson. Writer.
  40 St. Lukes Road. (Lived here in his last years and died 1922.)
Henry James. Writer.
  34 De Vere Gardens. 1886–1902.
Mohammed Ali Jinnah. Founder of Pakistan.
  35 Russell Street. (Stayed here in 1895.)
Louis Kossuth. Hungarian patriot.
  39 Chepstow Villas. 1802–94.
Andrew Lang. Man of letters.
  1 Marloes Road. 1876–1912.
Sir John Lavery. Painter.
  5 Cromwell Place. 1856–1914.
William Lecky. Historian and essayist.
  38 Onslow Gardens. 1838–1903. (Lived and died here.)
Lord Leighton. Painter.
  12 Holland Park Road. 1830–96.
Jenny Lind. (Madame Goldsmith.) Singer.
  189 Old Brompton Road. 1820–87.
Stéphane Mallarmé. Poet.
  6 Brompton Square. (Stayed here 1863.)
James Maxwell. Physicist.
  16 Palace Gardens Terrace. 1831–79.
John Stuart Mill. Philosopher.
  18 Kensington Square. 1806–73.
Sir John Millais. Painter.
  2 Palace Gate. 1829–96.
Sir Charles Parry. Musician.
  17 Kensington Square. 1848–1918.

Francis Place. Political Reformer.
21 Brompton Square. 1771–1854.

Sir Nigel Playfair. Actor Manager.
26 Pelham Crescent. 1874–1934.

Sir John Simon. Pioneer of public health.
40 Kensington Square. 1816–1904.

Sir Charles Stanford. Musician.
56 Hornton Street. 1852–1924.

Sir Leslie Stephen. Scholar and writer.
22 Hyde Park Gate. 1832–1904.

John Stuart. First explorer to cross Australia.
9 Campden Hill Square. 1815–66.

Dame Ellen Terry.
22 Barkston Gardens. 1847–1928.

William Thackeray. Novelist.
2 Palace Green and 16 Young Street and 36 Onslow Square. 1811–63.

Sir Hamo Thornycroft. Sculptor.
2a Melbury Road. 1850–1925.

Sir Henry Beerbohm Tree. Actor Manager.
31 Rosary Gardens. 1853–1917.

Lord Macaulay. Historian and man of letters.
Holly Lodge. (Now Watkins Buildings Queen Elizabeth College) Re-erected privately on new premises with supplementary plaque.

2. Other notable persons whose houses do not carry plaques.

Gilbert à Beckett. 1811–56. 19 Hyde Park Gate. Claimed direct descent from Thomas à Beckett. First editor of *Le Figaro*, immediate precursor of *Punch*. Principal leader writer of *The Times*.

Richard Ansdell. 1815–85. 7 Victoria Road. 1846–61. Animal Painter.

Charles Baker. Major General or Pasha Baker V.C. 47 Russell Street. 1893–97. Awarded the Victoria Cross during the Indian Mutiny. Concluded his active career as Chief of the Egyptian Public Security Department.

William Banting. 1797–1878. 4 The Terrace (Hornton Street). 1842–70. Undertaker. Cured of increasing fatness. Wrote a pamphlet for the public entitled 'A Letter on Corpulence'. 'To bant' became a household word.

Sir Frank Brangwyn. 1867–1956. 4 Stratford Studios, Stratford Road. 1892–8. Artist.

Hablot Brown. 'Phiz' 1852–82. 99 Ladbroke Grove and other addresses. Artist and illustrator. Collaborated with Charles Dickens.

Robert Browning. 1812–89. 29 De Vere Gardens. 1887–9. Poet.

Field Marshal Sir John Burgoyne. 1782–1871. 5 Pembridge Square. Distinguished engineer officer in the Peninsular and Crimean campaigns.

Sir Edward Burne-Jones. 1833–98. 41 Kensington Square. 1865–71. Painter.

Lord Byron. 1788–1824. As a young man lived in furnished lodgings in Queen Street (Hans Road).

Sir Austen Chamberlain. 1863–1937. 9 Egerton Place in 1921. Statesman.

Sir Winston Churchill. 1874–45. 28 Hyde Park Gate. (Died here.) Prime Minister 1940–5 and 1951–5.

Charles Haydon Coffin. 1862–1922. 76 Bedford Gardens. 1893–1922. Actor.

Marie Corelli. 1864–1924. 47 Longridge Road. 1892–1902. Novelist.

Thomas S. Eliot. 1888–1965. Lodged in Courtfield Gardens and 91 Emperor Place. 1938–40. American Poet.

Sir Jacob Epstein. 1880–1959. 19 Hyde Park Gate. 1928–59. Sculptor.

John Galsworthy. 1867–1933. Campden Hill Road. 16 Aubrey Walk and 14 Addison Road. 1897–1913. Novelist and dramatist.

Earl Lloyd George. 1863–1954. 2 Addison Road. 1928–38. Prime Minister 1916–22.

Thomas Hardy. 1840–1928. Lodged in Upper Phillimore Place, Wynstay Gardens and Campden Hill Road. 1887–99. Novelist and poet.

Sir Patrick Hastings. 1880–1952. 9 Young Street and 26 Victoria Road. 1908–18. Barrister. Attorney General (Lab.) 1924.

Herbert Hoover. 1874–1964. 39 Hyde Park Gate and Red House, Hornton Street. 1902–18. Engineer. President U.S.A. 1929–33.

Field Marshal Earl Kitchener. 1850–1916. 44 Phillimore Gardens. 1875–8. Secretary of State for War 1914–16.

John Lambert. 1619–33. Coleherne House. 1649–57. Famous Cromwellian General.

Wyndham Lewis. 1884–1957. Various addresses including 29A Notting Hill Gate. 1919–57. Artist, writer and critic.

David Low. 1891–1963. 33 Melbury Court. Political cartoonist.

Philip May. 1864–1931. Holland Park Road. 1864–1903. Humorous draughtsman.

Guiseppe Mazzini. 1805–72. 18 Fulham Road (formerly 2 Onslow Terrace). Lived in house for eleven years *c.* 1863. Italian Patriot.

Claude Monet. 1840–1926. 1 Bath Place. 1870. French Painter.

Henry Muddiman. 1629–92. Earls Court (died here 1692). King's journalist and founder of the London Gazette.

Fergus O'Connor. 1794–1855. 18 Notting Hill (now Pembridge Road). 1854–5. Chartist leader.

Arthur Onslow. 1691–1768. Kensington High Street. Speaker in five successive Parliaments.

General Sir James Outram. 1803–63. 10 Queen's Gate Gardens. 1862. Famous commander during the Indian Mutiny.

Samuel Palmer. 1805–81. 1A Victoria Road and 6 Douro Place. 1846–61. Artist and engraver.

Charles Keegan Paul. 1828–1902. 38 Ashburne Place. 1855–91. Author and publisher.

Beatrix Potter. 1866–1943. 2 Bolton Gardens. 1866–1913. Writer and illustrator of children's books.

Ezra Pound. 1885. 10 Kensington Church Walk. 1908–13. American poet. Broadcast for Fascists during Second World War. Detained after the War and declared insane in 1948.

General Sir Robert Baden Powell. 1857–1941. At intervals between 1861–1914 at 9 Hyde Park Gate, 15 Knightsbridge and 52 Princes Gate. Founder of the Scout movement.

First Marquis of Powis. 1617–96. 7 Kensington Square. Companion of James II in exile.

John Redmond. 1856–1918. 18 Wynstay Gardens. 1892–1918. Irish Political leader.

Baron Julius de Reuter. 18 Kensington Palace Gardens. 1867–99. Founder of Reuter's News Agency.

Lord Russell. 1832–1900. 2 Cromwell House, Cromwell Road. 1894–1900. Lord Chief Justice 1894–1900.

Eugene Sandow. 1867–1925. 61 Holland Park Avenue 1907–25. Expert in physical culture. Born of Russian parents. In 1909 offered to train, at own expense, recruits who were below standard for the Territorial Army. Trained thousands to become fit for service during First World War.

Luigi Schiovanetti. 1765–1810. 231 Brompton Road for many years. Line engraver.

Sir George Scott. 1811–78. 39 Courtfield Gardens (died here). Architect. (St. Mary Abbot's Church.)

Sir James Scott. 1785–1867. Campden Hill for several years. Astronomer.

Oswald Sickert. 1828–85. 14 Pembroke Gardens. 1878–85. Painter.

Princess Sophia. 1777–1848. York House, Church Street, for many years. Daughter of George III.

Alexis Benoît Soyer 1809–58. 3 Kensington Square. Famous chef and restaurateur. In 1851 opened his 'Symposium' in Gore House, previously the home of Lady Blessington.

Paul Spagnoletti. 21 Brompton Square. 1829–33. Conductor, Royal Opera.

Jonathan Swift. 1667–1745. Lodged at Kensington Gravel Pits 1712. Satirist. Dean of St. Patrick.

Angela Thirkell. 1900–61. born. 27 Young Street. Novelist.

Edward Trelawny. 1792–1881. 7 Pelham Crescent. Author.

Sir Anthony Van Dyke. 1599–1641. Said to have lived in Holland House for two years. Painter.

Madame Vestris. 1797–1857. Elm Place. 1838. Actress.

Chaim Weizmann. 1874–1952. 16 Addison Crescent. 1920–39. First President of Israel.

Marquis Wellesley. 1760–1842. Died in Kingston House 1842. Governor General of India.

* The dates against each name mark either their lifetime or the period in which they were resident in Kensington.

BIBLIOGRAPHY

Antique Collector, The: August 1959 issue.

Aspinall, A.: *Mrs. Jordan and her family*. Arthur Barker, London 1951.

Bailey, Sir Edward: *Geological Survey of Great Britain*. Thomas Murbie 1952.

Barker, Ashley: 'Lecture on Nineteenth-century Estate Development in South Kensington.' Kensington Society Annual Report 1966–7.

Bowack, John: *The Antiquities of Middlesex*. London 1705.

Brown, Miss E. P.: 'The Bird Life of Holland Park', *London Bird Report 1964*. London Natural History Society.

Brown, R. Weir: *Kenna's Kingdom. A Ramble through Kingly Kensington*. David Boyne, London 1881.

Bryan, M.: *Dictionary of Painters and Engravers*.

Butler, Edward N.: 'Kensington New Town', published in R. Watson's *Christ Church 1851–1951*. Victoria Road (privately.)

Cargill, David and Holland Julian: *Scenes of Murder, a London Guide*. Heinemann 1964.

Cecil, Hon. Mrs. Evelyn: *London Parks and Gardens*. Constable 1907.

Colby, Reginald: 'The Noble Origins of Earls Court'. *Country Life*, November 1968.

Corfield, W. Gordon: 'The Phillimore Estate'. Kensington Society 1961.

Croker, Thomas C.: *A Walk from London to Fulham*. Rewritten by Beatrice E. Horn Kegan, Paul, Trench, Trubner & Co. 1896.

Curl, J. S.: *The Victorian Celebration of Death*. David & Charles Ltd. 1972.

Curtis, W. H.: *William Curtis 1746–99. Botanist and Entomologist*. Warren & Sons. Winchester 1941.

Dictionary of National Biography.

Faulkner, Thomas: *History and Antiquities of Kensington. 1820*.

Ferguson, Rachel: *Passionate Kensington*. Cape 1939.

Fitzgerald, Bryan: *Lady Louise Connelly*. Staple Press, 1950.

Fletcher, H. R.: *Story of the Royal Horticultural Society 1804–1968*. Oxford University Press 1969.

Gladstone, Florence: *Aubrey House*. (Privately printed 1922.)

Gore, John (ed): *The Creevey Papers*. John Murray 1948.

Gover, J. E. D.: *Place Names of Middlesex, with collaboration of S. J. Madge. Allen Mawer and F. M. Sientor*. Cambridge University Press 1942.

Greater London Council: 'Blue Plaques, 1971'. *Survey of London*, Vol. XXXVII. North Kensington (General Editor, F. H. W. Sheppard). Athlone Press, University of London 1973.

Green, David: *Gardener to Queen Anne*. Oxford University Press 1956.

Harrods, Messrs.: *A Story of British Achievement 1849–1949*.

H.M.S.O.: *Bird Life in the Royal Parks. Short History of the Science Museum*. Reprinted 1955.

Home, Hon. J. A. (ed): *Letters and Journals of Lady Mary Coke*. 1889–96.

How, Harry: 'Illustrated Interviews'. *The Strand Magazine* 1892–93.

Howard, Philip: *The Royal Palaces*. Hamish Hamilton 1970.

Hudson, Derek: *Holland House in Kensington*. Peter Davies 1967.

—*Kensington Palace*. Peter Davies 1968.

Illustrated London and its representatives of commerce: London Printing & Engraving Co. 1893.

Jourdain, Margaret: 'Kensington Square'. *Country Life*. 1945.

Kennedy, Ludovic: *10 Rillington Place*. Gollancz 1961.

Kensington Public Library: *Campden Hill. Its historic houses and their inhabitants*.

Kilburn, Father Edmund: *A Walk around the Church of the London Oratory*. 10th Edition. Sands & Co. 1966.

Lean, E. Tangye: *The Napoleonists*. Oxford University Press 1970.

Liechtenstein, Marie: *Holland House*. Macmillan & Co. 1875.

Loftie, Rev. W. J.: *Kensington Picturesque and Historical*. Field & Tuer, The Leadenhall Press Co. 1888.

Lysons, Rev. D.: *The Environs of London 1810–11*.

Malan, A. H.: *Famous Houses of Great Britain*. G. P. Putnam & Son, New York 1902.

Millais, J. E.: *Life and Letters of Sir John E. Millais*. Methuen & Co. 1899.

Nares, Gordon: 'Aubrey House, Kensington'. *Country Life* 1957.

Notable British Trials: *Trial of Ronald True*. Edited by Donald Caswell 1925 and 1950. William Hodge & Co.

—*Trial of Neville George Clevely Heath*. Edited by Macdonald Critchley 1951. William Hodge & Co.

—*Trial of John George Haigh*. Edited by Lord Dunboyne. 1953. William Hodge & Co.

Old Inhabitant: *Kensington, Notting Hill and Paddington 1882.*

Oxford Companion of Art. Edited by Harold Osborn. Clarendon Press 1970.

Pasmore, H. Stephen: 'The History of Edwardes Square'. Annual Report of the Kensington Society. 1970–1.

—'Thomas Henshaw and the Manor of West Town, Kensington'. Abridged version of lecture to the Kensington Society 1964.

Peel, D. W.: *Garden in the Sky. The Story of Barkers of Kensington 1870–1957.* W. H. Allen. London 1960.

Pevsner, Nicholaus: *London except cities of London and Westminster.* (Buildings of England.) Penguin Books 1952.

Ponsonby of Shulbrede, Lord: 'Kensington Square'. *The Sunday Times* 1938.

Ridgeway, Brigadier. R.: 'A short history of Campden Hill Square 1932'.

Russell Barrington, Mrs.: *G. F. Watts. Reminiscences.* George Allen 1905.

Ryall, Ronald B. C.: 'Three of London's Waterways'. Lecture to the London Society. 1971.

Scott, Judith D. G.: The Story of St. Mary Abbots. Society for promotion of Christian Knowledge 1942.

Ship, Horace: *The English Masters.* George Newnes. 1955.

Sidgwick, Romney (ed): *Lord Harvey's Memoirs.* William Kimber 1952.

Stroud, Dorothy: 'The Thurloe Estate'. *Country Life* 1959.

Taylor, Gladys: *Old London Gardens.* Batsford 1953.

Timbs, John: *The Romance of London.* F. Warwick & Co. 1894.

The Times : 'Founding Father of Public Health'. 1963.

Toms, Stanley J.: 'When Mr. Derry met Mr. Toms'. *Kensington News,* September 1963.

Walford, Edward: *Old and New London,* Vol V. Cassell & Co. London.

Webster, F.: 'Royal Borough. Kensington'. *Municipal Review* 1953.

Wheatley, Henry B. (ed): *The Diary of Samuel Pepys.* G. Bell. London 1920.

Wroth, W.: *Cremorne and later London Gardens.* Elliot Stock 1907.

Wroth, W. and A.: *London Pleasure Gardens of the 18th Century.* Macmillan & Co. 1948.

INDEX